Regulating Government

About the Authors

Dwight R. Lee is Bernard B. and Eugenia A. Ramsey professor of private enterprise at the University of Georgia. Professor Lee received his PhD from the University of California at San Diego. He has taught at the University of Colorado-Boulder, Virginia Polytechnic Institute and State University, and George Mason University. He is an adjunct professor at the Center for the Study of Public Choice.

Richard B. McKenzie is professor of economics at Clemson University. He worked on this book while serving as John M. Olin Visiting Professor, Center for the Study of American Business at Washington University, where he remains an adjunct fellow. He is also a senior fellow at the Heritage Foundation.

Regulating Government

A Preface to Constitutional Economics

Dwight R. Lee
Richard B. McKenzie

Lexington Books

D.C. Heath and Company/Lexington, Massachusetts/Toronto

Library of Congress Cataloging-in-Publication Data
Main entry under title:

Lee, Dwight R.
  Regulating government.

  Includes bibliographical references and index.
    1. United States—Economic policy—
1981-   . 2. Business and politics—United
States. 3. Competition—United States. 4. Laissez-
faire. I. McKenzie, Richard B. II. Title.
HC106.8.L43   1987   338.973   86-45510
ISBN 0-669-13443-0 (alk. paper)

Published simultaneously in Canada
Printed in the United States of America
Casebound International Standard Book Number: 0-669-13443-0
Library of Congress Catalog Card Number: 86-45510

The paper used in this publication meets the minimum requirements of
American National Standard for Information Sciences—Permanence of
Paper for Printed Library Materials, ANSI Z39.48-1984. ⊚ ™

ISBN 0-669-13443-0

86 87 88 89 90 8 7 6 5 4 3 2 1

From the Jefferson Memorial

I am not an advocate for frequent changes in laws and constitutions. But laws and institutions must go hand in hand with the progress of the human mind as that becomes more developed, more enlightened; as new discoveries are made, new truths discovered, and manners and opinions change. With the change of circumstances, institutions must advance also to keep pace with the times. We might as well require a man to wear still the coat which fitted him as a boy as civilized society to remain ever under the regimen of their barbarous ancestors.

—Thomas Jefferson

Dedicated to Our Wives
Cindy D. Lee
and
Karen Albers McKenzie

Contents

Preface

Many proponents of social reform have argued repeatedly over the past half-decade that "America is now in a competitive fight for its economic life."[1] Their proposed solution has been a massive mobilization of Americans through a variety of governmental expenditure programs and tax incentives—that is, more regulation of people's social and economic activities by government. The proponents of reform generally advocate the centralization of economic powers in the hands of government, contained only by votes and the democratic political power structure as we know it. Unfortunately, they have given scant thought to how newly acquired economic powers might be misused and abused by the political power structure without changes in the way government itself is governed.

These reformers appropriately call their program of reforms a zero-sum solution, which in our view amounts to no solution at all. Indeed, the readers of this book will quickly learn that the proposed solution is a major source of the United States' economic problems. Instead, we advocate greater regulation *of* government, not regulation *by* government; this proposal offers a positive-sum solution—nothing less than a political route to the enhanced welfare of Americans.

While we speak to a new generation of concerned Americans, our arguments are not totally novel. They draw on the political philosophy that guided the Founding Fathers of this country who, it should be added, held deep-seated suspicions about the long-term viability of uncontained democracies.

Our arguments also are founded on much modern political-economic theory that explores the reasons for rules for government. Those familiar with modern social philosophy quickly will see the arguments as a summary statement of the emerging discipline of constitutional economics (sometimes called constitutional political economy). Those unfamiliar with that literature, however, will be relieved to know that this book is written for educated lay persons and policymakers, not solely for scholars.

---

[1]Lester C. Thurow, *The Zero-Sum Solution: Building a World-Class Economy* (New York: Simon and Schuster, 1985), 13.

Our purpose is straightforward. It is to explain in easily understood terms why containment of government powers through appropriately constructed constitutional rules offers hope for the improvement of our nation's economic well-being, as well as the preservation of our individual freedoms. Democracy is seen in this volume as absolutely essential to the maintenance of political stability. At the same time, we start with the proposition that democracy is a system of rules (or constraints) governing how collective decisions can be made and over what range of issues the collectivity will determine the use of resources. An important question addressed here is What rules can best achieve our various political and economic objectives over the long run?

The chapters repeatedly emphasize that political and economic powers must everywhere be dispersed and simultaneously contained. Our past works have separately argued for a dispersion of economic powers through markets and against the concentration of economic powers through government regulation of business. Our purpose in making those arguments has never been to argue that business powers should be unconstrained, and we do not mean to suggest here that government and business institutions should be constrained to a different degree. Neither do we view people in government as inherently bad or any worse than people in business.

On the contrary, our past arguments have been directed primarily at explaining how competition can be a more effective constraint on business than much government regulation can ever hope to be. Indeed, our opposition to much (but not all) government regulation of business has been founded on the fear that government powers to regulate will be used by the politically powerful business (and other) interest groups to further their ends to the detriment of the politically powerless. In this regard, we assume that people in government and business can be influenced by the same motivations.

We fiercely recommend competition as a means of containing economic and political power. Many benefits spring from competition among firms for consumer dollars, among politicians for political office, among governments for residents and tax bases, and among government bureaus and between government bureaus and private contractors for government budget dollars. By the same token, we fully acknowledge that competition cannot be introduced at all levels of political decisionmaking and other forms of constraints—namely, rules—often must be employed. This is because the self-seeking proclivities of people everywhere, in government and business, must be similarly checked, if for no other reason than to ensure that the nation's scarce resources are not diverted from constructive activity and into nonproductive and unproductive struggles to redirect the nation's income pool. The worry is that unchecked economic powers of government are unnecessarily tempting to current generations of voters to solve their own social problems at the expense of nonvoting future generations. For this reason, maintenance of rules for government (or, for that matter, for us as individuals) must be judged by how the rules affect human welfare over the course of time.

In so many ways, our arguments are relatively simple. They are familiar to us in our daily lives, grounded in the commonly acknowledged need for discipline. To take one of Julie Andrews's lines in the movie *Mary Poppins*, "Some people regard discipline as a chore. For me, it is a kind of order that sets me free to fly." We all need discipline in our personal lives, if for no other reason than to give us direction and to override the temptations of the moment. For similar reasons, governments need discipline. Discipline in the form of adherence to rules and principles can, in the short run, be confining, but in the long run, it can be a means of enriching our lives.

We frankly admit that our proposals for corrections in the American way confront a serious social dilemma: How do we give government authority to control people's behavior and transfer people's income and, at the same time, control the use of government's powers with rules? After all, rules are written on nothing more than paper and are enforced by people, many of whom are a part of the government that harbors the powers of control. Rules are subject to change and manipulation. Unfortunately, we do not have a complete solution to that dilemma. We know, however, that work on the solution first requires an appreciation by the electorate and the elected of the social value of rules for government that are reasonably permanent and confining. We call this appreciation the constitutional perspective. Without that perspective rules for government will not be worth the paper they are written on. Our effort here is geared mainly toward building an understanding of the constitutional perspective.

Acknowledgments

T his book has been several years in the writing. It has benefited greatly from comments and criticisms by many friends and colleagues across this country. We are, however, especially indebted to James Buchanan and Gordon Tullock, who as teachers, colleagues, and coauthors have guided our thinking in economic and social philosophy. The references to their work fill these pages. We are more directly indebted to William Mitchell, political scientist at the University of Oregon, and Laurence Moss, an economist at Babson College, for reviewing the entire final manuscript and for saving us from errors in judgment and substance.

We also have gained greatly from our respective associations with the Center for the Study of Public Choice at George Mason University the Heritage Foundation, and the Center for the Study of American Business at Washington University in St. Louis for stimulating our thinking and for providing an academic atmosphere conducive to completing this book. We have benefited greatly from the editorial and secretarial assistance of Richard Burr, Donna Cole, Joni Hallman, Sue Jones, and Debora Rosenthal.

This book brings together in substantially revised form a series of our papers on constitutional economics that were originally published elsewhere. We fully acknowledge that the original papers that form the bases of chapters 1 and 8 were developed for the Heritage Foundation, which sponsored the first academic conference that adopted the rubic constitutional economics. Chapter 1 was originally published as the introductory chapter to *Constitutional Economics: Containing the Economic Powers of Government* (Lexington, Mass.: D.C. Heath and Company, 1984). A portion of chapter 8 was originally written for the Heritage Foundation for its *Backgrounder* series under the title "Incentives for a Balanced Budget" (August 1982).

Chapter 5 was originally published as *The Political Economy of Social Conflict or Malice in Plunderland* by the International Institute for Economic Research (August 1982), and chapter 6 was a monograph titled *Inflation and Unemployment: The Case for Limiting Political Discretion* distributed by the International Institute for Economic Research (September 1983). Chapter 7 originally appeared as an article, "Constitutional Reform: A Prerequisite for Supply-Side Economics," in the *Cato Journal* (Winter 1983/84), which has given its permission for republication here. And a portion of chapter 9 was an article in the *Cato Journal* titled "Social Security: The Absence of Lasting Reform in the Reform Movement" (Fall 1983). We are pleased that the publishers and editors have granted us permission to include these works in revised form here.

Finally, we are extraordinarily pleased and proud to dedicate this book to our wives, Cindy D. Lee and Karen A. McKenzie, who have added immeasurably to our lives and have made possible the completion of this book.

1

The Constitutional Perspective

Has it not . . . invariably been found that momentary passions, and immediate interests, have a more active and imperious control over human conduct than general or remote considerations of policy, utility or justice?

—Alexander Hamilton[1]

In May 1787, fifty-five delegates from the thirteen original states began to assemble in Philadelphia for the purpose of reconstituting the government of the United States. The assembled delegates labored through four months of secret sessions to produce a document that the states then had to ratify.

To sweat through the sessions and to accomplish what they did, the delegates who gathered that summer at the convention had to be visionaries in the sense that they must have possessed a strong and abiding concern for what they wanted the country to be. They also had to be men of practical affairs because they must have understood the need for compromise and the limited capacity of any group as diverse as the one in assembly to achieve agreement on the basic framework for government, an objective of no mean order.

The acknowledged task of the delegates was to establish a new political order, one that would improve upon the Articles of Confederation adopted several years earlier. Because government of necessity impinges on the uses of economic resources and prescribes economic relationships of people in their private and public dealings, however, any established political order is necessarily an economic order. That is to say, any political order sets bounds on what people can do in their public and private dealings and prescribes rules by which collective decisions on the use of the country's resources will be made. For this reason, the Constitution adopted in Philadelphia in September 1787 can be interpreted as an economic document as well as a political one.

The subject of this book is constitutional economics, a twist of words that on the surface may seem odd. The field of economics may appear to be far

---

[1] *The Federalist,* No. 6 (New York: Modern Library, n.d.), 30.

removed and only tangentially concerned with constitutions, which are essentially political documents. The phrase itself is relatively new, but it aptly reflects a growing concern among economists who believe that every now and then, people must follow the lead of the fifty-five delegates to the Constitutional Convention and reassess their political and economic institutions, not by way of a continuous stream of ad hoc policies but by way of fundamental adjustment to society's basic document.

Accordingly, constitutional economics is fundamentally concerned with the framework for social processes—that is, the structure of and interrelationships among political and economic institutions—all of which are designed to allow people, individually and collectively, to pursue desired ends. The underlying theory of *constitutional economics is a theory of the rules within which political and economic processes will be allowed to operate through time.* The analysis is largely one step removed from specific policies; it is principally concerned with appropriate rules for making public policy decisions, necessarily governmental activities, not with the policy decisions themselves. And because rules typically define the boundaries of behavior, constitutional economics is concerned with the regulation of government, not regulation by government.

While the phrase may be new, the theory underlying constitutional economics is not. The analysis of this book builds on the painstaking and growing volume of work of other economists, social philosophers, and political scientists, dating back to Adam Smith and extending forward to Friedrich Hayek and James Buchanan.[2]

Obviously, constitutional economics is not economics as usual. Granted, one of its major concerns is assessing the efficiency of the economy, as is true of all economic analysis. The thrust of what is generally sought by scholars in the field, however, is social improvement through the development of rules under which government, and therefore the people in government, must operate. Because the central concern is social improvement through institutional design, the constitutional economists cannot avoid normative questions (normally sidestepped in traditional economic discussions). That means the constitutional economist must start with a basic value, for example, individual freedom, and proceed to assess logically the future of individual freedom under different institutional designs—that is, sets of economic, political, and procedural rules for government to follow.

We will expand on all these points, but in the remaining pages of this opening chapter, we hope to whet your appetite by outlining several of the basic premises and concerns underlying the paradigm of constitutional economics.

---

[2]Many of these scholarly works are cited in this chapter. This chapter is founded upon one of these works, Richard B. McKenzie, ed., *Constitutional Economics: Containing the Economic Powers of Government* (Lexington, Mass.: Lexington Books, Inc., 1984).

Later chapters will consider the following in detail:

the logic of rules for government (chapter 2) and constraints on the economic powers of government embedded in the U.S. Constitution (chapter 3);

the federal republic as a structural constraint on the economic powers of state and local governments (chapter 4);

the politicization of society that is likely to accompany the breakdown of constitutional barriers to what government can and cannot do in the economy (chapter 5);

the constraints on the monetary powers of government (chapter 6);

the inherent difficulties of other schools of economic thought, namely, Keynesian and supply-side economics in guiding government policies (chapter 7);

the constraints on the fiscal powers of government (chapter 8);

the constraints on the authority of government to redistribute the nation's income (chapter 9).

The final chapter will summarize the approach of constitutional economics and the conclusions drawn.

Although somewhat different from the conventional economic approach to economic and political issues, the analysis of all these issues, grouped for convenience under the rubric of constitutional economics, is founded on assumptions about individual behavior that are readily accepted in standard economic analysis. Indeed, we assume, as do other economists, that people are motivated by personal interests, many of which are completely selfish but others of which are altruistic. Our purpose is to apply this self-interest postulate to the political setting. In doing that we place the analysis of the political sphere on an equal footing with standard economic analysis of market behavior.

As already noted, constitutional economics approaches many economic problems in a way that sets it apart from traditional economics, the type of economics developed in major introductory textbooks.[3] The purpose of this chapter is to contrast conventional with constitutional economics and to reveal in nontechnical language how constitutional economists tend to perceive the world.

---

[3]See, for example, Campbell McConnell, *Economics: Principles, Problems, Policies* (New York: McGraw-Hill Book Company, Inc., 1984); and Paul Samuelson, *Economics* (New York: McGraw-Hill Book Company, 1983). The McConnell textbook is the most widely adopted book in the history of the economics profession; the Samuelson textbook historically has been a major seller.

Admittedly, by setting out to describe the constitutional perspective, we are venturesome. The old adage that you can set all economists end to end and still have them go off in all directions applies in a restricted way to the study of constitutional issues. Constitutional economists are not in full agreement over how best to model the world in which we live. Frankly, all we can attempt to do here is search various writings of economists who have worked on constitutional issues for common themes on how they approach their subject matter, contrasting their constitutional perspective with the more traditional policy perspective.

The Policy Perspective

Economists do a great many things, and conventional economic analysis has contributed much to our understanding of the complexity of the social world in which we live. A common (but by no means the exclusive) concern of the economist has been with establishing, from conceptual and statistical perspectives, the efficiency or inefficiency of various governmental policies, such as minimum wages and budget deficits. The lessons of such studies are relatively simple but important and, judging by the extent to which citizens are oblivious to them, relatively difficult for many to grasp. The important point is that most of these studies assume that the rules of the political game by which policies are chosen are assumed to be given to (or fixed in) the investigation. The task of conventional analysis is to evaluate the consequences of policies chosen within more or less fixed political rules. In short, the professional competence of the economist typically has been directed toward illustrating the gains that can be had by or the loss that will be imposed upon the public from many government initiatives or policies organized under established political and economic institutions.

Public choice economics, a growing subdiscipline within economics, has broadened the limits of economic inquiry over the past two decades by focusing on the types of policies that can be expected to emerge under any other form of government, principally democratic government. Public choice economics attempts to explain the political attractiveness of policies such as minimum wages and farm subsidies, in spite of what are believed by economists to be their obvious inefficiencies.

Why does bad economics so often make good politics? That is the type of question that has attracted a growing share of the professional attention of economists as well as political scientists who have begun to employ the theories and statistical methods of economists.

Conventional economics, to a considerable extent, subsumes a property rights structure within which trades are consummated and the efficiency of short-term government policies (which can be readily extended or repealed by Congress or state legislatures) is judged. Trades occur because people own things (have rights to things) and see an opportunity to trade the things that they own and appreciate less for the things that they like more and are owned by others. A gain is recorded by both trading parties—the buyer and seller—or else it would not have occurred. (Indeed, the argument often is circular, with appeals being made to the existence of trades for confirmation of the presence of mutual gains.)

The consequences of government intrusions into the marketplace are evaluated by the extent to which they encourage or disrupt mutually benefi-cial trades. Such government intrusions are not judged by economists on the basis of whether the property rights should exist and how those rights should be distributed in the first place. In this context, the morality of property is not a particularly pressing issue. Property, as an institution, is largely taken as a given, settled before the economic analysis commences.[4]

Similarly, the rules within which government must operate and select its policies, whether efficient or inefficient, are subsumed. In traditional econom-ics courses, the beginning student is likely to hear little about the institutional rules (for instance, how votes are taken) by which Congress and state legisla-tures must play the political game or about how those rules affect the types of policies chosen. The policies are again subsumed—given to the economist to evaluate as efficient or inefficient, effective or ineffective.

The typical economist is concerned with the effects of minimum wages on employment, prices, and fringe benefits, not with the institutional setting within which minimum wage laws are repeatedly selected or with how that institutional setting can be modified (or manipulated) to prevent the selection of such laws. Within such a methodological framework, the economist can assume the role of the impartial, amoral analyst—that is to say, a social scien-tist whose personal values of what society should be are left suspended from the work underway.[5] He or she generally is concerned with predicting the effects policies will have, *given the distribution of property rights and the decisionmaking institutions.*

If minimum wages are imposed by government, the economist-qua-scientist can predict that employment will fall in the affected industries, teenage crime

---

[4]Concern with property rights has not been absent from professional discussions. Over the past two decades, concern over the theory of property rights has attracted a growing list of econo-mists. We should include much of this work in constitutional economics.

[5]Economists typically make a sharp distinction between normative and positive economics. Normative economics is concerned with what should or ought to be. Positive economics is concerned with what is. [For a discussion of the perceived distinction between normative and positive economics, see Milton Friedman, "The Methodology of Positive Economics," in *Essays in Positive Economics* (Chicago: University of Chicago Press, 1976), 1-35.] Most economists tend to think of themselves as positivists, predicting consequences of policies. When being asked to make a judgment on which policies should be adopted, they tend to believe that their professional mantle must be dropped.

will rise, prices of some goods will rise, and fringe benefits within the affected labor markets will decrease. If quotas are imposed on imported textiles, the prices of domestic and foreign textiles will rise, domestic textile employment will rise, national income will fall, and the profits of textile magnates will increase. Such predictions have no particular moral content; they are simply statements of what will tend to happen.

The issue of the rightness of government actions, and the implied redistribution of property rights, rarely is discussed by economists *as* economists. Economists have simply made their predictions and allowed others, who may lean on economic analysis, to decide whether the policies are good or bad.

The Constitutional Difference

The perspective of constitutional economics tends to be significantly different from that of traditional economics. Its focus is on the institutional setting—the rules of the game—within which trades are made and public policies are adopted.

Critical to constitutional economics is the simple question, On what grounds can government be justified? If government is deemed necessary, what rules should it follow? How should it operate? Who should be in control? And how should the implied powers of government be contained? When such questions are the focus of analysis, the analyst cannot escape moral or ethical concerns by professing to deal exclusively with predictions.

The constitution is an institutional framework for government inscribed on parchment; it is a setting for permissible government action, what the government can and cannot do. One must wonder how such a topic can be discussed openly and reasonably without some initial ethical stance on what is fundamentally important to people and, therefore, what is to be achieved by institutional design, the central reason for the discussion in the first place. As the late and eminent economist-social philosopher Frank Knight wrote some years back,

> The predicament in which free society finds itself at the moment arises precisely out of the fact that any free society must, by virtue of its nature as a free society, reach agreement, by discussion, on fundamental values, wherever "serious" conflicts of interest arise. For . . . it is only as conflicts of values or of "rights" that conflicts of interests can be discussed, and any solution of such a problem is in the nature of the case a value or mode of rightness.[6]

Presumably, we choose our institutional framework as a device for settling disputes among competing interests. The framework is, by its nature, one

---

[6]Frank H. Knight, in "Fact and Value in Social Science," ed., *Freedom and Reform: Essays in Economics and Social Philosophy* (Port Washington, N.Y.: Kennikat Press, 1947), 243-44.

in which specific ends or policies are left for future decisions—that is, the postconstitutional policy stage. At the constitutional stage of discussion, we can only project forward, appraise the categories of disputes that may arise, and determine how best to resolve the disputes that do arise. At the constitutional stage, we determine the rules of the game that will be played out in future time periods.[7]

Rules that effectively regulate government spring from a desire to have government, and what it can do for the well-being of people, and from a necessity to contain what government can do—to ensure that government will not emerge as a counterproductive social force over time. To make public policy decisions, rules must be followed. We must know how the decisions will be made—for example, by majority vote. The relevant question is Which rules are best? The answer does not always lie in the status quo. Nor does the answer lie in no rules, because such an answer fails to define government or what constitutes governance.

At the constitutional analytical level we cannot be fully informed on the exact policies that will be chosen, so our ability to assess the consequences of the selected rules is necessarily limited. Certainly, our ability to assess the costs and benefits of the rules by which unknown government programs are selected far into the future will be severely circumscribed. Costs and benefits depend on people's evaluations of alternatives, what they are willing and unwilling to do. At the constitutional-institutional stage of decisionmaking, we do not know what all those unknown people (some of whom are unborn) may want to do. Although positive economic analysis may permeate our discussion over the types of rules considered and cost-benefit analysis of a rough-and-ready sort may be included in the constitutional discussion, the discussion cannot, by its nature, be completely economic, completely detached and amoral. We are, as Knight argues at length, concerned with the distribution of power, and such decisions must have some moral fiber.[8] Constitutional economics is not—and cannot be—a strict science in the sense that the analysis is value free or that all the conclusions can be assessed with the same empirical standards applied to policy-oriented propositions founded on more short-term propositions.

---

[7]Surely, as John Rawls has stressed in *A Theory of Justice* [(Cambridge Mass.: Harvard University Press, 1971), chapters 1-4], the justice of the game will depend on the fairness of the social setting in which the rules of the game are determined. In the case of parlor games, we judge games not by the results—someone has to win—but by the agreement on the rules before the game begins. If we allow the game to begin and then proceed to change the rules, people's judgments over which rules should be adopted will be influenced by how they are faring under the old rules. Everyone will want to change the rules to improve his chance of winning. The morality of such rules must then be questioned.

[8]Frank H. Knight, "Freedom as Fact and Criterion," in *Freedom and Reform*, 1-18.

Individual Freedom and Agreement

Constitutional economists have, accordingly, been open about the normative basis of their analysis. They have tended to be strong supporters of individual freedom. Individual freedom has tended to be a fundamental value by which rules are judged. The type of freedom that is supported is not the freedom to do as one pleases. The limited availability of resources to produce goods and services imposes severe restrictions on us all. Rather, the type of freedom supported is, to the maximum extent possible, freedom from coercion either through direct brute, physical force or indirect force by way of government action. Individual freedom is perceived as maximum protection from others directly or indirectly through the government institution that is the subject of social design.

Anarchy, writes James Buchanan, is ideal for ideal people who have no intersecting, competing private interests or, if they do, are able to resolve all conflict potential without the aid of a mediating third party such as government.[9] For passionate people, the type of people we all know, some mediating force often is necessary, however, just to keep people off each other's back and to give them a modicum of freedom from the coercion (brute, physical force) of others.

Government is designed to resolve the very practical problems of the intersecting interests of real people who want the same things and are inclined to impose their will on others to get what they want. But the creation of government does not automatically solve the problem of passionate people, for such people may just as well work their will through government as through physical force. *The point of constitutional constraints on government is to prevent people from doing through government that which they would do in the absence of government. The very purpose of constraints on government is the same as the purpose of government.*

John Locke once observed,

> The end of law is not to abolish or restrain but to preserve and enlarge freedom; for in all states of created beings capable of laws, where there is no law, there is no freedom. For liberty is to be free from restraint and violence of others, which cannot be where there is no law. . . . For who could be free, when every man's human might [may] domineer over him?[10]

Constitutionalists take to heart Locke's central point: If we seek to enlarge individual freedom (to get people off each other's back) by erecting government,

---

[9]James M. Buchanan, *The Limits of Liberty: Between Anarchy and Leviathan* (Chicago: University of Chicago Press, 1975), ix.

[10]John Locke, *The Second Treatise of Government,* Thomas P. Peardon, ed. (New York: Liberal Arts Press, 1954), 32-33.

then we must be just as concerned with ensuring freedom from government, meaning the people who may control government.

The great dilemma confronting constitutional economists and society in general is how to ensure, to the greatest extent possible, such freedom. What do we do? How do we protect ourselves from each other by government and, at the same time, remain protected from the power handed over to government? What types of protection do we need? More importantly, on what types of protection do we agree? Buchanan writes in full:

> Precepts for living together are not going to be handed down from on high. Men must use their own intelligence in imposing order on chaos, intelligence not in the scientific problem-solving but in the more difficult sense of finding and maintaining agreement among themselves. Anarchy is ideal for ideal men; passionate men must be reasonable. . . . These are men and women who want to be free but who recognize the inherent limits that social independence places on them. Individual liberty cannot be unbounded, but the same forces that make some limits necessary may, if allowed to operate, restrict the range of freedom far below that which is sustainable.[11]

Again, in constitutional economics, there is the presumption that individual freedom is important to people, or else there would be little purpose for talking about constitutional design for government. Although often obscured behind the veil of analytical jargon, individual freedom is the prior ethical value by which institutional designs (sets of rules) are evaluated.[12] We make no apologies for the lack of impartiality evident in how we make our points throughout the book.

All that has been said does not mean that constitutional economics is devoid of positive-economic content. We can predict the type of world (what Friedrich Hayek calls patterns of outcomes) that will emerge when people are given freedom to do as they, not government, want to do. Similarly, we can predict the type of world that likely will emerge if people are given the freedom to do as they wish, on a policy-by-policy basis, through government. That sort of comparative institutional analysis enables the constitutionalist to recommend, for public consideration, the types of rules by which government will be regulated. (To repeat, in constitutional economics there is an abiding concern for government regulation, but the focus is on regulation of government, not regulation by government, although the two concerns necessarily run hand in hand.)

In evaluating constitutional principles, agreement among people over the framework is the only reasonable test we know that can be used. The test for

---

[11]Buchanan, *The Limits of Liberty,* ix.

[12]As Knight succinctly stated, "Freedom means freedom to use power, and the only possible limitation on the use of power is intrinsically ethical." Knight, "Freedom as Fact and Criterion," 14.

social improvement in conventional economics is the existence of mutually beneficial trades. Voluntary trades necessarily imply unanimous consent between and mutual benefit to the trading parties, a clear-cut social improvement. In constitutional economics, trades are not generally possible. We can look to the same criteria, agreement, for judging the social worthiness of the rules tendered.

As noted, cost-benefit analysis can be of only limited usefulness, simply because the costs and benefits are not precisely known to anyone at the constitutional stage. Even if cost-benefit analysis of various future government courses of action were available with tolerable accuracy at the constitutional stage, the information would have to be filtered through the minds of the people who seek to form a stable union. And these constitutional participants would, without doubt, be basing their decisions on rough calculations of what might happen in the future if this or that rule were adopted. Clearly, if all agree on a given constitutional provision, the provision must be construed as being desirable.

This does not mean that the concept of public interest is vacuous.[13] To the constitutionalist, however, the only meaningful notion of public interest is that to which individuals would assent if they were impartial and reasonably well informed on the arguments, pro and con.

Agreement has both conceptual and practical dimensions. At the conceptual level, economists play intellectual games, attempting to ascertain as best they can, by logical devices, rules to which people would ascent if they were impartial over the outcome of the discussion and understood the arguments for the rules. The concern is with achieving a rational consensus.[14]

At the practical level, agreement is more difficult to achieve. This is because in real-world political settings, people are not always impartial and reasonably well informed. The rules adopted can affect the welfare of the participants in the debate, and the debaters invariably will attempt to pass rules that further their own particular interests. Still, the intellectual exercises, reflected in what is written in the following chapters, are important and useful. They can guide the debate by suggesting appropriate changes in rules and can help us understand how progress can be made in achieving the consensus we seek.

Models of Man and Government

Throughout this chapter we have emphasized that conventional, postconstitutional economic analysis is concerned with predicting how people in markets

---

[13]For an extended discussion of the congruence of private and public interests, see Geoffrey Brennan and James M. Buchanan, *The Reason of Rules: Constitutional Political Economy* (Cambridge, Mass.: Cambridge University Press, 1985), chapter 3.

[14]The mode of analysis is most accurately represented by Rawls, *A Theory of Justice,* and Buchanan, *The Limits of Liberty.* The constitutionalist's methodology is most completely developed in Brennan and Buchanan, *The Reason of Rules.*

will react to various government policies. To make those predictions, a rather dismal model of man is employed. He is called *homo economicus* (or economic man), often characterized as a greedy, grubbing, utility maximizer who weighs off, in minute detail, the costs and benefits of every action. Whatever he does is done for private gain, as he perceives private gain.

Economic man buys clothes, has sex and then children, gets married, breaks laws, seeks elected office, and lies because of the favorable balance between costs and benefits for every action. He is the sort of person who, presumably, would sell his grandmother into slavery if the expected benefits of such a sale exceeded the expected costs (including the costs associated with imprisonment and being ostracized from his family).

Among economists such a model is adopted for one or both of two principal reasons. Some economists may believe that this is the way man, the purposeful actor, must behave (what else can motivate people to purposeful action if it is not some form of calculated net gain?). Others adopt the economic man model simply as a device for making predictions. By modeling man as a maximizer, we can make reasonably correct predictions of how people in general will behave in different market settings, distorted by one public policy or another.

The value of the model cannot be denied. We note the many contributions conventional economics has made to our understanding of markets and government intervention in them. Nonetheless, we question its descriptive relevance. By simple introspection, we detect that human behavior is guided by more than gain and pain calculations.

Constitutional economics frequently employs a similarly dismal model of government behavior. It is a model of government that, because of the assumed motivations of people who control and run government, is a complete revenue maximizer, one that will not leave a dime in the public's pocket if it is not restricted from doing so. It is a model of government as the pocket-picker, the Leviathan (to use Thomas Hobbes's characterization).

To prevent this government from following its natural inclinations, rules must be devised, and the rules can be either procedural (meaning restrictions on how decisions are made) or substantive (meaning limitations on the range of decisions that can be made). We have noted that democracy is nothing more than a set of rules concerning how government decisions can be made, and many, if not most, of those rules are designed to restrict, not facilitate, the range of government activities.

Clearly, requirements in the United States that bills be passed by both houses of Congress, be endorsed by the president, and not be overturned by the Supreme Court if they are to be law are an obstacle course that intentionally obstructs government actions. If one were concerned about a revenue-maximizing government, such restrictions would appear desirable because they reduce the number of bills that can be passed.

The simple majority voting rule is another procedural restriction on what government can do. A voting rule requiring only a very small fraction of yes votes from eligible voters before an expenditure can be made would likely result in the passage of far more money bills, and far more taxes collected, than a simple majority voting rule. A voting rule requiring more than 51 percent would, of course, restrict the passage of expenditure and tax bills.[15]

Substantive rules include provisions such as the First Amendment, which prohibits in very rigid terms the government from infringing on basic human freedoms. The balanced budget/tax limitation amendment, discussed in chapter 8, would be another substantive restraint on government. (We will see in this book that constitutional economists have other substantive and procedural restraints in mind.) All the rules that form democracy as a political order are a testimonial to the fact that unchecked, open-ended democracy cannot be trusted.

Once we acknowledge that democracy is, by definition, constraints on collective decisionmaking, the logical question then becomes what constraints should be imposed and how we should arrive at them. Even the persons who object to the rules we might select cannot object to the legitimacy of the question.

In the pursuit of constraints on government, is it reasonable to model government as a revenue maximizer and, on that basis, to recommend additional fiscal and monetary rules for government, when in fact we know that government is constrained in part by other rules of democracy? That is a very natural and reasonable question, and it is one we will address at length in the following chapters. As in the case of *economic man* models of conventional economics, Leviathan government may be a reasonably accurate description of the way governments are prone to behave. Very likely, however, it is a partially inaccurate and incomplete description.

There is, however, a more fundamental reason for the Leviathan government model: Our primary purpose in devising a social structure is self-protection from what may happen in the future (since at the constitutional level of discussion, we cannot know for certain what will in fact happen).

Many people are not completely self-serving in the economic sense, and government may never be fully peopled with self-serving types who exploit their position to the maximum degree possible to further their own narrow ends. Admittedly, Congress and the government bureaucracy include many men and women who are honestly concerned about the welfare of society. We must ask, however, "From whom or what do we seek protection?" Clearly, the concern is with Leviathan government, or its real-world approximate, and with narrow, self-interested economic men and women who might—just might—gain control of the reins of government at some future point in time. It is then that we need, for certain, bounds on government.

---

[15]For more on the role of voting rules in determining the cost of government, see James M. Buchanan and Gordon Tullock, *The Calculus of Consent; The Logical Foundations of Constitutional Democracy* (Ann Arbor, Mich.: University of Michigan Press, 1962), especially parts II and III.

Geoffrey Brennan and James Buchanan compare the process of securing a social contract—a constitution—with the process of developing a home construction contract.[16] When we seek to have a home built, we naturally check with friends and associates about prospective builders in the area. We want to ensure that the builder has the necessary technical skills to build the house, but we also are interested in the builder's integrity. If the house plans call for the studs to be of a certain quality and spaced at certain distances, we want to know that his word on abiding by the plans is meaningful, independent of whether the contract is enforceable. In short, we want to make sure that the builder we choose will give us our money's worth, if not more.

The builder may be one of the more respected people in the community, but in devising a contract our talks with attorneys will likely proceed as if we think the builder is a moral reprobate, inclined to shirk on every oral commitment he may have made and to engage, to the extent possible, in what has been called post-contractual opportunism, which amounts to taking advantage of every loophole in the contract.[17] We want the contract to protect us from shirking and opportunism if it occurs, even though we hope and expect it will not.

Similarly, in devising a constitution, we often find the Leviathan model of government useful because it helps us define those rules that will provide the self-protection we as a collective body of people seek. If we use a less austere view of government, our analysis may leave us unprotected.

The Self-Generating Market

Through much of the literature on constitutional economics, we can detect a common intellectual thread, a devotion to markets that are as free as possible from government intrusion. Most of the economists writing in this area have read much of Adam Smith and his scholarly legacy. They recognize his concern for the wealth of nations as a commitment to the future of humankind and the wealth that successive generations will have available to them. Additionally, they understand that the diversity of people imposes severe limitations on the ability of centralized authority.

The flow of humanity around any busy street corner in almost any major city is bound to teach us an important lesson: People differ greatly in color, abilities and talents, inclination to work and play, and tastes and background. We plod along each day with only imperfect knowledge of what we want to

---

[16]See Geoffrey Brennan and James M. Buchanan, *The Power to Tax* (Cambridge, Mass.: Cambridge University Press, 1981). The methodology employed also is repeated and advanced in Brennan and Buchanan, *The Reason of Rules.*

[17]See Benjamin Klein, R.A. Crawford, and A.A. Alchian, "Vertical Integration, Appropriable Rents and the Competitive Contracting Process," *Journal of Law and Economics* 21 (October 1978), 297-326.

do at the time and down the road, knowing that the continuously evolving circumstances of our daily existence are not, and cannot be, the same as the circumstances of others who pass to our left and right and follow in our steps. But we cope as best we can, doing what we can for ourselves and enlisting, where possible, the cooperation of others.

Social organization must ultimately spring from the diverse humanity that can be observed in microcosm from the street corner. The philosophical foundation of individualism, which permeates much writing in constitutional economics, is part ethical and part pragmatic. We have noted a fundamental ethical proposition: The individual, as a legal and social entity, independent of personality, is important. To say that a person is important is to say that he is deserving of rights and of the protection of those rights from the encroachment of others.

The pragmatism of individualism stems from the problem we encounter on the street corner: We know little about the people who pass us by. Any statement of rights must be a constitution of liberty,[18] encompassing general propositions concerning what people can and cannot do, including what they can and cannot do through government. Such a constitution is born in what Hayek has termed our constitutional ignorance. None of us can know very much about others' behavior, so none of us can plan very well the lives of many others.

Government control of people's lives can be opposed, therefore, on both ethical and practical grounds. Government control is an encroachment on the rights—the legal being—of some people by others, that is, by those who run the government. Even though well intended, government control must be the manipulation of some people's lives by people who really do not and cannot know what others want, given their different interests and circumstances.

We may know little of what people want to do with their lives in specific, concrete terms, but we do know that they have interests and, if given the freedom to do so, will pursue them. In the pursuit of those interests, they will seek to do many things for themselves, but they also will, where advantageous, form groups and firms. Trades are inevitable, as people discover differences in their individual evaluations of the resources and goods they have. Competition is inevitable as people seek to make the best deals they can. The markets that self-generate may not be perfect in the sense that they meet the economist's criterion of perfect competition,[19] but they will enable people

---

[18]Friedrich A. Hayek, *The Constitution of Liberty* (Chicago: University of Chicago Press, 1960).

[19]Perfect competition is a highly idealized market structure in economic theory involving four primary assumptions: There are numerous buyers and sellers in the market; all producers are selling a homogeneous product; no one buyer or seller can influence the price by altering his purchases or sales; and entry and exit is completely free. Clearly, no real-world market can meet the criteria of perfect competition. Further, the perfectly competitive model of markets fails to capture the essence of competition, which is to transmit information on what people are able and willing to do for each other. It would appear to us that any reasonable critique of markets must be made in terms of their viable alternatives—such as collective delivery systems, which have handicaps of their own—to satisfy that objective.

to improve their lot, which is all they are supposed to do anyway. They will enable people to overcome partially and imperfectly their constitutional ignorance, for market competition forces trading parties to reveal what they want and are willing to do.

Government plays an inevitable role in helping markets emerge. After all, government defines and enforces property rights, if nothing else. But in making the case for government and markets, as we have done here and do in greater detail in the following chapters, we also create the problems of separating the public and private affairs of people, of regulating governments, and, through that, of regulating markets.

Concluding Comments

The constitutional intellectual setting is a perspective from which we can look out imperfectly into the unknown of future events and attempt to set up bounds on people's rights, which is another way of saying set up limits on individual freedom. Unlimited freedom is a contradiction in terms. If all people have rights, then the rights of all are limited; freedom is limited, by definition. Government is necessary, as we argue in detail in the next chapter, but it is an institution through which people operate. The establishment of individual rights necessarily entails limits on what people can do through government.

Constitutional economics is primarily concerned with establishing those rules for government; conventional economics is primarily concerned with the efficiency of economic policies once those rules are set in place. The two approaches necessarily compliment one another. Admittedly, constitutional economics is beset with critical problems that have no easy resolution. Rules cannot possibly cover all circumstances and are ultimately subject to interpretation by people, most notably judges. The limited inclusiveness of rules, especially those that comprise a social contract, necessarily leaves open the prospects for opportunistic behavior—for violations of the spirit, if not the letter, of the rules and for taking advantage of loopholes in rules. One must wonder if any set of specific rules can ever work very well in the absence of a commonly acknowledged set of higher, ethical rules of behavior.[20]

Because rules must ultimately be interpreted by judges, constitutional reform often means a substitution of the judicial process for the legislative process as a means of governance. "Unfortunately," writes Judge Robert Bork, "we do not have at hand a general principle by which we may determine which subjects are best controlled by judges and which by elected representatives."[21] Frankly, such a caveat suggests only that we should investigate

---

[20]For an elaboration of this problem with rules, see Terry L. Anderson and Peter J. Hill, "Constitutions and Ideology: Substitutes or Compliments," a paper presented at Allied Social Sciences Association annual meeting, December 1986.

[21]Robert H. Bork, "A Lawyer's View of Constitutional Economics," in McKenzie, ed., *Constitutional Economics,* 227.

arguments for and against using the legislative and judicial processes for insights into how social decisions can best be made.

The rest of this volume explores how constitutional economics can contribute to the formulation of long-term policies, which we call constitutional rules, principles, or precepts. We may not develop the "general principle" that Judge Bork says is lacking, but we may understand more about the relative importance of rules in social decisionmaking.

2
The Reason for Rules

> When tribunals and regulations proliferate, when legislators become
> administrators and judges become legislators, and laws become orders
> instead of rules, government becomes not only arbitrary but ineffective.
> —Shirley Robin Letwin[1]

I n the absence of scarcity there would be no need for rules. Each of us
could consume as much as we wanted of everything we wanted without
having to interact with, or have an impact on, anyone else. A world
without scarcity, however, is a utopian dream. No matter how proficient we
become at transforming the raw ingredients of nature into those things we
value, our desired consumption always will exceed our productive capability.
Because of resource and technical limits, we are faced with an abundance of
scarcity. Because of scarcity, individuals must interact with one another, and
rules will emerge to order this interaction.

A universal response to scarcity is division of labor. By concentrating on a
few productive activities, individuals can take advantage of differences in natural abilities and the skills that develop through training to produce more than
if they attempted to produce everything they wanted.[2] Because of specialization, individuals produce much more of a few things but much less of most
things than they want to consume personally. Each of us is dependent on the
productive efforts of millions of others for almost everything we consume.
Without specialization we would be destitute. But if we are to realize the
benefits of specialization, we must have some structure of rules that allows the
billions of people scattered around the world to interact with each other in a
cooperative way.

---

[1]"A Case Study of the United Kingdom," *The Mont Pélerin Society, General Meeting Paper,* 1982.

[2]The importance of the division of labor in the creation of wealth is emphasized by Adam Smith,
who began his book *The Wealth of Nations* with the sentence, "The greatest improvement in the
productive powers of labor, and the greater part of the skill, dexterity, and judgment with which it
is any where directed, or applied, seem to have been the effects of the division of labor" (An
Inquiry into the Nature and Causes of the Wealth of Nations [New York: Modern Library, 1937],
p. 3).

Because of scarcity, cooperation is desirable, but it is also because of scarcity that competition is inevitable. Each of us wants more than we have, and the only way to get more is by competing against others for limited resources. People often mistakenly blame competition for social ills and argue that these ills would be cured if competition somehow were eliminated. Competition is not the cause, but rather the consequence, of the ultimate social ill, scarcity. Since there is no foreseeable way of eliminating scarcity, the important question is not how to eliminate competition but how to structure the rules for social interaction in such a way that competitive behavior leads to productive and cooperative results. Competition can be either productive or destructive depending on the rules that define permissible behavior limits on our dealings with each other.

One organizational possibility is to have no rules, or more accurately, the rule of force. Everyone would be free to do whatever he wanted as long as he possessed the power to force his will on others. Competition in this setting takes the form of unrestrained brute force. There is much to object to here. There would be little freedom in the meaningful sense of "independence of the arbitrary will of another."[3] If one person has physical power, he can force others to work for him, to be his slaves. But the master today has little assurance that he will not be someone else's slave tomorrow.

In addition, the rule of force is not likely to motivate productive and cooperative competition. There would be no incentive to devote one's effort entirely, or even significantly, to the production of wealth, since it would be subject to forcible expropriation by others. Successful competition would depend as much on developing the skills needed for plundering and defending against plunder as it would on developing wealth-producing skills. Even if one survived, one's standard of living would be low. With limited resources being devoted overwhelmingly to predation and predator-avoiding activities, little would be produced, and poverty would be the norm. Life in this Hobbesian jungle would indeed be "solitaire, poor, nasty, brutish, and short."[4]

Freedom from rules is simply not a viable social possibility. In a world without rules, there would be little genuine freedom or prosperity.

---

[3]For this definition of freedom and a strong justification for it, see Friedrich A. Hayek, *The Constitution of Liberty*, (Chicago: University of Chicago Press 1960), especially chapters 1 and 2.

[4]These are the words seventeenth-century philosopher Thomas Hobbes used to describe life in a world without government (in a state of nature). It was the unattractiveness of this setting that, in Hobbes's mind, explained why individuals opt for the alternative of an all-powerful government and the surrender of their independence in the process. See Thomas Hobbes, *Leviathan* (London: J.M. Dent, Everymans Library, 1943).

For Hobbes there was no middle ground; either anarchy or Leviathan (complete control by government) were the alternatives. A primary concern of constitutional economics is that of exploring how this middle ground can be achieved and maintained in the face of unrelenting pressures toward the Hobbesian Leviathan. For a seminal work in constitutional economics and a detailed discussion of the problems in maintaining this middle ground, see James M. Buchanan, *The Limits of Liberty: Between Anarchy and Leviathan* (Chicago: University of Chicago Press, 1975).

Social Order at the Cost of Freedom

Emergence from the Hobbesian jungle, or state of nature, which finds a "war of each against all," is necessary if we are to realize the benefits of a civil social order. Underlying any beneficent social order are rules that will impose limits on individual behavior. All rules necessarily serve to restrain freedom of action to some extent. When rules or laws are generally applied, the limits placed on each individual can, by limiting the actions of others, expand the freedom of all. When they become too detailed and numerous, however, rules can destroy freedom just as effectively as no rules at all. Traditionally, there has been a strong tendency toward too many rules. Societies have been obsessed by the horrors of disorder. Plunder, riot, murder, and mayhem have been the common experience, and loss of freedom has been seen as the unavoidable price for order. The prevalent human condition throughout the history of civilization has been subjugation to rigid and brutally enforced rules specifying the type and location of one's work, travel, entertainment and religious practices, and even one's social status. The overriding problem of society has been that of maintaining order, and only the most limited amount of freedom is considered compatible with this objective.

While a rigid social order based on detailed rules concerning every aspect of behavior may be preferable to the chaos that would prevail in the no-rules setting, one need not look very hard for its shortcomings. The first problem is to find those worthy of exercising the authority that must be present in a controlled society. To give someone, or some group, the power to impose and enforce an extensive set of rules on society is to yield a power that is subject to enormous abuse. As we will see as this chapter progresses, the power that any government possesses, no matter how limited and democratic the government, is likely to be abused. The sweeping authority that government needs to maintain detailed control of society is sure to be abused. Those who are in positions of authority will be in a position to use their power to advance their interests at the expense of their subjects and seldom will be able to resist the temptation to do so. The only possible advantage an all-powerful government has over anarchy is that the exercise of government authority typically is very visible. Moving from the anarchy of no rules to the detailed control of a Leviathan government is to substitute one thief in the light for many thieves in the night.

The costs in terms of sacrificed freedoms is much that same regardless of whether the freedoms are sacrificed to anarchy or to unlimited government. Someone who finds himself forced to toil for the benefit of others is not likely to care who his masters are—the physically dominant brutes in the jungle or the politically dominant brutes in the goernment. Even if a benevolent dictator, who exercised Leviathan power with compassion, were in charge, the problem of productivity would remain. Individuals will not work as creatively and diligently for objectives that are handed down by authority, no matter how noble these objectives may be, as they will for personally chosen goals. To allow individuals to pursue personal objectives has been seen, throughout most of human history, as a move away from the control needed if social order and predictability are to be maintained.

Traditionally the social choice has appeared to be between some combination of two unfortunate states: the regimentation of detailed rules and the disruption of social disorder. Society could have less of one only at the cost of having more of the other. There appeared to be no realistic hope that individuals living together in a world of scarcity could simultaneously have fewer rules and more social order. Not until the seventeenth and eighteenth centuries did moral and political philosophers begin to give serious consideration to a structure of rules that offered genuine potential for finding a way out of this social dilemma.

The Rule of Private Property

The writings of John Locke, Adam Smith, Bernard Mandeville, and a few other philosophers gave birth to the idea of the potential compatibility between individual freedom and social order. Crucial to this idea was a fundamental shift regarding the role of rules in accomplishing their purpose. Previously the role of social rules was to force particular results that were seen as necessary for the maintenance of a productive social order. Fields had to be tilled, cloth had to be woven, cattle had to be tended, and particular services had to be rendered. Concentrating authority in the hands of a ruler who could require these things to be done was seen as the only guarantee that they would be done. The fundamental insight of the aforementioned moral and political philosophers was that establishing general rules of behavior that ignored particular outcomes could create an environment in which the social order was maintained while individuals were given what was in the seventeenth century unprecedented freedom of action. Furthermore, as a happy by-product of this freedom, productivity would be increased.

Underlying this new view of rules was the belief that individual goals and aspirations are not only important in their own right, but that the social energy generated when people are given the freedom to pursue their personal advantages can, under certain rules and institutional arrangements, promote rather than disrupt a productive social order. Crucial to all this are rules that clearly define individual rights by providing assurance to individuals that they can plan and carry out their activities with the confidence that others will not arbitrarily confiscate the return on their efforts. Lacking such elementary rights, people have little motivation to be productive and no basis for them to interact with each other in a civil manner.

With this in mind, the institution of private property and the rules that guarantee individuals the right, within broad limits, to utilize their private property for their own purposes can be seen as a crucial ingredient in a productive and civil society. Speaking to the productivity of property rights, Adam Smith argued that "[c]ommerce and manufactures can seldom flourish long in any state . . . in which the people do not feel themselves secure in the possession of their property. . . ."[5]

Jean Jacques Rousseau, the eighteenth-century French philosopher, emphasized the connection between civil order and property when he wrote, "The first man who, having enclosed a piece of ground, bethought himself of saying, 'this is mine,' and found people simple enough to believe him, was the real founder of civil society."[6] Once a system of property rights is in place, with individual rights to property well defined and mutually respected, the groundwork has been laid for meaningful individual freedom, genuine human rights, and cooperative interaction among millions of people, each competing for a larger claim on limited resources.

The ownership of property gives individuals assurance that their decisions are controlling over some range of human action. In the absence of such assurance, individual freedom has no operative meaning because all facets of one's life are subject to the control of others. This concept of individual freedom is closely aligned to human rights, which are often, though erroneously, seen as threatened by an emphasis on the importance of property rights. If human rights mean anything, they mean the right of individuals to use some resources for purposes of their own choosing—to be able to own resources and exercise control over them as private property. Rather than human rights and property rights conflicting, they are in fact mutually reinforcing. In a society where human rights are not valued, property rights soon cease to be respected. And unless property rights are respected, the notion of human rights will be nothing more than a meaningless pretense.

Human rights and the individual freedom that necessarily accompanies these rights are highly valued objectives quite apart from any instrumental function they may perform. Benefits are, however, realized from the personal freedoms that, though secondary to personal freedom itself, are crucial to the discussion of constitutional economics. There is no more effective way of generating socially productive energy than by giving individuals the freedom to pursue their personal advantage as they see it. It must be emphasized that the freedom to pursue personal advantage does not guarantee socially beneficial outcomes. In many, if not most, settings it does not. As we have seen, in the Hobbesian jungle actions motivated by self-interest will be destructive of wealth and ultimately of individual freedom itself.

It is true, however, that socially desirable outcomes materialize when people are free to advance their personal advantages within the rule of private property. When private property rights are well defined and respected, if one

---

[5]Smith, *The Wealth of Nations,* 862.

[6]J.J. Rousseau, *The Social Contract* (London: J.M. Dent & Sons, 1958), 192.

individual wants something that he does not own, he will have to pay the owner for it. Therefore, under the rule of private property, the important form of competition among people attempting to promote their own purposes involves being willing to outbid each other for goods, services, and resources. Because of this competition, the price an individual must pay for a product will be at least as high as what others are willing to pay. This means that the prices people have to pay in the marketplace for privately owned goods reflect the value of those goods in their best alternative uses. Faced with these prices, people are motivated to acquire products and resources only if they believe that the ways in which they will use them are at least as valuable as the ways in which others will use them.

This price competition has important implications for the possibility of a cooperative and productive social order in which individuals are free, within broad limits, to pursue their own ends. For any society to be productive, it must be a society in which people are able to communicate and cooperate with each other. Directing scarce resources into their most valuable employments is a necessary task in a productive society, and it requires cooperative communication among competing resource users. The productivity that comes from specialization requires cooperative interaction among people who have produced what others want and who want what others have produced.

It is exactly this type of communication and cooperation that is motivated by the price competition that occurs under the rule of private property. As has already been noted, the market prices that materialize from private ownership and exchange are the means by which millions of people communicate the value they place on different resources. Similarly, our willingness to pay the market price for a product provides others with information on its value to us.

This process of price competition does more than allow people to communicate with each other; it motivates people to communicate honestly. Honesty can be expected to prevail because it is in no one's interest to be dishonest with respect to the prices they ae willing to pay. It is in the self-interest of market participants to assess carefully the value they will realize from different products, and they have no motivation to communicate their desire for more of a product unless it is honestly worth more to them than the market price. Further, each participant in this communication process is motivated to give the concerns of others as much consideration as his own. When an individual decides that the value of a product is not worth the price, he is in effect saying, "others are telling me honestly that the product is worth more to them than it is to me, so I will consume less so they can consume more."

This system of communication, honesty, and consideration obviously does not work with perfection. For example, because of transaction costs, market prices will not always reflect accurately the value of products and resources to others. Some people will purchase products that are worth somewhat more than others. Because it is sometimes difficult for consumers to determine quality, it is occasionally possible for sellers to realize temporary advantages by dishonestly representing their products.[7] Even in the face of these imperfections, however, the advantages we realize from private property, market exchange, and price competition are impressive. Because the information and incentives generated by market competition allow each of us to interact cooperatively and honestly with billions of people around the globe, we are able to specialize our efforts, put resources to their most productive uses, and thus generate enormous wealth.

Surely even more important than the wealth that is generated under a system of private property and market exchange is the individual freedom that this system permits. Under the rule of private property, people can be given a large measure of freedom because this rule makes people accountable for their actions. Every time an individual puts a resource to some use, he imposes a cost on society. That cost is measured in terms of the value of the resource in alternative uses. When the individual owns the resource in question, he is fully acountable for this cost, since by using the resource himself, he has to sacrifice the amount others are willing to pay for it. Given this accountability, there is no harm, and in fact much benefit, in giving people wide freedom to employ (use themselves or sell to others) resources as they choose.

In cases where important resources are not privately owned, people find themselves clamoring, often with good reason, for detailed restrictions on individual choice. It is difficult to imagine, for example, dividing up and parceling out the atmosphere as private property. Therefore, people are not accountable for the cost they impose on others when they use the atmosphere as a dump for their auto exhaust, industrial smoke, and so on. The result is a constant tendency toward excessive air pollution and huge federal and state bureaucracies whose purpose is to reduce pollution by imposing a host of detailed restrictions on our behavior. Another example concerns the blue whale, which because of its size and migratory habits, is not easily owned as private property. Again, in the absence of the rule of private property, those who slaughter blue whales are not accountable for the very real cost of this slaughter. From a natural population that is estimated to have been approximately 200,000, blue whales have been killed to the point where there are fewer than 10,000 remaining. People who otherwise place great value on

---

[7]By transaction costs we mean the cost of things such as acquiring information on the availability, price, and quality of different products. Because information is never perfect, these costs are never zero and will be higher for some products and in some markets than others. But there are ongoing incentives to keep these costs as low as possible in open markets because doing so expands markets and opportunities for private gains. Similarly, product misrepresentation never will be completely eliminated, but this problem is mitigated by market forces. Many market arrangements reduce the sellers' potential to gain by fraud because both buyers and sellers benefit from such arrangements. For a useful discussion of these arrangements, see Ben Klein and Keith Leffler, "The Role of Market Forces in Assuring Contractual Performance," *Journal of Political Economy* (August 1981), 615-41.

individual freedom are, with strong justification, urging that international controls be placed on whalers.

It cannot be overemphasized that, in a very real and direct way, the institution of private property protects our personal freedoms. The reason for this goes beyond the fact that without private property the government faces no barrier to violating individual freedom. In the absence of private property and the accountability that goes with it, there will be widespread sympathy for controls over a considerable span of individual behavior. Social order requires that people be accountable for their actions, and in absence of accountability through the general rule of property, one can be sure that more detailed rules will be imposed on individual behavior. It should come as no surprise that in those countries in which reliance on private property and exchange is officially frowned upon, one is most likely to find blatant violations of basic human rights and freedom.

The rule of private property aims at no particular ends. Rather, it establishes a system of accountability within which people can be left free to pursue their own ends, whatever they may be, without concern over the maintenance of social order. The way to judge this system is not in terms of particular results but in terms of how well the process it establishes allows people to interact freely, honestly, and with consideration for others. This does not mean that particular results are unimportant. But the social outcomes that materialize are more likely to be advantageous when the emphasis is on a process of accountability that allows maximum individual freedom. As F.A. Hayek has pointed out, "If we knew how freedom would be used, the case for it would largely disappear. . . . Our faith in freedom does not rest on the foreseeable results in particular circumstances but in the belief that it will, on balance, release more forces for the good than for the bad."[8]

The advantage of a system based on the rule of private property is that it allows the freedom necessary to accomplish desirable things that no one could have predicted or programmed ahead of time. As will become clear as this book unfolds, attempts to force particular outcomes, no matter how desirable those outcomes may be, typically work to undermine the proess that is our best hope for maintaining an orderly and prosperous society.

The Need for Government

The advantages we realize from observing the rule of private property are general advantages. The rule of private property is not designed to allow particular individuals to benefit at the expense of others.[9] Rather, it is to allow

---

[8]Hayek, *The Constitution of Liberty*, 31.

[9]It is widely believed that the free market economy, which is based on private property, is a system designed to favor the business community. This is in fact not true, as evidenced by the constant efforts of business to substitute government control for the market process. For a detailed discussion of the love-hate relationship between business and government, see chapter 5 of this book.

for a process whereby people can interact cooperatively and productively to the benefit of all. The price that must be paid for these benefits is a measure of restraint on the part of all of us. Unless we refrain from attempts to infringe upon the property rights of others, the advantages we receive from the process of specialization and exchange will be diminished for all as we move back toward the Hobbesian jungle.

Although collectively we are worse off when property rights are violated, it is possible for individuals to improve their situation by taking the property of others. Of course, the individual who steals, plunders, and fails to honor his contractual obligations will find that he is living in a slightly less productive and orderly society than before. But just as the benefits from a productive and cooperative society are general, so it is that the costs of reduced productivity and order are spread over the entire population. The thief will bear such a small percentage of this general cost of his thievery that he can safely ignore it. If all others continue to respect the property rights of others, the successful thief can receive all the general advantages of living in a productive order while at the same time realizing the additional advantage that comes from plundering the wealth of others.

Being the only parasite on a healthy organism is a very advantageous situation. But when there is a multitude of parasites all attempting to free ride on the same organism, no one benefits. The organism eventually dies, and so do the parasites. This does not provide sufficient motivation, however, for anyone to stop being a parasite and return to productive activity. Everyone knows that denying himself the immediate gains from plunder will be insufficient to preserve the process of productivity and exchange if it is being destroyed because others are failing to respect property rights. Indeed, in a world where everyone is engaged in plunder, it would be the height of folly to confine one's own effort to productive activity. In the absence of external constraint on individual behavior, the process based on private property will tend to break down as first the few and then the many find it to their personal advantage to infringe upon the property rights of their fellows.

Another way of looking at this problem is to liken respect for property rights to what economists refer to as public goods. A public good is one that, when provided for the benefit of one individual in the community, is simultaneously made available for all. The difficulty that arises with public goods is that each individual in the community can hope to benefit from the public goods paid for by others. If, for example, national defense is provided, each individual in the community will benefit whether he contributes or not. Conversely, if others are not contributing, each individual knows that his contribution will make little difference and will generate benefits that are worth less to him than they cost. The tendency is for people, acting individually, to contribute too little for public goods.

The productive social order that comes with respect for private property rights is a public good in the ame sense as national defense. As with any public good, individuals must pay for it. In this case, individual payments take the form of restraint in the face of temptation to transgress the rights of others. Since individuals know that they can benefit from the productive social order that is being paid for by the restraint of others, whether they restrain themselves or not, when they are left entirely to individual action we can expect too little respect for private property rights (too little purchase of a productive social order).

When faced with the problems of providing valuable public goods, individuals generally will agree to pay their share of the cost if, through their agreement, everyone else can be made to pay his share as well. Collective agreement has the potential for making everyone better off.[10] For obvious reasons, however, collective agreements of this type require some mechanism for enforcement. Without the power to impose penalties on individuals who refuse to carry their share of the burden in providing a public good, shirking and free riding will soon become prevalent, agreement or not. The authority to exercise this power comes from the institution of government.

Government is the repository of coercive, or police, power, and it is the legitimate role of government to exercise this power to enforce a society's rules of the game. In this capacity government is to play the part of an impartial referee who knows the rules of the game, observes the play of the participants, and imposes penalties on those who violate the rules. Inevitably, judgment calls must be made, but the good referee makes those calls as evenhandedly as possible, with no desire to affect the outcome of the game one way or the other. The good government, as the good referee, does not strive for particular results but rather is concerned with enforcing a set of agreed upon rules that allows outcomes to unfold from the interplay of competitors who are free to operate within the limits established by those rules.

By enforcing the rule of private property, government is performing as a referee and requiring that those who benefit from the productive social order contribute their part to maintaining it. Those who persist in violating the property rights of others will, when government is doing its job, find themselves imprisoned, or removed from society. This has the effect of turning the public good provided by respect for private property into a price-excludable public good; those who do not pay the price are excluded from the benefits. In this case paying the price requires respecting the property rights of others.[11]

---

[10]The problems associated with reaching collective agreements are an important concern in the branch of economics known as public choice. For a complete discussion of these problems and how they are confronted with various success by different types of democratic institutions, see James M. Buchanan and Gordon Tullock, *The Calculus of Consent: The Logical Foundations of Constitutional Democracy,* (Ann Arbor, Mich.: University of Michigan Press, 1962). This book played a key role in initiating the field of public choice.

[11]In some cases it is relatively easy to exclude nonpayers from enjoying the benefits of a public good. For example, a football game provided for one person in the stadium is available simultaneously for the enjoyment of everyone else in the stadium, but those who refuse to pay at the gate can be denied admission. In such cases as this, public goods can be provided by private entrepreneurs. The only way of denying people the benefits of public goods such as national defense and a productive social order is by excluding them from society. Clearly, we do not want to grant an individual entrepreneur the authority to remove people from society. We all will rest more comfortably if this power is exercised collectively in accordance with rules that apply generally.

With the government enforcing the rule of private property, we can all benefit from the productivity and freedom that comes from harmonious interaction with our fellow citizens in the game of specialization and exchange. Without government enforcement, we would soon find ourselves back in the insecurity and poverty of the Hobbesian jungle.

Up to this point, we have been discussing primarily the protective or rule-enforcement role of government. The government has to enforce general rules if desirable public goods, including social order, are to be provided. In this capacity the government makes no choices in the sense of weighing the benefits and costs of alternatives. Conceptually, it must determine whether the rules are being obeyed and take predetermined measures if they are not. The discussion has, however, touched on a further function of government. Public goods other than social order exist, and the government also is the institution through which members of the community choose which of these goods to finance publicly, how extensively they should be funded, and whether they should be provided through public or private arrangements. In this capacity government is called upon to make genuine economic choices and when public provision of goods is chosen, to engage in directly productive activities.[12]

The government is more than just the referee; to some extent it is a participating player as well. In this capacity as a player in the game, the government must be subject to rules just as the other players are. This situation presents some rather difficult problems. The fact is that the government is necessarily exempt from certain rules that apply to all other players in the game. The government, in one sense, has the authority to violate property rights by forcing citizens to pay for certain public goods. One can argue that this is not really a violation of property rights, since everyone is part of the collective process in which the decision to provide public goods is made and goods are provided in return for the payment made. This may be, but it remains true that the government's legal power to compel people to make payments places it outside the rules that apply to other individuals and organizations.

Not only does the government enter into the game under a less restrictive set of rules than is imposed on nongovernment players, but it is government that enforces the rules on everyone, including government. Letting a player in any game be the judge of his own infractions creates an opportunity for abuse that few can be expected to resist completely. Of course, the government is not a single player but rather a collective of the members of the community. Even so, in their role as political decisionmakers, individuals will coalesce around certain objectives and will be tempted to take whatever action is necessary to realize their objectives. Whether acting individually or in groups,

---

[12]Buchanan makes a clear distinction between the rule enforcement role of government and its role as economic decisionmaker and provider of goods. See Buchanan's discussion titled "The Protective State and the Productive State" in chapter 4 of the *The Limits of Liberty*.

people find fewer things easier to do than justifying in their minds those actions that advance their interests. As a player in the game, the government must be called on violations of the rules just as all other players are. But how can we be sure that the government will be sufficiently diligent in calling infractions and imposing penalties against itself?

It is comforting to believe that by getting good people to serve in government, this problem will be taken care of. Comforting it may be, but it is not very realistic. The reason for government power in the first place is that we cannot rely on good people voluntarily ignoring their own advantages to advance the general good. It was Jefferson's observation that "[i]n questions of power, let no more be heard of confidence in man, but bind him down from mischief by the chains of the Constitution." James Madison also saw this problem clearly when, in arguing for ratification of the U.S. Constitution, he wrote:

> If men were angels, no government would be necessary. If angels were to govern men, neither external nor internal controls on government would be necessary. In framing a government which is to be administered by men over men, the great difficulty lies in this: you must first enable the government to control the governed; and in the next place oblige it to control itself.[13]

A productive and orderly society depends on rules, and those rules must be enforced by government. In a fully productive society, government also will engage directly in economic activities under the constraint of rules that, though less restrictive, are similar to those imposed on others. It is important that these rules be obeyed. No society will long remain free and productive unless they are. But how do we impose the discipline necessary for government to enforce these rules on itself? What problems must be considered in this crucial effort?

The Threat of Government

The power needed by government if a productive social order is to be maintained can easily be used to undermine that order. The existence of government power presents both a threat to and an opportunity for each of us. On the one hand, government can impose costs on us without providing offsetting benefits, in effect violating our property rights. On the other hand, it is possible for each of us to use government power to acquire benefits for which others will have to pay, thus creating an opportunity to realize personal gain by engaging in political efforts that are completely nonproductive. Ideally, government action of this type will be kept to a minimum. But doing so is no easy task.

---

[13]Federalist 51, *The Federalist Papers*.

Constantly demanding our attention are particular problems that it appears we could solve if only government would force particular people to behave in particular ways. This type of government action invariably imposes a cost on some to the advantage of others. What is of real significance and so difficult to keep in mind is that any government that attempts to force particular results can, by undermining the general process that allows for both freedom and a productive social order, create many more problems than it solves.

For the sake of illustration, assume that the government is performing its enforcement function perfectly: Everyone respects the rule of private property, and the process of specialization and exchange allows for the cooperative and productive social interaction discussed earlier in this chapter. Assume that this market process also is working perfectly: Individual freedom within the rules results in all resources being put to their most valuable use, and the maximum amount of wealth is being produced and widely shared. Even with this perfection, it would still be true that this is a world of scarcity, and people would find cause for complaint.

For example, when the process of specialization and exchange is working perfectly, producers in their use of resources are completely responsive to the desires of consumers. When consumer preferences change, purchasing decisions increase the profits of those who are producing goods that are now demanded more and reduce the profits of those who are producing goods that are now demanded less. When a new technology creates new goods that consumers value more than existing goods, or allows existing goods to be produced more economically, consumer choice will reward those producers who quickly put the new technology to use and punish those who do not. This process, which provides ongoing incentives to provide consumers with greater value at less sacrifice, is the basis of economic progress. Over the long run this economic progress has bestowed material wealth (and individual freedom) that would never have been realized had government attempted to create progress directly rather than establish the setting in which it can occur spontaneously. But long-term progress necessarily requires temporary dislocations that impose genuine costs on those who are dislocated.

Progress comes from destroying particular jobs. In a world of scarcity there will always be more work to do than can possibly be done. The hard problem is not finding jobs for people but finding those jobs in which their contribution is most valuable. With progress, some existing jobs and skills are always becoming obsolete as new opportunities arise that make more valuable use of human effort. We collectively benefit from this destruction of particular jobs because it releases labor that can be used more productively elsewhere. If, for example, we had to rely on the same telephone technology that was in use at the turn of the century, more than half the adult population would have to be employed as telephone operators to process current telephone traffic.

This is all true, but it will be small comfort to the individual who finds his job eliminated and his skills obsolete. Such an individual usually can find another job, but it may take time, require moving away from family and friends, and accepting a much lower salary than he previously earned. From this individual's perspective, his particular problems would best be solved by having the government interfere with the process of social interaction that puts his job at the mercy of consumer preferences and technical progress. The government could do this by protecting the firm for which the individual works against competition, by covering the firm's losses with subsidies or loan quantities, or by taking over the firm and running it as a nationalized enterprise. In either case the communication between consumer and producer would be broken as consumers were forced to buy, through their taxes, products they would not voluntarily buy and prevented from buying products they would rather have. The government is, in effect, violating the property rights of some (consumers) to provide selective benefits to others (such as politically influential producers).

If the government uses its coercive powers to give a particular firm and its employees preferential exemption from the rules of the game, the value that comes from playing the game is reduced; the incentive to innovate and use resources efficiently is diminished. Like the thief who violates the rules of private property, those who benefit from government infringement of the same rules will live in a somewhat less productive and orderly society. As with the thief, however, those who receive all the benefits from violating the rules suffer only a small part of the cost. The cost of a less productive and orderly society is spread over everyone. This cost will do little to dampen individuals' enthusiasm for using government to bend the rules in their favor. Restraining government temptations to bend the rules to promote particular ends provides a public good. But as we have seen, individuals have little motivation to make personal sacrifices to provide public goods.

So we see that there are pressures for government to provide too little of the public good that comes from respecting property rights. For similar reasons there are pressures for government to finance excessively other types of goods. Most goods that government finances are not pure public goods. For example, the federal government provides much of the financing for flood control projects. Such a project certainly provides benefits to everyone in a region protected from floods, but it is hard to make a compelling case that everyone in the entire country benefits. Because the benefits are quite focused geographically, a flood control project does not provide a public good for the country at large. State and local governments commonly finance the construction of sports arenas and golf courses. These are not public goods under even the most lenient interpretation. Only those who watch sporting events or play golf receive the benefits provided by these facilities. Governments finance many goods that provide selective benefits. In doing so they are imposing costs on the general public to provide benefits for a selected few.

Obviously, a group that will receive most of the benefits from a publicly financed good will favor such financing. Through government financing everyone in the community can be forced to bear the cost of a good that primarily benefits the favored group. Government financing of nonpublic goods allows special interest groups to benefit in the same way a thief does—by receiving private benefits at the expense of others. Not only will special interest groups want the government to provide many nonpublic goods, but since their taxes pay only some fraction of the total cost, they will want much more extravagant sports arenas, golf courses, and flood control levies, for example, than if they had to pay the entire bill. Special interests can be expected to pressure government to finance many goods that are not public goods and to finance them excessively.

To the extent that government can yield to pressures to provide differential benefits to favored groups, government poses a threat to each of us. While we may be on the receiving end with some government programs, this advantage will likely be more than offset by our being forced to pay for the benefits of others.

Restricting Democracy

It is one thing for an individual or group to want differential benefits from government and another for them to be successful in obtaining them. The hope of a republican,[14] or democratic, form of government is that by giving the people the right to be heard on the issues, government will remain responsive to the citizens' general interests and concerns. To the extent that this hope is realized, only genuinely public goods will be provided and only when they are worth more than they cost. Government will perform its refereeing function by preventing some from obtaining gains at the expense of others. In comparison with alternative political arrangements, democratic institutions can do a tolerable job of restraining government. But as desirable as democracy is in comparison to the alternatives, allowing government to do anything agreed to by a majority of the voters, or by a majority of their elected representatives, does not provide an adequate constraint on government power.

It is easy to imagine, for example, a majority of the people in a community deciding to impose a tax on the remaining members of the community but not on themselves. The fact that such a selective tax received a majority vote in an honest election would not justify it. Few of us would want to live in a society in which, if we found ourselves in the minority, we would be at the complete mercy of the majority. Again we fall back on the importance of general rules of

---

[14]We are not referring to the Republican party. A republican form of government is one in which the supreme power rests with the citizens through their right to vote.

the game that apply to all and that cannot be violated just because a majority would like to do so. We all feel safer, in the case of taxes, for example, subjecting ourselves to majority rule knowing that when our neighbor votes to increase our taxes, he also is voting to increase his own.[15]

We will never have a tax system that finds everyone who is similarly situated facing the same tax burden. This is true even though there is an objective measure of tax burden—that is, how much individuals actually pay.[16] But even if horizontal equity in taxation were ensured, there would remain the very real potential for democracy to be abused on the expenditure side. When it comes to government expenditures, there is really no way of requiring that everyone who is similarly situated receives the same benefits. When the expenditure is for a public good, many people benefit simultaneously, and there is no obvious way of apportioning the expenditure over individuals. Even if a publicly provided good is equally available to everyone, there will be wide differences in the value different people place on it. For this reason, it is often difficult to know whether a good is truly a public good or one that focuses benefits on a relative few. If government is obligated to respond to the preferences of the majority, it is difficult to imagine a rule that restricts some from voting themselves benefits not shared by others.

It will be useful at this point to look at a simple example. Consider three people in a community—Jones, Roberts, and Simons—all of whom share the tax burden equally. Assume that there are three public projects that are being considered and will be financed through taxation if they receive majority support. The projects are a swimming pool, a library, and a playground. The total costs of the pool, library, and playground are $30,000, $45,000, and $15,000, respectively. If the projects are approved, each individual will face a tax cost of $10,000 for the pool, $15,000 for the library, and $5,000 for the playground. These tax burdens are shown in parentheses in the relevant cells of table 2-1. Table 2-1 also contains the value each member of the community

---

[15]Tax rates, of course, vary from individual to individual, but an important objective in structing tax systems is horizontal equity—that is, everyone with the same income faces the same tax liability. The importance of this objective comes, in part, from the protection it provides against political majorities. Although horizontal equity has never been fully realized, the public is typically, and justifiably, offended by blatant deviations from this objective. When, for example, Congress effectively exempted its members from the income tax in late 1981, there was a widespread and angry reaction from the public. The public has always been suspicious of tax loopholes that allow some to pay less tax than others, even though their income is the same. While it did not generate the same hostility, the so-called windfall profits tax, which was applied only to oil companies, is another flagrant violation of horizontal equity in taxation. For a discussion of horizontal equity in taxation, see Richard A. Musgrave and Peggy B. Musgrave, *Public Finance in Theory and Practice: Analytical Foundations of a Fiscal Constitution,* (Cambridge: Cambridge University Press, 1980).

[16]Although an objective measure, the tax paid is far from a perfect measure of the tax burden. One problem arises from the fact that tax incidence is not necessarily imposed on the party that seemingly pays the tax. See Ibid., chapters 16-20.

Table 2-1
Direct Democracy and Costly Benefits

	Jones	*Roberts*	*Simons*
Pool	$12,000 ($10,000)	$11,000 ($10,000)	-$500 ($10,000)
Library	0 ($15,000)	$16,000 ($15,000)	$20,000 ($15,000)
Playground	$7,000 ($5,000)	-$1,000 ($5,000)	$8,000 ($5,000)

places on the projects. For example, Roberts enjoys swimming and reading and values the pool and library at $11,000 and $16,000, respectively. Roberts, however, would be willing to pay $1,000 to prevent the noisy playground, which is to be constructed across the street from his house, from being built; the playground is worth minus $1,000 to him.

If the three projects are voted on individually, they will each receive a majority of the vote. Each project will carry by a vote of 2 to 1, with Jones and Roberts voting in favor of the pool, Roberts and Simons voting in favor of the library, and Jones and Simons voting in favor of the playground. In each case, the majority was able to capture net benefits by imposing costs on the minority. But, as is easily seen from table 2-1, each voter was in the minority on one vote and lost more in this minority position that he gained from his majority positions. On balance everyone is worse off: Jones receives $19,000 worth of benefits, Roberts $26,000 worth of benefits, and Simons $27,000 worth of benefits, but each has to pay $30,000 in taxes.

This is a simple example, of course, and was constructed to show that majority voting can lead to undesirable results. Quite clearly, this will not always be the case. But because majority voting allows people to obtain benefits without having to pay all the cost, it is not unusual to find projects being approved that are worth less than they cost (as is the case for each project in the above example). This does not have to happen all that frequently for everyone in the community to find himself worse off under the political rule of unrestrained majoritarianism.

The above example was one of direct democracy. Each issue was put to the direct vote of the citizens. But few issues are decided by direct vote, as it would cost an exorbitant amount to hold the number of elections direct democracy would require. The standard way out of this difficulty is through representative democracy. Citizens from different geographic regions elect someone, by majority vote,[17] to represent their views on those issues that are to be decided politically. These elected representatives make up a legislature

---

[17]This assumes that only two candidates are being considered. In the case of three or more party candidates, it is, of course, possible that less than a majority of voters can elect a representative.

that decides on the fate of different issues through majority vote.[18] What is of interest here is that although all decisions require majority support of the relevant voters, it is possible for a minority of the citizens to control final decisions.

Another simple example will be helpful. Assume that there are 7 political districts and each district contains 100 voters. Each district elects one person to represent it in the legislature. To keep the example as simple as possible, assume that one issue (whether the government should finance a large dam) is of overriding importance to all citizens. In districts 1-4, 51 voters in each district favor the dam, while 49 voters oppose it. These districts will elect a representative who supports the dam. In districts 5-7, all 100 voters in each district oppose the dam and will elect a representative who does the same. The dam will be financed because the legislature will approve it by a margin of 4 to 3, even though, as can be seen from table 2-2, the citizens disapprove of the dam 496 to 204. In this example, the support of 29 percent of the voters was enough to override the wishes of the remaining 71 percent. As the number of voters in each district and the number of districts increases, we move toward a situation where if as few as 25 percent of the population desire a government spending program, they can obligate the 75 percent who oppose the program (slightly more than 50 percent of the voters in slightly more than 50 percent of the districts) to pay for it.

We do not deny that this example was constructed to exaggerate the small percentage required for control in a representative democracy. It is highly improbable that we would find political opinions distributed in as extreme a way as that shown in table 2-2. Note that in rearranging political

Table 2-2
Representative Democracy and Minority Control

District	Voters		Representatives	
	Favoring	Opposing	Favoring	Opposing
1	51	49	1	
2	51	49	1	
3	51	49	1	
4	51	49	1	
5	0	100		1
6	0	100		1
7	0	100		1
Total	204	496	4	3

---

[18]This is an extremely simplified version of a representative democracy. Some of the complications that typically exist in representative democracies, and the reasons for these complications, will be discussed later in this chapter and in subsequent chapters.

districts, political strategists often attempt to fix political boundaries to get as close to the table 2-2 pattern as possible. For example, if the Republican party had control of redistricting in a state, it would be motivated to shape some districts so that they contained almost nothing but Democrats. These districts would be conceded to the opposition. This would leave too few Democrats when spread over the remaining districts to control any of them. This can easily result in a majority of the state's representatives being Republicans, even though the majority of the state voted for Democrats. The practice of shaping political districts to give one political party more influence than is warranted by actual citizen support is known as gerrymandering.[19]

We also should point out that the ability of the minority to dominate the majority was constrained in the earlier example by the assumption that each district had the same number of voters. If the number of voters differs from district to district, it is possible for tiny minorities to control the decision. Referring to table 2-2, assume, for example, that there are only 3 voters each in districts 1-4, with 2 of the 3 favoring the dam. With the information relevant to districts 5-7 remaining as shown in table 2-2, we would still find the representatives favoring the dam 4 to 3, even though the citizens oppose it 304 to 8. To avoid this problem, members of at least one legislative body commonly represent districts containing approximately the same number of voters.[20]

The desire to prevent the minority from overriding the majority also can explain the existence of bicameral legislatures (legislatures containing two representative bodies) and why the number of representatives in each body is determined differently. But even bicameral legislatures cannot guarantee that a minority will be unable to control political decisions.[21]

Unrestrained democracy, whether direct or representative, can be abused. When the use of government power is completely responsive to a majority vote, the path is clear for some to acquire preferential treatment at the expense of others. This abuse is fundamentally inconsistent with the hope that government will enforce impartially the general rules that must be enforced if free and productive interaction is to be encouraged among the members of society. This abuse also is inconsistent with the objective of limiting government's direct participation in the game to financing those public goods that

---

[19]This name was inspired by Massachusetts governor Elbridge Gerry, whose political party neutralized much of the opposition's influence in 1812 by creating a district in Essex County shaped much like a salamander.

[20]Each district represented in the U.S. House of Representatives contains approximately the same population. After each ten-year census, these districts are rearranged (gerrymandered) to maintain this balance.

[21]Simple examples can be constructed to establish this fact. Also, very small interest groups can exert a controlling influence on legislatures, bicameral or not, as will be discussed in the next chapter.

would not be provided by market activity and that provide benefits that exceed their cost. The easier it is to use the government to enforce the rules of the game selectively or to finance nonpublic goods to favor the politically influential, the more people we can expect to spend their talents and resources becoming politically influential. People will find that the best way of promoting their personal advantage is by using government to capture existing wealth rather than by producing new wealth. The result is a less productive society. The greater government's involvement in who gets what and how much, the greater the control that must be exercised over individuals. Accountability must depend more on detailed government rules on what people can and cannot do and less on the general rule of private property. The result is less individual freedom.

The abuses and tendencies of unqualified democracy are real. A tyranny of the majority can be just as cruel and stifling as any other tyranny. But this does not justify throwing over the ideals of democracy. If we are to come out of the Hobbesian jungle, people must subject themselves to some degree of government control. The ideal of democracy is that this government control be subject to the ultimate control of the people and used only for the good of the people. As Abraham Lincoln said in the Gettysburg Address, "government of the people, by the people, for the people. . . ." Unfortunately for the implementation of this democratic ideal, "the people" do not comprise a homogeneous group of like mind. It is not the case, as some would like to believe, that there exists a general will of the people that can be determined through democratic processes.[22] A multitude of objectives and concerns attach themselves to differences in location, occupation, income, age, and so on. In most cases, responding to the general will of one group will require violating the general will of another.

To realize the advantage of a government that is responsive to the general interests of its citizens while protecting a broad range of individual rights against the infringement of government, democracy must be restrained. There must be a division between what government can do in response to majority preference and what government cannot do regardless of the wishes of the majority. This division, while it will always be somewhat obscure, should be made as clear as possible. Even in activities over which it is agreed that government should have control, it will be desirable to temper the majority with restrictions on the range of possibilities. For example, raising revenue is a legitimate function of government, but the majority should not be able to

---

[22]The view that there is a general will and that it is government's duty to discover and act in accordance with this general will is given strong expression by Rousseau in *The Social Contract*. The influence of Rousseau and the notion of the general will has been an important source of support for unfettered democracy. For a discussion of Rousseau's influence and a critical appraisal of unqualified democracy, see Felix Morely, *Freedom and Federalism* (Indianapolis: Liberty Press, 1981), chapters 2-5.

impose a tax that applies only to the minority. Neither should the majority be able to exempt itself from rules that it is the legitimate function of government to enforce.

Restricting democracy is the same thing as regulating government. Government in one form or another is essential if we are to benefit from rules—rules that are essential to our escape from the Hobbesian jungle. But escape from the tyranny of anarchy can be nothing more than a headlong rush into the tyranny of Leviathan unless rules also are imposed on government. Democratic processes are one such set of rules. But unless democracy is qualified and restricted in ingenious ways, it will not be enough to control government. The framing of a political constitution (the fundamental rules and principles of a government) is, in a democracy, the means of providing democratic rule both the appropriate rein and the necessary restraint to motivate government to do those things it should do and prevent it from doing those things it should not. Without this combination of motivation and constraint, there is little hope for the individual freedom with accountability that is the essence of the productive free market economy. To understand and appreciate the free market economy, one also must understand and appreciate the delicate balance between government force and restraint that must be maintained in any desirable political order. This study of political economy is at the heart of constitutional economics.

Concluding Comments

The Founding Fathers of the United States were familiar with the writings of Locke, Smith, Mandeville, and other leading sixteenth- and seventeenth-century moral and political philosophers. They were convinced that an orderly and productive society did not depend on government enforcement of detailed rules of individual behavior or attempts to force particular ends. They hoped to achieve a productive social order by establishing general rules of social interaction that gave individuals a broad measure of freedom to pursue their personal ends as they saw fit. The foundation of these general rules was the rule of private property, which ensured that freedom would be coupled with accountability and would thus channel self-interest into socially productive activities.

The overriding concern of the Founding Fathers was that of granting government sufficient power to enforce the general rules and raise needed revenue while denying government the power to go beyond its legitimate functions. The dominant fear was that government would abuse the power that is inherent to government and in so doing undermine the social process of freedom and productivity that depended on general rules and minimal government. This fear of an overpowerful and overreaching government manifested itself in abhorrence of the idea of giving unchecked power to either a single individual, as in a monarchy, or to the people, as in a pure democracy. The Founding Fathers were not, as a group, advocates of unrestrained democratic rule. They did support the view that in those activities where the exercise of government power was essential, it should be subject to the control of the citizens, acting through their elected representatives. But a primary objective was to prevent government power from being put to every purpose that a majority of the voters happened to favor.

The result was a government structure that provided a combination of limits and freedom on individual behavior that led to an amazingly productive economic system. The importance of the U.S. Constitution to the economic success enjoyed by the American people cannot be overstressed. Similarly, many current economic problems can be traced to the erosion of certain political principles that the Founding Fathers intended to lock constitutionally in place. In the next chapter, we take a closer look at the U.S. Constitution, its economic consequences, and its diminishing influence.

3

The U.S. Constitution and Its Economic Consequences

Agreement to submit to the will of the temporary majority on particular issues is based on an understanding that this majority will abide by more general principles laid down beforehand by a more comprehensive body.

—Frederich A. Hayek[1]

The concerns that led to the colonists' break with Great Britain were very much in the public mind when the Constitutional Convention met in Philadelphia during the summer of 1787. The well-known pre-Revolution rallying cry, "No taxation without representation," reflected a clear understanding of the dangers that accompanied any exercise of government power not answerable to those who are governed. That the government established by the Constitution would be democratic in form was not in doubt. Unchecked democratic rule, however, was anathema to the most thoughtful of the Founding Fathers. A grievance against English rule rivaling that of taxation without representation concerned the sovereign authority assumed by the English Parliament in 1767. In that year Parliament decreed that, through its democratically elected members, it had the power to pass or strike down any law it desired. The colonists had brought with them the English political tradition, which dated back at least to the Magna Carta of 1215. That tradition declared that the people have certain rights that should be immune to political trespass regardless of momentary desires of a democratic majority. The concern was not only that the colonists were not represented in Parliament but, more fundamentally, that Parliament assumed unlimited power to meddle in the private lives of individuals whether represented or not.

Although the Founding Fathers were determined to establish a government that was democratic in the limited sense that political decisions could not ignore citizen input, they had no intention of creating a government that was fully responsive to majority interests. In many ways the Constitution is designed to frustrate the desire of political majorities to work their will

---

[1] *The Constitution of Liberty* (Chicago: University of Chicago Press, 1960), 180.

through the exercise of government power. The most obvious example of this is the first ten amendments to the Constitution, or the Bill of Rights. These amendments guarantee certain individual freedoms against political infringement regardless of majority will.[2] If, for example, freedom of speech and the press was dependent on majority vote, many unpopular but potentially important ideas would never be disseminated. How influential would the public protest over the Vietnam War have been if the ability to voice concern over U.S. involvement during the early days of the war had been decided by majority vote? How effectively would a university education expose students to new and controversial ideas if professors had to submit their lectures for majority approval?

Other examples exist of the undemocratic nature of the government set up by the Constitution. There is very little that can be considered democratic about the Supreme Court. Its nine members are appointed for life, and their decision can nullify a law passed by Congress and supported by the overwhelming majority of the American people. In a five-to-four decision, one member of the court, completely insulated from the democractic process, can frustrate the political will of a nearly unanimous public. The arrangement whereby the president can reverse the will of Congress through his veto power is certainly not a very democratic one. Neither is the Senate, where the vote cast by a senator from Montana carries weight equal to the vote by a senator from California, even though the California senator represents a population more than fifty times larger than the Montana senator. The senators from the twenty-six least populated states can prevent a bill from clearing Congress, even if it has incontestable popular support in the country at large. Congress is actually less democratic than just indicated once it is recognized that popular bills can be prevented from ever being considered in the full House of Representatives or Senate by a few representatives who serve on key congressional committees.

It is safe to say that the chief concern of the framers of the Constitution was not that of ensuring a fully democratic political structure. Instead they were concerned with limiting government power to minimize the abuse of majority rule. In the words of R.A. Humphreys, "they [the Founding Fathers] were concerned not to make America safe for democracy, but to make democracy safe for America."[3]

In this chapter, we examine how the concerns of the founders affected the structure of the U.S. Constitution and how the Constitution has affected

---

[2]Without the assurance that a bill of rights was to be incorporated in the Constitution at the earliest possible moment, it is doubtful that the Constitution would have been ratified by the required number of states. The Constitution was ratified when New Hampshire became the ninth state to approve it on June 21, 1788. The Bill of Rights was presented to the first Congress by James Madison in September 1789, and ratification was complete on December 15, 1791.

[3]R.A. Humphreys, "The Rule of Law and the American Revolution," *Law Quarterly Review* 53 (1937), 80-98. Also quoted in Hayek, *The Constitution of Liberty,* 474.

U.S. economic performance. At the heart of this discussion is the importance of limiting the power and discretion of government. We also will be concerned with the unrelenting political forces pushing against constitutional limits on government and how, over time, these forces have diminished the influence of these limits. With the breakdown in constitutional constraints on government have come shifts in the political and economic incentive structure, causing unfortunate consequences for economic freedom and productivity.

Background to the Constitutional Convention

Fear of the arbitrary power that could be exercised by a strong central government, democratically controlled or otherwise, was evident from the Articles of Confederation. The Articles of Confederation established the national government of the thirteen colonies after they declared their independence from England. There is some exaggeration in this use of the term national government, since the articles did little more than formalize an association (or confederation) of thirteen independent and sovereign states. In the congress established by the articles, each state had one vote, although each state could send several representatives; these representatives were chosen by the state legislatures. While this congress was free to deliberate on important issues and pass laws, it had no means of enforcing them. The Articles of Confederation did not even establish an executive branch of government, and congressional resolutions were nothing more than recommendations that the state could honor if they saw fit. The taxes that states were assessed to support the Revolutionary War effort often were ignored, and raising money to outfit and pay the American army was a frustrating business.[4]

Once the war was over, the confederation became even weaker. Many saw it as nothing more than a temporary association of the thirteen states for the purpose of waging war. The power the congress did have during the hostilities began to disappear soon after they were over, as it became difficult even to bring together a quorum. Those who drafted the Articles of Confederation had been determined to avoid creating a strong central government capable of infringing upon the rights of the people and the prerogatives of the individual states. They were completely successful in this determination.

---

[4]Invariably it was those states suffering from British occupation that were most likely to contribute to the war effort. Even when a state did respond to its tax assessment, it typically did so with state IOUs rather than currency. When American soldiers were paid at all, it was commonly in notes backed only by the hope that the states would honor their obligations.

By 1786, five years after the was was over, concern had shifted to providing the central government the power needed to form a viable union out of the separate states and to mitigate the power being exercised by the state governments. Without the power to enforce revenue assessments against the states, the congress found it impossible to raise the money necessary for an army or navy. Under the articles, the congress had no power over individuals except through the states, and there was little the congress could do to discourage individual states from making pacts with foreign powers and engaging in intrigues against one another. There were well-founded fears that the union was vulnerable to the ongoing conflicts among European countries and their schemes for expansion. Without a stronger central government than that provided by the articles, little could be done to protect the new nation, as a union of states, against external threats.

The shift in favor of a stronger central government during the 1780s did not mean that the founders were less concerned over the dangers of arbitrary government power than they had been. Rather, they had discovered that weak central government provided no guarantees against the abuse of government power. In the ten years between the Declaration of Independence and the call for the Constitutional Convention in 1786, the state governments had demonstrated their ability to misuse power. Majority coalitions motivated by special interests found it relatively easy to control state legislatures and trample on the interests of minorities. Debtors promoted questionable banking schemes with legislative assistance, which seemed to reduce the real value of their debt obligations. States often resorted to the simple expedient of printing money to satisfy their debts. Trade restrictions between the states were common as legislators responded to the organized interests of producers while ignoring the general concerns of consumers. In 1786 the five middle states met in Annapolis, Maryland, to discuss ways to reduce trade barriers among the states. At this meeting the call was made for a larger meeting in Philadelphia to discuss the more general problems of the Articles of Confederation. That meeting became the Constitutional Convention.

Advantages of an Inefficient Political Process

James Madison, Alexander Hamilton, and other leaders at the Constitutional Convention did not wish to alter the Articles of Confederation but to replace them entirely with a central government that was more than an association of sovereign state governments. If the new nation was to be viable and prosperous, the new government would have to be strong enough to impose some uniformity on financial, commercial, and foreign policy and to establish some general protections for citizens against the power of state governments. In the words of James Madison, we needed a "general government" sufficiently strong to protect "the rights of the minority, which are in jeopardy" in all cases where a majority are united by a common interest or passion."[5] This position was not easy to defend. Many opponents to a genuine national government saw little merit in the desire to strengthen government power at one level in order to prevent the abuse of government power at another level. Was there any way around this apparent conflict? Many thought not, short of giving up hope of a union of all the states. There were those who argued that the size and diversity of the thirteen states, much less that of the larger continent, were simply too great to be united under one government without sacrificing the liberty for which they had just fought.[6]

Madison, however, saw no conflict in strengthening the national government to control the abuses of state governments. In his view the best protection against arbitrary government authority was through centers of government power, which were in effective competition with one another. The control that one interest group, or faction, could realize through a state government would be largely nullified when political decisions resulted from the interaction of opposing factions within many states. As Madison said,

> [t]he influence of factious leaders may kindle a flame within their particular states but will be unable to spend a general conflagration through the other states. . . . A rage for paper money, for an abolition of debts, for an equal division of property, or for any other improper or wicked project, will be less apt to pervade the whole body of the Union than a particular member of it. . . .[7]

A central government strong enough to unite a large and diverse set of states would weaken, rather than strengthen, the control that government in general could exercise.

To the framers of the Constitution, weakening government in the sense just discussed meant making sure that it was unable to extend itself beyond a relatively limited role in the affairs of individuals. This does not imply, however, impotent government. The referees in a football game, for example, are

---

[5]Max Ferrand, ed., *Records of the Federal Convention of 1787*, vol. 1 (New Haven, Conn.: Yale University Press, 1937), 57 and 134-35. Madison elaborated on the abuse of state power in an October 1787 letter to Jefferson: "The Mutability of the laws of the states is found to be a serious evil. The injustice of them has been so frequent and so flagrant as to alarm the most steadfast friends of republicanism. I am persuaded I do not err in saying that the evils issuing from these sources contributed more to the uneasiness that produced the Convention, and prepared the public mind for a general reform, than those which accrued to our natural character and interest from the inadequacy of the Confederation to its immediate objects." Quoted in Bernard H. Siegan, *Economic Liberties and the Constitution*, (Chicago: University of Chicago Press, 1980), 31.

[6]See Herbert J. Storing, *What the Anti-Federalists were for: The Political Thought of the Opponents of the Constitution* (Chicago: University of Chicago Press, 1981).

[7]*The Federalist Papers*, No. 10 (New York: New American Library, Mentor Books 1961), 84.

not the strongest participants on the field and have limited control over specific outcomes in the game. Yet in enforcing the general rules of the game, the referees are potent indeed. Government, in its role as referee, obviously cannot lack the authority to back up its decisions if the economic and social process is to remain orderly and productive. In addition to performing its refereeing function, the government also should provide certain public goods. Again that is a duty that requires a measure of authority—the authority to impose taxes up to the limit required to provide those public goods that are worth more than they cost.

In granting government the power to do these things, the Founding Fathers knew that they were creating a power that had to be carefully controlled. But how could this control be imposed? In the case of providing for public goods, for example, it is impossible to draft a consititution that would identify those particular goods, or even classes of goods, that government should provide. Space exploration exhibits public-goods characteristics, and as such government support for a space program may be justified. The Founding Fathers, of course, could not have anticipated that space exploration would be an acceptable government responsibility. Even if a complete list of goods acceptable for government financing could have been included in the Constitution, there would have remained the problem of determining how much financing should be provided for each, something that would be impossible to determine without specific knowledge of population size, age distribution, wealth, the state of technology, and so on.

Furthermore, different levels of government can provide goods and a decision must be made in each case as to which level is most appropriate. On the one hand, some public goods provide benefits over the entire country. National defense is the best example here. Clearly, it would not be reasonable to impose the entire cost of national defense on those living in California or any other region of the country. First, it would violate any rule that was generally accepted as fair, and second, we could be sure that too little national defense would be provided. National defense is best provided by the national government. On the other hand, some public goods provide benefits over only relatively small areas. For example, city street repair primarily provides benefits to those who live within the jurisdiction of a local government. It would not be sensible to require everyone in the country to pay for the repair of potholes in Dull Center, Wyoming. Pothole repair is best taken care of by government at the local level. The choice between local and national provision is not, however, always so easy to determine, and it would be unrealistic to attempt to spell out in a constitution which level of government should provide a detailed list of public goods. (The problem of dividing government responsibility among several levels of government is considered in greater detail in chapter 4.)

More generally, a constitution cannot limit government in a reasonable way by enumerating a list of specifics concerning what government can and cannot do.[8] In the previous chapter, we argued that the economy cannot perform properly if the government attempts to force specific economic outcomes. Economic decisions are best made when the government establishes general rules of conduct and allows outcomes to unfold from the spontaneous interaction of economic decisionmakers operating within those rules. It is the process that is important here. Similarly, the political performance necessary for an efficient economic process cannot be realized by attempting to impose a particular set of do's and don'ts on government. Instead, a general set of constitutional rules are required within which government decisions are made, with specific government outcomes determined through the resulting political process. Those at the Constitutional Convention hoped to establish a political process, through constitutional reform, that brought government power into action only when needed to serve the broad interests of the public.

This hope was not based on the naive, though tempting, notion that somehow individuals would ignore their personal advantages and concentrate on the general advantage when making political decisions. While noble motives are seldom completely absent in guiding individual behavior, either private or public, the Founding Fathers took as a given that most people, most of the time, would maintain a healthy regard for their private concerns. The only way to prevent self-seeking people from abusing government power was to structure the rules of the political game in such a way that it would be costly for them to do so. The objective of the framers was to create a government that was powerful enough to do those things that received political approval and also to establish a political process that made it exceedingly difficult to obtain political approval for any action that did not have wide public support.

The national government was not, constitutionally permitted to exercise some powers. The national government was created by the states, and until the Constitution, all government power resided in the states. Through the Constitution the states relinquished some of their powers—such as the power

---

[8]Because of the problem of attempting to incorporate specific dos and don'ts in a constitution, there was resistance to including in the Constitution a list of the individual rights that government could not violate. Alexander Hamilton expressed strong exception to attaching a bill of rights to the Constitution on the grounds that the purpose of the Constitution was to protect a broader set of individual rights than could be enumerated and having listed some, the others would be more vulnerable to the argument that they were not protected. In *The Federalist,* No. 84, Hamilton argued that "bills of rights . . . are not only unnecessary in the proposed Constitution but would even be dangerous. They would contain various exceptions to powers which are not granted; and, on this very account, would afford a colorable pretext to claim more than were granted. For why declare that things shall not be done which there is no power to do?" The Bill of Rights was not included in the Constitution until after it was ratified by the states, a ratification that may not have been realized without the assurance that the Constitution would be so amended. To protect against the problem that concerned Hamilton, the ninth article in the Bill of Rights states, "The enumeration in the Constitution of certain rights, shall not be construed to deny or disparage others retained by the people."

to impose taxes on the citizens, establish uniform rules of naturalization, raise an army and navy, and declare war—to the national government. In addition, the states agreed to refrain from exercising powers such as the powers to coin money, pass laws impairing the obligations of contracts, and pass retroactive laws. (Of the powers that did remain in the state, some of them were located in local governments.) Thus the powers that government could exercise were limited, and the powers that did exist were diffused over three levels of government.

The Constitution further diffused power at the national level by spreading it horizontally over three branches of government, with the power of each acting as a check and balance on the power of the others. These branches are the legislative, executive, and judicial. The legislative branch, which includes the House of Representatives and the Senate, is empowered to pass bills into law. The executive branch, which consists of the president, vice president, and numerous administrative agencies, executes the laws passed by the legislative branch, with the president being the commander in chief of the army and navy. The judicial branch, composed of the Supreme Court and the federal district courts, adjudicates controversies that come under its jurisdiction.

For a bill to become a law, it must first be approved by a majority of both houses of the legislature. The next step is receiving the approval of the president. If the president vetoes the bill, it must be approved by two-thirds of both the House and the Senate to remain alive. Even if a bill clears these obstacles and becomes a law, it can be nullified by the judicial branch. In response to a legal challenge, the federal courts (with the Supreme Court being the court of last resort) can find that the legislative and executive branches overstepped their authority under the Constitution in passing the law and thus rule it unconstitutional.[9] This separation of power creates a political process that was deliberately designed to make it difficult for the national government to enact viable legislation.

The intent of the Founding Fathers was to create a mixed government in which power was dispersed vertically through different levels of government and horizontally across given levels of government. The thought was to have government power so fragmented that it would be extremely difficult for any narrowly motivated faction or group to gain sufficient control to work its political will. Only those objectives widely shared and consistent with constitutional limits would be realized through the use of government power.

---

[9]The power of the federal courts to rule laws enacted by state legislatures unconstitutional was clearly implied by the Constitution. The Constitution did not, however, clearly empower the federal courts to nullify laws passed by Congress. It was not until Chief Justice Marshall's ruling in *Marbury v. Madison* in 1803 that the federal courts established the right of judicial review over federal as well as state legislation. The background and importance of the *Marbury v. Madison* decision is provided by James MacGregor Burns, *The Vineyard of Liberty* (New York: Alfred A. Knopf, 1982), 183-93.

The beauty of the political process established by the Constitution is that it is cumbersome and inefficient. According to Forrest McDonald, the process is

> [s]o cumbersome and inefficient . . . that the people, however virtuous or wicked, could not activate it. It could be activated through deals and deceit, through bargains and bribery, through logrolling and lobbying and trickery and trading, the tactics that go with man's baser attributes, most notably his greed and his love of power. And yet, in the broad range and on the average, these private tactics and motivations could operate effectively only when they were compatible with the public good, for they were braked by the massive inertia of society as a whole.[10]

Or, as Clinton Rossiter has said of the Founding Fathers' motive in creating the system of checks and balances, "Liberty rather than authority, protection rather than power, delay rather than efficiency were the concern of these constitution-makers.[11]

While the Constitution did not, indeed could not, lay out in detail exactly what government could and could not do, it did create a system that offered hope that government would confine its role to that of the impartial referee except in those instances where collective action was needed to provide for public goods worth more than they cost. The national government had the power to enforce the general rules of the game that protected basic human rights and freedom of commerce. The judicial system stood ready to invalidate any attempt on the part of either a state or the national government to extend its authority beyond those limits that were clearly established by the Constitution. Given the obstacles of getting legislation passed, the hope was that government would agree to provide only those goods that provided general benefits in excess of their costs to all in the relevant jurisdiction. The national government would provide national public goods, and the state and local governments would provide local public goods.

The Success of the Constitution

It is hard to argue with the success of the U.S. Constitution. The history of the United States in the decades after the ratification of the Constitution was one

---

[10]Forrest McDonald, *E Pluribus Unum: The Formation of the American Republic 1776–1790* (Indianapolis: Liberty Press, 1979), 316.

[11]Clinton Rossiter, *Seedtime of the Republic: The Origin of the American Tradition of Political Liberty* (New York: Harcourt, Brace and World, 1953), 425. The Constitution does not attempt to dictate to the individual states the particular structure of their governments, other than to guarantee to every state a republican form of government. In actuality, however, each state has a government characterized by much the same system of checks and balances that exists in the national government. A more complete discussion of federalism, or the interaction among the different levels of government, is provided in chapter 4.

of limited government and individual liberty, major increases in the size of the United States in terms of population and geography, and unprecedented growth in economic well-being. With the major exception of (and, to a large extent, in spite of) the unfortunate legacy of slavery and the Civil War, millions of diverse peoples were able to pursue their individual objectives through harmonious and productive interaction with one another. The opportunities created by the process of specialization and exchange made possible by limited and responsible government motivated an outpouring of productive effort that soon transformed a wilderness, populated largely by the malcontents, misfits, and outcasts of Europe, into one of the more prosperous nations in the world. The role the U.S. Constitution played in this transformation was an important one and can be explained in terms of both negative and positive incentives.

Broadly speaking, there are two ways an individual can acquire wealth: He can capture existing wealth through nonproductive transfer activities or create new wealth through productive activities. A major strength of the Constitution was that it established positive incentives for the latter activities and negative incentives for the former.

The most obvious form of nonproductive transfer activity is private theft. The thief simply takes through force or stealth something that belongs to someone else. A primary purpose for establishing government is to outlaw private theft. But the power that government necessarily possesses if it is to enforce laws against private theft is a power that affords individuals or groups the opportunity to benefit through public theft (legal transfer activity, to phrase it more gently). The more vague and ineffective the limits on the scope of government authority, the less difficult it is to acquire legal transfer through political activity and the larger the number of people who will find this activity offering them the greatest profit opportunity.

While those who are successful at the transfer game can increase their personal wealth, in some cases significantly, it is clear that the country at large cannot increase its wealth through transfer activity. What one person receives is what another person, or group, loses. No net wealth is created, and for this reason transfer-seeking activity is often referred to as a zero-sum game. In fact, it is more accurately described as a negative-sum game. The attempts on the part of some to acquire transfers, and the predictable efforts on the part of others to protect their wealth against tranfers, require the use of real resources. These resources could have been productively employed creating new wealth rather than wasted in activities that do nothing more than redistribute existing wealth. For every dollar that one person receives from a transfer activity, the rest of the community sacrifices more than a dollar.[12] The net result of transfer activity to society at large is not zero-sum, it is negative-sum.

---

[12]See Gordon Tullock, "The Welfare Costs of Tariffs, Monopolies, and Theft," *Western Economic Journal* 5, no. 3 (June 1967), 224-32. This article was one of the first to recognize the social costs associated with attempts to use the government to acquire transfers. This rent seeking is the subject of a growing literature. Some of the more important contributions to this literature are contained in James Buchanan, Robert Tollison, and Gordon Tullock, *Toward a Theory of the Rent-Seeking Society* (College Station, Texas: Texas A&M University Press, 1980).

A major virtue of the U.S. Constitution was that it discouraged people from playing the transfer game. By establishing a governmental apparatus that was very difficult to put in motion for narrowly motivated purposes, the Constitution dampened the incentive to use government as a means of acquiring the wealth of others. This is not to say that the government was not used as a vehicle for transfer in the early days of the Constitution. Every political decision results in some redistribution of wealth, and no government structure will ever completely insulate the political process against the transfer activities of some.[13] But the opportunity for personal enrichment through political activity was limited. Most people found that the best way to increase their wealth was through wealth-producing activities.

It was here that the political structure established by the Constitution created positive incentives. Not only did the Constitution establish a climate in which it was difficult to profit from transfer activities, it also created a setting in which productive effort was rewarded. By providing protection against the arbitrary taking of private property (the fifth article of the Bill of Rights), people were given assurance that they would not be denied the value generated by their efforts. This clearly provided people with a strong incentive to apply themselves and their property diligently. In the words of M. Bruce Johnson, "America was a place where if you were ready to sow, then by God you could reap."[14] But the motivation to work hard is not enough for a productive economy. Also needed is information about which objectives effort and resources are best directed toward, as well as incentives to act on this information. In this regard we saw in the previous chapter that protecting private property provides the foundation for a system of communication and interaction that guides effort and resources into their most valuable employment. To complete this system, the concept of private property rights must be expanded to include the right to transfer one's property to others at terms regulated only by mutual agreement of those who are party to the exchange. The lower the cost of entering into transactions of this type, the more effectively the resulting market prices will allow people to communicate and coordinate with each other to the advantage of all. The U.S. Constitution lowered these transaction costs by reducing government's authority to prevent people from entering into mutually acceptable exchange and by putting the weight of the national government behind the sanctity of the contracts that resulted from these exchanges.

In what has become known as the contract clause of the Constitution, the states are forbidden from passing any "law impairing the obligation of contracts. . . ." In the same clause, the states also are forbidden from imposing tariff duties on imports or exports (unless absolutely necessary for enforcing

---

[13]For a discussion of the use of government to transfer wealth throughout U.S. history, see Jonathan R.T. Hughes, *The Government Habit: Economic Controls from Colonial Times to the Present* (New York: Basic Books, 1977).

[14]M. Bruce Johnson, ed., *Resolving the Housing Crisis: Government Policy, Decontrol, and the Public Interest* (San Francisco: Pacific Institute for Public Research, 1982), 3.

inspection laws). In the commerce clause, the national government was given the power to regulate commerce "among the several states." Although the commerce clause can be interpreted (and has been in recent decades) as providing the central government the authority to substitute political decisions for market decisions over interstate commerce, the U.S. Congress ignored this possibility until it passed the Interstate Commerce Act in 1887. Prior to the Civil War, the commerce clause was used by the Supreme Court to overrule unconstitutional state laws that attempted to regulate commerce. After 1868 the Supreme Court used the doctrine of due process as expressed in the Fourteenth Amendment to strike down many government attempts to regulate things such as prices, working hours, working conditions, and pay.

In summary, the Constitution created an environment in which individual advantage was best served by engaging in positive-sum activities. The specialization and exchange facilitated by the constitutional rules of the game contribute to a system in which individuals can improve their own position only by serving the interests of others. When private property is protected against confiscation, an individual becomes wealthy only by developing skills, creating new products, or innovating better technologies and thereby providing consumers with more attractive options than they would otherwise have. In a truly free enterprise economy, with the minimum government role envisioned by the framers of the Constitution, the rich are the benefactors—not the exploiters—of the masses. Wealth through exploitation becomes possible only when unrestricted government allows negative-sum transfer activity to become more profitable than positive-sum market activity. We will have more to say on this subject in chapters 5 and 9.

Constitutional Erosion and the Rise of Political Piracy

The early success of the Constitution and the economic system that developed under it can be explained by the fact that relatively few people felt any urgency to worry about politics. Political activity offered little return, as there was little chance to exploit others and little need to prevent being exploited by others through political involvement. People could get on with their private affairs without having to worry about the machinations and intrigues of politicians and bureaucrats in faraway places. But this very success can, over time, undermine itself as a politically complacent public increases the opportunities for those who are politically involved to benefit from political chicanery.

Motivating people to maintain the political vigilance necessary to protect against the abuse of government power is always a difficult task. The individual who becomes involved in political activity incurs a direct cost. By devoting time and resources to the attempt to realize political objectives, he is sacrificing alternative objectives. The motivation to become politically active will be compelling only if the expected political outcome is worth more to the individual than the necessary personal sacrifices. This typically will not be the case when the objective is to prevent government from undermining the market process that it is government's proper role to protect. The benefits that are realized when government limits its role to that of the impartial referee and provider of a few genuine public goods are general benefits. These benefits accrue to everyone in the community whether they personally work to constrain government or not. Exercising vigilance over the political process is equivalent to purchasing a public good, and there is little reason to expect that there will be much in the way of individual motivation to make the purchase.

An example will be helpful. Assume that a state legislature is considering a bill that would make selling cheese made with vegetable oil rather than butter fat illegal. If passed into law, this bill will hamper the system of specialization and exchange by preventing consumers from purchasing a product they may prefer. Also, by reducing the competition faced by producers of cheese made from dairy products, the law will increase the price consumers pay for this cheese. This bill, if it becomes law, clearly will be detrimental to consumers' interests. But what motivation will any individual consumer have to oppose it? The answer is not much. Each consumer buys literally thousands of different products, and a slight increase in the price of cheese is unlikely to be seen as an important concern. Even if an individual knew he could defeat the cheese bill through a diligent lobbying effort, it would not pay him to do so. He would incur all the cost of this effort, which would greatly exceed the benefit he would receive from lower cheese prices. Most of the benefit from a successful campaign against the bill would be received by the other cheese consumers, even though they contributed nothing to the campaign. The motivation for political involvement is small in this situation, particularly when it is noted that an individual lobbying effort is unlikely to be successful.

Of course, a concerned cheese consumer could attempt to organize all other cheese consumers for a lobbying effort. Mass opposition to the bill would convince the state legislators to oppose the restrictive cheese bill, and with the lobbying cost being spread over everyone, each would realize a net gain. But no one will see a compelling reason for joining such an organization. No individual will gain much regardless of the success of the organization. Also, each individual knows that this success is, for all practical purposes, independent of his decision to join or not. Each person can continue with his personal pursuits knowing that he will benefit fully from the lobbying effort if it is successful and that his involvement would have made no difference if it is not. Rational apathy will prevail, and an organizational effort aimed at overcoming this apathy will have a difficult time getting off the ground.

Over the broad range of political issues, people quite rationally do not want to get involved. When it comes to politics in general, people are not only rationally apathetic, but they also are rationally ignorant.[15] This is not to say, however, that everyone will be apathetic and uniformed about all political issues. It is possible to predict the circumstances that will motivate political activism. Often a relatively small number of individuals will receive most of the benefit from a particular political decision, while the community at large bears the cost. Members of such a special interest group will find it relatively easy to organize for the purpose of exerting political influence. The number of people to organize is comparatively small; indeed, the group is probably already organized around a common interest, and the political issues that effect this common interest will be of significant importance to each member of the group. Of course, the free-rider problem exists in all organizational efforts, but the smaller the group and the narrower the objective, the easier it is to get everyone to contribute his share. Also, the benefits to effective effort can be so great to particular individuals in the group that they will be motivated to work for the common objective even if some members of the group do free ride. Not surprisingly, then, narrowly focused groups commonly will have the motivation and ability to organize for the purpose of pursuing political objectives.[16] When people organize politically, it is almost always to advance their narrow personal interests, not to protect the diffused general interest. The dairy industry in Wisconsin, for example, recently prevailed upon the state legislature to outlaw selling cheese made with vegetable oil,[17] so our example is not a fanciful one.

In the absence of constitutional boundaries on government power to limit the political effectiveness of special interest groups, the unorganized general interest is largely unprotected. Special interest groups, or factions, will not be nullified through mutually offsetting competition against each other as James Madison suggested.[18] Rather, factions can go largely unchallenged as they compete, not against each other but against an unorganized, apathetic, and defenseless public.

The constitutional limits on government seem to have imposed effective restraints on political piracy for many years after the Constitution was ratified. There are undoubtedly many explanations for this. The vast frontier rich in

---

[15]See Anthony Downs, *An Economic Theory of Democracy* (New York: Harper and Brothers, 1957).

[16]According to Milton Friedman, "The most potent group in a democracy such as ours is a small minority that has a special interest which it values very highly, for which it is willing to give its vote, regardless of what happens elsewhere, and about which the rest of the community does not care very strongly." Milton Friedman, "Special Interest and [His] Law," *Chicago Bar Record* 51 (June 1970), 434-41.

[17]See "Fake Food," *The Wall Street Journal*, 20 July 1981, 1.

[18]Madison, *The Federalist*, no. 10.

natural resources offered opportunities for wealth creation that, for most people, overwhelmed the opportunities for personal gain through government transfer activity. Also, it can take time for politically effective coalitions to form after the slate has been wiped clean, so to speak, by a social upheaval of the magnitude of the Revolutionary War.[19] Widespread public attitudes also were an important consideration in the control of government. Much has been written about how the pervasive distrust of government power among the American people shaped the framing of a Constitution that worked to limit government.[20] What might be more important is that the Constitution worked to limit government because the public had a healthy distrust of government power. For example, in the 1860s the Baltimore and Ohio railroad had its Harpers Ferry bridge blown up many times by the Confederate army and occasionally by the Union army, and each time the railroad rebuilt the bridge with its own funds without any attempt to get the government to pick up part of the tab. Or consider the fact that in 1887 President Grover Cleveland vetoed an appropriation of $25,000 for seed corn to assist drought-stricken farmers with the statement, "It is not the duty of government to support the people."[21] There is little doubt that Cleveland's view on this matter was in keeping with broad public opinion.

The constitutional safeguards against government transfer activity have lost much of their effectiveness over the years. The western frontier disappeared, and a long period of relative stability in the political order provided time for factions to become entrenched in the political process. Of more direct and crucial importance, however, in the move from productive activity to transfer activity was the weakening judicial barrier to the use of government to advance special interests. The 1877 Supreme Court decision in *Munn v. Illinois* often is considered to be a watershed case. This decision upheld a lower court ruling that the Illinois state legislature had the authority to determine the rates that could be charged for storing grain. This decision, by sanctioning an expanded rule for government in the determination of prices, increased, at least marginally, the payoff to political activity relative to market activity and established an important precedent for further such increases.

In *Chicago, Milwaukee and St. Paul Railroad Co. v. Minnesota*, decided in 1890, the Supreme Court imposed what appeared to be limits on state regulation of economic activity by ruling that such regulation must be reasonable. Unfortunately, this reasonableness doctrine put the effectiveness of judicial restraint on government at the mercy of current fashion in social

[19]Mancur Olson, *The Rise and Decline of Nations* (New Haven, Conn.: Yale University Press, 1982).

[20]Gordon S. Wood, *The Creation of the American Republic: 1776–1787* (Chapel Hill, N.C.: University of North Carolina Press, 1969), especially chapter 1.

[21]Quoted in A. Nevins, *Grover Cleveland: A Study in Courage* (New York: Dodd Mead, 1944), 332.

thought. What is considered unreasonable at one time may be considered quite reasonable at another.[22] It was unreasonable for the Baltimore and Ohio railroad to consider requesting government funds to repair its Harpers Ferry bridge, destroyed by government forces, during the Civil War. In the 1980s it was considered reasonable for Chrysler Corporation to request and receive a federal government bailout because Chrysler was not competing successfully for the consumer's dollar.

The idea of reasonable regulation significantly undermined the concept of a higher constitutional law to be enforced because it established protections needed for the long-term viability of a free and productive social order. Once the notion of reasonable regulation stuck its nose into the judicial tent, it was just a matter of time before the courts began seeing their task as that of judging particular outcomes rather than overseeing the general rules of the game. Illustrative of this changing emphasis was the legal brief submitted by Louis Brandeis, then an attorney for the state of Oregon, in the 1908 case *Muller* v. *Oregon*. At issue was the constitutionality of an Oregon law that regulated the working hours of women. The Brandeis brief contained only two pages addressing constitutional considerations and more than one hundred pages of social-economic data and argumentation attempting to establish the unfortunate consequences of women working long hours. It was a judgment on the reasonableness of a particular outcome—women working long hours—rather than constitutional considerations that were judged of paramount importance and led to a Supreme Court ruling in favor of Oregon. When the constitutionality of legislation stands or falls on the reasonableness of the particular outcomes it hopes to achieve, opportunities increase for people to increase their wealth through nonproductive political activity.

In the 1911 case *United States* v. *Grimand*, the Supreme Court handed down a decision that significantly increased the private return on obtaining transfers through political influence. Prior to this decision, Congress had increasingly moved toward granting administrative agencies the authority to promulgate specific rules in order to implement the general policy objectives outlined by Congress. In *United States* v. *Grimand*, the Court empowered these admistrative rulings with the full force of law. After this decision, the cost of successfully using government authority to transfer wealth decreased significantly, as special interest groups seeking preferential treatment could concentrate their influence on a few key members of a particular administrative board or agency. The typical result of this has been the development of

---

[22]In spite of the two decisions just cited, between 1897 and 1937, the Supreme Court used the due process clause of the Fourteenth Amendment to reach decisions that served to protect the market process against political intrusions. See Siegan, *Economic Liberties and the Constitution.* Unfortunately, this pattern of judicial decisions was not solid enough to prevent these decisions from being ignored or overruled when the political climate and prevailing notions of reasonableness changed.

symbiotic relationships between bureaucratic agencies and their special interest clients. A special interest group can thrive on the benefits transferred to it by the ruling of a bureaucracy, and the bureaucracy's budget and prestige will depend on a thriving special interest group demanding its services.[23]

What we have observed over the years is a slow, somewhat erratic but unmistakable breakdown in the protection the Constitution provides the public against arbitrary government power. Those who want to get on with the task of creating new wealth have much less assurance today than they did in the past that significant portions of the wealth they create will not be confiscated by government and transferred to those who have specialized in political influence.

Maintaining constitutional constraints on government transfer activity is a task requiring constant vigilance. Once a breakdown in these constraints begins, it can initiate a dynamic of increasing government transfers that is difficult to control. Any change that makes it easier to obtain transfers through government will motivate some people to redirect their efforts away from productive enterprises and into transfer enterprises. As this is done, those who continue to create new wealth find that the payoff for doing so is somewhat diminished as more of this wealth is being taken from them. This again will reduce the relative return to productive activity and motivate further attempts to use government power to benefit at the expense of others. Further, the burdens and inefficiencies created by one government program will be used as justification for yet additional government programs, which will create new burdens and inefficiencies.[24] This dynamic can lead (according to Anderson and Hill, it already has led) to what is best characterized as a transfer society.[25] A rough and ready measure of the degree to which we have,

---

[23]The relationship between the U.S. Department of Agriculture and the farm block is but one of many illustrative examples that could be cited here. It is clear that those employed by the Department of Agriculture strongly support the agricultural price support and subsidy programs that transfer billions of dollars from the American consumer and taxpayer to the nation's farmers. [Most of this transfer goes to the largest and wealthiest farmers. See Bruce L. Gardner, *The Governing of Agriculture*, Lawrence, Kansas: Regents Press of Kansas, 1981.] By expanding these programs, the Department of Agriculture can justify bigger budgets and more employees, something it has been quite successful at doing. In 1920, when the farm population was approximately 31 million, the Department of Agriculture employed 19,500 people. By 1975 the farm population had declined to less than 9 million, but the Department of Agriculture had increased its employment to 121,000 people. This trend toward fewer farmers relative to agricultural bureaucrats has continued into the 1980s.

[24]Our federal farm programs are a perfect example of this process. See ibid. Early on James Madison recognized the possibility of this type of legislative chain reaction. In *The Federalist*, no. 44, Madison states "that one legislative interference is but the first link of a long chain of repetitions, every subsequent interference being naturally produced by the effects of the preceding."

[25]For a detailed and compelling analysis of how the breakdown in constitutional limitations on government activity has moved the United States away from positive-sum economic activity and toward negative-sum activity, see Terry L. Anderson and Peter J. Hill, *The Birth of a Transfer Society* (Stanford, Calif.: Hoover Institution Press, 1980).

in recent years, increasingly become a transfer society is given by changes in the ratio of engineers to lawyers. Although exceptions exist, engineers generally are concerned with the production of wealth, while the litigation and lobbying activities that occupy lawyers are more concerned with the transfer of wealth. In 1960, 4.94 engineers graduated in the United States for every lawyer. This ratio has declined steadily ever since, and in 1977 only 2 engineers graduated for every lawyer.[26] While this measure, by itself, is not compelling, it is illustrative of a pattern of change in the structure of economic activity that does reflect increasing emphasis on transfer activity.

Once we start down the road to a transfer society, we can easily find ourselves trapped in a situation of which almost everyone will disapprove but which no one will be willing to change. An analogy that may be helpful is that of piracy. When all ships are employed productively shipping goods, a large amount of wealth can be generated. But if sanctions against piracy are eased, a few shippers may find it to their personal advantage to stop shipping and start pirating the merchandise being shipped by others, even though this reduces the total wealth available. This piracy by the few will reduce the return others receive from shipping, and some of them will then find the advantage in becoming a pirate. Eventually the point may come where everyone is sailing the seas looking for the booty that used to be shipped legally but is no longer. No one is doing well under these circumstances, and all would be much better off if everyone would return to shipping goods legally. Yet no one individual will be willing to return to productive shipping knowing, as he does, that everyone else is a pirate.

Obviously, we have not yet arrived at a point of being a full-blown transfer society; not everyone has become a political pirate. Plenty of people remain productive, and they still receive a large measure of protection against the confiscation of the returns on their efforts by the constitutional limitations that remain on government power. But there can be no doubt that these limitations are less effective today than they were in the past. This erosion is in large measure due to a change in the prevailing attitude toward government. The fear of unrestrained government power that guided the Founding Fathers has been largely replaced with the view that discretionary government power is a force for social good. If there is a problem, government supposedly has the obligation and ability to solve it. Such public attitudes have a decisive influence on the effectiveness of constitutional limitations. Simply writing something down on a document called the Constitution does not make it so. The Constitution is in many respects a legal fiction. It was because of this that de Tocqueville, writing in the 1830s, predicted that the Constitution eventually would cease to exercise effective restraint on government. Acording to de Tocqueville, "The government of the Union depends almost entirely upon

---

[26]See James Gwartrey and Richard Stroup, "Cooperation or Conniving: How Public Sector Rules Shape the Decision," *Journal of Labor Research* 3, no. 3 (Summer 1982), 247-57.

legal fictions." He continued that it would be difficult to "imagine that it is possible by the aid of legal fictions to prevent men from finding out and employing those means of gratifying their passions which have been left open to them.[27]

But controlling our passions is what constitutional government is all about. In the absence of government, we are in the Hobbesian jungle in which controlling our passion for immediate gratification and applying our efforts toward long-run objectives simply increase our vulnerability to the predation of those who exercise no control over their passions. Granting government the power to enforce general rules of social interaction is a necessary condition if a productive social order is to emerge from a state of anarchy. But without strict constitutional limits on the scope of government activity, the existence of government power will only increase the scope of effective predation. The notion that government can solve all problems becomes a convenient pretense for those who would solve their problems not in cooperation with others but at the expense of others. Unlimited government reduces the personal advantage to the productive pursuit of long-run objectives as surely as does anarchy. Government can be little more than the means of moving from the anarchy of the Hobbesian jungle to the anarchy of the political jungle.

The American experience, however, demonstrates convincingly that with a healthy fear of government power, a realistic understanding of human nature, and a certain measure of luck, a constitution can be designed that, over a long period of time, will effectively constrain government to operate roughly within the limits defined by the delicate balance between proper power and prudent restraint. A fundamental concern of constitutional economics is that of understanding how, through institutional arrangements and reform, this delicate balance can be maintained.

Concluding Comments

The United States is a wealthy country today in large part because our Founding Fathers had what can quite accurately be described as a negative attitude toward government. They had little confidence in the ability of government to promote social well-being through the application of government power to achieve particular ends. In their view, the best government can realistically hope to achieve is the establishment of a social setting in which individuals are free, within the limits of general law, to pursue their own objectives.

This negative view of government contrasts sharply with the dominant view today—the view that government is the problem solver of last resort and has an obligation to provide a solution to any problem not taken care of by the

---

[27]Quoted in Morley, *Freedom and Federalism,* 138-39.

private sector. Unfortunately, this positive view of government is less conducive to positive consquences than the negative view of the founders. According
to Hayek,

> The first [view] gives us a sense of unlimited power to realize our wishes,
> while the second [view] leads to the insight that there are limitations to what
> we can deliberately bring about, and to the recognition that some of our
> present hopes are delusions. Yet the effect of allowing ourselves to be
> deluded by the first view has always been that man has actually limited the
> scope of what he can achieve. For it has always been the recognition of the
> limits of the possible which has enabled man to make full use of his powers.[28]

The exercise of government can, without doubt, be used to accomplish
particular ends. Neither can it be denied that many of the specific outcomes
realized through government programs provide important benefits and advance worthy objectives. As is always the case, those accomplishments are
realized at a cost, and the pervasive truth about government accomplishment
is that those who benefit from them seldom are the ones who pay the cost.
Indeed, much of the motivation for engaging in political actions is to escape
the discipline imposed by the market, where the rule of private property holds
individuals accountable for the cost their decisions impose on others. This
market discipline is the hallmark of the process of specialization and exchange
that channels individual efforts into a cooperative pattern of positive-sum
productivity.

The escape from market discipline is the inevitable consequence of
reducing the constitutional limits on the use of government power. The
immediate and visible benefits that are generated by wide-ranging government discretion are paid for by a shift in the incentive structure that, over the
long run, will reduce the amount of good that can be accomplished. More,
much more, has been accomplished by the American people because our
Founding Fathers had a strong sense of the limits on what can be accomplished by government.

We now turn out attention to some specific issues of current interest that
can be usefully discussed from the perspective we have developed. A careful
discussion of these issues will reinforce the wisdom of that perspective by
illustrating that over the long run we can accomplish more if we constrain
government to do less.

---

[28]Friedrich A. Hayek, *Rules and Order*, vol. 1 of *Law, Legislation and Liberty* (Chicago: University
of Chicago Press, 1973), 8.

4

The Compound Republic

The political theory of a compound republic [is founded upon] . . . propositions which assert, among others, that: (1) every man is presumed to be the best judge of his own interest; (2) no man is a fit judge of his own cause in relation to the interests of others; (3) no body of men are fit to be judges and parties at the same time; (4) ambition must be made to counteract ambition; (5) authority should be assigned so that the persons, from whose agency the attainment of an end is expected, ought to possess the means by which it is to be attained; and (6) the constant aim is to divide and arrange the several offices in such a manner that each may be a check on the other.

—Vincent Ostrom[1]

When President Ronald Reagan declared in his first State of the Union address that the federal aid system had developed into a bewildering "maze of interlocking jurisdictions and levels of governments," he stirred the political caldrons.[2] To remedy the more glaring problems of fiscal federalism, the administration offered a New Federalism, a complicated proposal encompassing a reduction in the funding level of many federal grants to state and local governments, a swap in responsibility for a number of aid programs between the states and the federal government, and a regrouping of many categorical (specific purpose) grants into a smaller number of block (general purpose) grants.

The reaction from most government quarters to the president's proposal was immediate and gave the impression that the president was intent upon destroying the union. Cries of foul play were especially loud from those that had grown accustomed to receiving 20, 35, or an even greater percentage of their revenues from Washington. State and local officials did not object to the trust fund the president proposed to establish, the proceeds from which were to be distributed among the states. As might be expected, however, almost all

---

[1]*The Political Theory of a Compound Republic: A Reconstruction of the Theory of American Democracy as Presented in The Federalist,* rev. ed. (no information on the place of distribution, duplicated; review copy, 1983), 65.

[2]Text of an Address by the President on the State of the Union before a Joint Session of Congress, Office of the Press Secretary, The White House, 26 January 1982, 6.

wanted the federal government to retain full funding responsibility for most of the expensive grant-in-aid programs, such as Medicare and Aid to Families with Dependent Children.

The ensuing public debate in Congress and the media focused largely on the financial capacity of state and local governments to handle additional fiscal responsibilities and on the possible resulting hardship on the citizenry, especially the poor. Academic economists debated the impact of federal aid reductions on state and local expenditures. Some predicted that state and local expenditures would fall by less than the drop in federal aid; others argued that state and local expenditures would fall by the same amount or even more than the decrease in federal aid.

Most analysts concurred with the president, concluding that no mortal could understand, much less rationalize, a federal grant-in-aid system that, in 1981, covered more than five-hundred programs, some of which attempted to solve the "simplest of problems,"[3] such as filling potholes in country roads. Most listeners to the president's address understood what the president meant when he said that because of the complicated, overlapping grant system, people "do not know where to turn for answers, who to hold accountable, who to praise, who to blame, who to vote for or against."[4] Still, a stalemate over what should be done emerged in Congress. Some change occurred, but only grudgingly. Regardless of how much change has actually occurred, the president's New Federalism had one important side-effect: It reignited a long-standing debate over what kind of country we are and want to be.

By analyzing the considerable difficulty of assigning government responsibilities among several levels of governments (specifically, between the national government and state governments), this chapter extends our discussion of constraints on government. The fact that government responsibilities cannot always be precisely defined and distinguished imposes severe limitations on our ability to constrain government activities at all levels. As we will show, those who supported (the Federalists) and opposed (the Anti-Federalists) the adoption of the U.S. Constitution appreciated the difficulty of this task.

The Constitution of the Federal Republic

We noted in chapter 3 that the Founding Fathers were not democrats in the sense that they believed simple, unrestrained majoritarian rule should be the

---

[3]Ibid.

[4]Ibid.

order of public decisions.[5] Indeed, they harbored an intense fear that unchecked majoritarianism would be no better than dictatorship, a "tyranny of the majority" over the minority. We also stressed earlier that the checks and balances of the three branches of the national government served, in the eyes of the framers, as important constraints on majoritarian rule. Indeed, much of the debate in the Constitutional Convention was concerned with the issue of how a national government could be created to pursue fully acknowledged national goals and at the same time be delimited by rights retained by the states. For instance, Patrick Henry held nothing but contempt for the centralized, national government that he thought was being created by the Constitution.[6] In fact, many of the Anti-Federalists took issue with the Federalists on this point. Although many of the Anti-Federalists saw the need to improve the Articles of Confederation, they nonetheless believed the Constitution to be a misguided leap toward the creation of the nation-state and therefore destructive of the states' independence.

Judging by the standards of their opponents in the ratification debate, the Federalists were nationalists (proponents of an expanded Federal government) in the sense that they sought to establish a stronger central government than the one that existed under the Articles of Confederation. Under the confederation the central government was dependent on what were more or less subscription gifts from the state legislatures for its operating revenues. The confederate government had no power of direct taxation and no power

---

[5]In his often quoted essay in *The Federalist* papers, James Madison spoke for most of the framers:

> [In] a pure democracy, by which I mean a society consisting of a small number of citizens, who assemble and administer the government in person . . . there is nothing to check the inducements to sacrifice the weaker party or an obnoxious individual. Hence it is that such democracies have ever been spectacles of turbulence and contention; have ever been found incompatible with personal security or the right of property; and have in general been as short in their lives as they have been violent in their deaths. Theoretic politicians, who have patronized this species of government, have erroneously supposed that by reducing mankind to a perfect equality in their political rights, they would, at the same time, be perfectly equalized and assimilated in their possessions, their opinions, and their passions.

James Madison, *The Federalist,* no. 10 (New York: Modern Library, n.d.), 58.

[6]Virginia's Patrick Henry vigorously opposed the adoption of the Constitution in part because of what he believed was this mistaken view of the country implied in the preamble:

> [W]hat right had they to say, *We, the People?* My political curiosity, exclusive of my anxious solicitude for the public welfare, leads me to ask, who authorized them to speak the language of *We, the People,* instead of *We, the States?* States are the characteristics, and the soul of a confederation. If the States be not the agents of this compact, it must be one great consolidated National Government of the people of the United States.

Herbert J. Storing, *What the Anti-Federalists Were For: The Political Thought of the Opponents of the Constitution* (Chicago: University of Chicago Press, 1981), 12.

to force state governments to pay their share of central government revenue, an arrangement that left the central treasury largely incapable of financing a national militia to fend off foreign invasions, Indian assaults on frontier settlers, and domestic uprisings, such as Shay's Rebellion in the mid-1780s.

As we have pointed out, the confederate government also had no power to nullify state legislation that impeded interstate commerce, jeopardized private property rights through state and local regulation, threatened the independence of the press and the freedom of religion, and corrupted debt through the rampant production of state and bank currencies:

> That most of us carried into the Convention a profound impression produced by the experienced inadequacy in the old Confederation . . . as to the necessity of binding the states together by a strong Constitution, is certain. The necessity of such a Constitution was enforced by the gross and disreputable inequalities which had been prominent in the internal administrations of most of the states. Nor was the recent and alarming insurrection headed by Shay in Massachusetts without a very sensible effect on the public mind. Such indeed was the aspect of things, that in the eyes of all the best friends of liberty a crisis had arrived which was to decide whether the American Experiment was to be a blessing to the world, or to blast for ever the hopes which the republican cause had inspired. . . .[7]

If the Founding Fathers were not interested in pure democracy, what was their goal? The desire to contain political power placed them on the horns of a fully recognized social dilemma, which has only partial and imperfect institutional solutions. As Madison wrote in a letter to Jefferson,

> Wherever the real power in a Government lies, there is the danger of oppression. In our Governments the real power lies in the majority of the community, and the invasion of the private rights is *chiefly* to be apprehended, not from the acts of Government contrary to the sense of its constituents, but from the acts in which the Government is the mere instrument of the major number of the Constituents.[8]

Their solution to the social, institutional dilemma was twofold. First, they stated carefully (or as carefully as time and circumstances at the convention

---

[7]Letter from James Madison to J.G. Jackson, in Max Farrand, ed., *The Records and Proceedings of the Federal Convention of 1787*, vol. 3 (New Haven, Conn.: Yale University Press, 1937), 449. For more on how states invalidated property rights and obstructed trade prior to the Constitutional Convention, see Bernard H. Siegan, "The Economic Constitution in Historical Perspective," in Richard B. McKenzie, ed., *Constitutional Economics: Containing the Economic Powers of Government* (Lexington, Mass.: D.C. Heath and Company, 1984), 39–54.

[8]James Madison, *The Writings of James Madison*, vol. 5, Gaillard Hunt, ed. (New York: 1900–1910), 272.

allowed) what the national government could and could not do, as in the Bill of Rights (which, although not incorporated into the original Constitution, was planned prior to ratification). Second, they established a "compound republic" which would, in Madison's view, cure the excesses of democracy and at the same time grant people some, albeit indirect, control over their political destinies.[9]

Again, the primary but not exclusive reason for giving most people the right to govern themselves is that the dispersion of political rights is the only effective means of denying any one person or group governmental power over others. Having distributed political rights to the masses, the convention then faced the problem of checking the central, exploitive tendencies of factions (or the "factious spirit") that Madison believed had "tainted our administrations."[10] Madison wrote,

> By faction, I understand a number of citizens, whether amounting to a majority or minority of the whole, who are united and actuated by some common impulse of passion, or of interest, adverse to the rights of other citizens, or to the permanent and the aggregate interests of the community.[11]

Madison reasoned that "there are two methods of removing the causes of faction: the one, by destroying the liberty which is essential to its existence; the other, by giving to every citizen the same opinions, the same passions, and the same interests."[12] The latter option was impractical; the former was unacceptable, even though "liberty is to faction what air is to fire, an ailment without which it instantly expires."[13]

By giving the national government the power of direct taxation and by defining its powers in very general terms (to, for example, "provide for the national defense and general welfare"), the Anti-Federalist's feared that the newly constituted government would soon emerge as a Leviathan, the epitome of the form of coercive government the Federalists sought to avoid. The Anti-Federalists also feared that the harmful effects of factions in states, which was a central concern of the Philadelphia conventioneers, would be magnified under the national government proposed in the Constitution.

According to the Federalists, a free interstate market would encourage the creation of offsetting factious interests (especially commercial interests

---

[9]For a thorough discussion of the purpose of the compound republic, see Ostrom, *The Political Theory of the Compound Republic.*

[10]Madison, *The Federalist,* no. 10, 54.

[11]Ibid.

[12]Ibid., 55.

[13]Ibid.

that would countervail against the entrenched agrarian interests of the period). The republican form of government disperses political power among the competing factional interests, reducing the harm that any faction can do if it is ever able to exert its will: "The influence of the factious leaders may kindle a flame within their particular state, but will be unable to spread a general conflagration through the other states."[14]

Again, the creation of workable majorities would be made more difficult because republican government increases the number of factions that would be represented in any political debate at the center of power, making it less likely that any one faction would have a controlling influence on Congress: "[H]owever small the republic may be, the representatives must be raised to a certain number, in order to guard against the cabals of a few; . . . however large it may be, they must be limited to a certain number, in order to guard against the confusion of a multitude."[15]

Embedded in those claims are rudiments of a theory of an optimum-size government, one that is big enough but not too big. Presumably, Madison would consider a polity composed of only two factions of unequal size as being too small. The smaller of the two groups would likely suffer the political abuse of the larger group. Madison seemed to consider the union of thirteen states a workable size, one with enough offsetting factions that the fear of political abuse to each group would be minimized but one that would not be so large that public policy would be conducted in a disorderly manner.[16]

Contrary to the concerns of the Anti-Federalists, the Federalists argued that the citizenry need not be unduly concerned with the concentration of power in a central government, whatever its size, as long as the political integrity of states was maintained with strict limitations on the powers of the central government (see the Tenth Amendment). With the maintenance of states as political entities, people would continue to direct their allegiance to their respective states where a "local spirit will infallibly prevail."[17]

---

[14]Ibid., 61. Madison added as explanation, "A religious sect may degenerate into a political faction in a part of the Confederacy; but the variety of sects dispersed over the entire face of it must secure the national councils against any danger from that source." Ibid., 61–62.

[15]Ibid., 59–60. The Anti-Federalists argued that the republican form of government proposed in the Constitution would encourage one area of the country to exploit other areas economically. The Anti-Federalists, in other words, wanted a weak central government or, barring that, several much smaller republics, each made up of three or perhaps four or five states, not thirteen or more states. Madison, in making his argument concerning the reduced influence of factions within a large number, was attempting to turn the Anti-Federalists' argument on its head and to encourage the adoption of the Constitution. See Storing, *What the Anti-Federalists Were For,* especially chapters 3 and 5.

[16]We must wonder whether Madison (and those who shared his views on government) would have felt that an extension of the Union to fifty states was too large or that an increase in the number of factions within states, encouraged by population growth and the commercial development of the country, would reduce the need to centralize regulatory and preemptive power held by the national government.

[17]James Madison, *The Federalist,* no. 46, 307.

"Should an unwarranted measure of the federal government be unpopular in the states," Madison reasoned, there existed a number of "powerful" internal checks, which included civil disobediance: "The disquietude of the people; their repugnance and perhaps, refusal to cooperate with the officers of the Union; the frowns of the executive magistry of the State; the embarrassments created by legislative devices . . . would form, in a large state, very serious impediments." These checks would be overpowering "where the sentiments of several adjoining States happened to be in unison."[18]

In addition, while the Constitution (article I, section 8) gave the central government the power of direct taxation, the Federalists tended to believe that the power and influence of the federal government would always be held in check by its limited ability to raise revenue. Because a significant portion of the population grew its own food, made its own clothes and furnishings, and was paid in kind, direct income taxation was largely impractical. "Tax laws," wrote Alexander Hamilton, "have in vain been multiplied; new methods to enforce the collection have in vain been tried; the public expectation has been uniformly disappointed, and the treasuries of the States have remained empty."[19]

In short, many of the Federalists shared Hamilton's faith that the fiscal powers of the federal government would be largely circumscribed by the limits of the tariff revenues it could collect on imports. The Anti-Federalists were not as confident that the fiscal limitations of the central government would be as severe as those faced by the states. To them it was just a matter of time until the fiscal powers of the federal government would supersede those of the states.

The Founding Fathers operated with a tolerably clear theory of government, not unlike the one commonly used in modern public choice theory and in this book, which is based on the fear that unchecked government, initially designed to "preserve and enlarge liberty" would achieve its own contradiction, the denial of liberty to those who do not govern. To safeguard individual rights, political and property rights would be dispersed among the citizenry. As these rights were exercised in the political process, the competing ambitions of citizens would be largely offsetting and negating, except where truly public purposes, defined by a commonality of interests, are at stake. A national government, with fiscal powers of its own, was needed to pursue truly national goals.

Once established, however, the excesses of such a national government would be restrained naturally by its limited taxing capacity and could be further restrained by the construction of a compound republic. In the compound republic the number of factions would be large enough—but not too large—so that the competing interests of the representatives would again form an effective check on government through the factious spirit.

---

[18]Ibid., 308-9.

[19]Alexander Hamilton, *The Federalist*, no. 12, 71-72.

This compound republic would impose a double check on the federal government. Majorities would be difficult to achieve and concurrent majorities would be required. The majorities in the two houses of Congress, each house with a different political base, would have to reflect different majority wishes in the states.[20]

Did the Founding Fathers achieve their goal? The answer, in our view, is mixed. The central problem faced by the founders was one of properly dividing governmental powers betweeen a central government and states. The question of "Who should do what?" has no clear answer but could be "fended off with a series of practical arrangements."[21] While modern political theorists have tended to praise the framers as rare visionaries, Herbert Storing writes that the founders were "typically not very sanguine about the long-range viability of such arrangements, so much praised by later generations of scholars, historians, and statesmen; but they saw no other course. The Federalists accepted it mainly because of the strength of the Federal feeling in the country. Some of them saw it as a reasonable, permanent basis for government, but many of them saw their plan as a more or less temporary arrangement in the course of building a genuine national government.[22]

Through the years, others have expressed serious misgivings. Anti-Federalist Thomas Watt warned that trying to extend democratic principles to a territory the size of the United States would be as useless as trying "to rule Hell by prayer."[23] Writing to a friend in the middle of the nineteenth century, British historian Thomas Babbington Macaulay reaffirmed the framers' position on majoritarian rule but questioned the longevity of the U.S. system:

> "I have long been convinced that institutions purely democratic must sooner or later, destroy liberty, or civilization, or both. . . . It is quite plain that your government will never be able to restrain a distressed and discontented majority. For with you the majority is the government, and has the rich, who are always a minority, absolutely at its mercy."[24]

---

[20]In general, Madison concluded that while people may not be angels, government can be so constructed that "ambition counteracts ambition." The proposed solution was to break up power through a compound republic:

> "In the *compound republic* of America, the power surrendered by the people is first divided between two distinct governments [the federal and state governments], and then the portion allotted to each is subdivided among distinct and separate departments. Hence a double security arises to the rights of the people. The different governments will control each other, at the same time that each will be controlled by itself."

James Madison, *The Federalist,* no. 51, 330–40.

[21]Storing, *What the Anti-Federalists Were For,* 37.

[22]Ibid.

[23]As quoted in Storing, *What the Anti-Federalists Were For,* 47.

[24]From the letters of Lord Thomas Babbington Macaulay, May 23, 1857.

Macaulay noted that the day will come in the state of New York when the people, the majority of whom have not "had half a breakfast, or expect to have more than half a dinner," will be asked to vote either for a statesman who stands for protection of private property rights and "preaching patience" or a demagogue, "ranting about the tyranny of the capitalists and usurers, and asking why anybody should be permitted to drink champagne and to ride in a carriage." He asked pessimistically, "Which of the two candidates is likely to be preferred by a working man?" and concluded,

> There is nothing to stay you. Your Constitution is all sail and no anchor. . . .
> As I said before, when society has entered on this downward progress, either
> civilization or liberty must perish. Either some Caesar or Napoleon will seize
> the reins of government with a strong hand; or your republic will be as
> fearfully plundered and laid waste in the twentieth century as the Roman
> Empire was by barbarians who came from without, and that your Huns and
> Vandals will have been engendered within your country by your own insti-
> tutions.[25]

While Macaulay's fears have not been realized, there is a touch of realism in what he predicted many years ago.

Federalism and Public Goods

The central, most perplexing economic problem encountered in the construction or reconstruction of a compound republic is one fully recognized in the 1780s: "The perfection of the federal republic consists in drawing the proper lines between those objects of sovereignty which are of a general nature, and which ought to be vested in the federal government, and those which are of a more local nature and ought to remain with the particular governments. . . ."[26] Explaining the difficulty of drawing political boundaries requires that we, as modern analysts of federalism, reintroduce the concept of public goods.

A public good, by definition, cannot be easily sold in the marketplace because people benefit from its provision whether voluntary payment is made or not. Therefore, few people are willing to pay for units of the public good received; most people are inclined to free ride on its provision by others. Few sellers are willing to provide truly public goods, such as national defense, which we have previously discussed, when their production costs are not covered. Therefore, although public goods may be highly valued in a community or country, they may go unproduced or underproduced unless government intervenes in the market. Other often cited examples of public goods (and

---

[25]Ibid.

[26]"The Fallacies of the Freeman Detected by a Farmer" (April 1788), in Herbert J. Storing, ed., *The Complete Anti-Federalists* (Chicago: University of Chicago Press, 1981), 8.

services) include some forms of police and environmental protection, poverty relief, laws and justice systems and education.[27]

From another perspective, we might say that private provision of public goods is difficult to achieve because the benefits are received by people who do not buy units of the goods—that is, the benefits are said to be external to the purchaser.[28] If a person provides or buys a unit of national defense, benefits are received by nonbuyers because there is no means by which they can be excluded. Getting these nonbuyers to pay for the benefits received can be a difficult, if not impossible, task for the supplier.

In the case of private goods (the kinds of goods found on store shelves), the provision and receipt of benefits are separable. The customer can be denied the benefits of, say, a candy bar unless payment is made. Because of these external benefits for which charges cannot be levied by private sellers, producers are likely to face a demand for their product that underrepresents community desires. As argued, the good is underproduced.

The argument for public support of education is founded on external benefits: The student who buys education provides (external) benefits to the general community, for which a charge cannot be levied in a marketlike context. Therefore, students would buy privately less education than they would buy if they were able to charge people in the community for the (external) benefits they received. In this sense, in the absence of government coercion to extract taxes and produce schooling through direct production of public schools (or subsidies for private schools), education is underproduced, or so the argument goes.

Recognition of the conceptual existence of public goods and external benefits does not mean that government should or must provide a class of goods. Difficult problems abound. First, which goods should be classified as public is not always clear. Many policymakers claim that, in addition to national defense and education, garbage collection, roads, fire protection, parks, concerts, and building codes are public.

Further complicating the situation, when government subsidies are involved, private, not community, interests can motivate claims of publicness.

---

[27]The paradox of the public goods is best articulated by economist Mancur Olson:

> Almost any government is economically beneficial to its citizens, in that the law and order it provides is a prerequisite of all civilized economic activity. But despite the force of patriotism, the appeal of national ideology, the bond of a common culture, and the indispensability of the system of law and order, no major state in modern history has been able to support itself through voluntary dues and contributions. Philanthropic contributions are not even a significant source of revenue for most countries. Taxes, *compulsory* payments by definition, are needed. Indeed, as the old saying indicates, their necessity is as certain as death itself.

Mancur Olson, *The Logic of Collective Action: Public Goods and the Theory of Groups* (Cambridge, Mass.: Harvard University Press, 1965), 13.

[28]External benefits also may be created by the purchaser of a public good. The supplier can be the effective buyer in the case of self-produced goods.

Even if we accept the general proposition that a class of goods called national defense is public, we are left with the thorny issue of what constitutes national defense. Tanks are commonly acknowledged to be a strategic part of national defense, but are candles as well? The candle industry has argued that candles deserve protection from foreign competition because they are a critical light source in a national military emergency.

Second, once government is given the authority to produce public goods, we cannot be confident that the quantity actually produced will be more appropriate for the needs of the nation than the quantity produced with no government involvement. Given private investments to garner public subsidies and the influence of special (private) interests in the political process, too much may be produced. Since public provisions of public goods requires the community to forgo other goods, public and private, the misallocation of resources may be just as severe with too much production.

Third, provision of certain public goods may benefit some while adversely affecting others. Music jamborees in city parks are a good example of a local public good that some may dislike and others enjoy. Public welfare programs may benefit certain nonpoor at the same time they impose discomfort on a segment of the nonpoor. If the externality argument were taken completely seriously, taxes would have to be imposed on those, and only those, who benefit from provision of the goods at the same time a subsidy was provided to those who object to the provision of the goods. Strict adherence to the public goods theory of income redistribution would require that the poor and those who object to public welfare be compensated through government. (We will discuss this point further in chapter 9).

Fourth, the benefits of various public goods and services vary in the extent to which they are externalized across the population and landscape. Some public goods and services, such as street lights, are highly localized, affect few people, and cover a relatively small geographic area. The benefits of other public goods, such as national defense are spread across the country.

How do we divide the responsibility for the provision of these goods? How do we design a federal system so that appropriate checks are placed on government to do what, and only what, it is supposed to do? Should we think of the United States as a unified whole or as a collection of largely independent parts? Does such a perceptual distinction make a difference? These are the questions that are fundamental to the development of a federal republic.

The Distribution of Government Responsibilities

Theoretically, the division of government responsibilities has been drawn with clarity: The economically optimum constitution of government would partition government responsibilities according to the spatial coverage of the externalities of the good. If there are no externalities, which is the case in the production of candy bars, provision should be strictly private—that is, the good should be provided through strictly voluntary arrangements, such as trades. National goods have externalities that extend to the boundaries of a country, and should be the responsibility of the national government. Regional goods, those that go beyond the boundaries of a single state, should be the responsibility of regional governments. State goods should be the responsibility of state governments, and local goods the responsibility of local governments.[29]

A perfect mapping of government responsibilities would, from economist Albert Breton's perspective, occur when the external benefits extend only to the boundaries of the government providing the good. Mancur Olson calls that arrangement of government responsibilities one of fiscal equivalence.[30]

Practically, this ideal is difficult to achieve. We might all agree that the federal government must fund or subsidize the production of national goods. This is because in the production of such goods without federal funding, states and communities might be inclined to free ride, contributing little or nothing to their production within their borders and the national goods could be underproduced.

Problems abound however, in setting the real-world limits of various levels of government. We noted earlier that the concept of external costs and benefits were largely subjective concepts. People naturally will disagree over what goods have national externalities. Again, we might all agree that national defense, as a generalized activity, is a national good, but exactly what kind of defense is the nation going to procure? Clearly, considerable disagreement exists over the division of the country's defense between nuclear and strategic forces. Does not education have a national defense component? The private, as well as the public, interests of people and their representatives will influence their votes over how government responsibilities are divided among various levels of government.

Rationalizing all of the more than five-hundred federal grant programs in existence at the beginning of this decade on the basis of public goods and externalities is not easy. On the one hand, many state and local programs

---

[29]Albert Breton, "A Theory of Government Grants," *Canadian Journal of Economics and Political Science* (May 1965), 175-87. Breton's description of an economically optimum constitution is strikingly similar to a plan devised by an Anti-Federalist:

> All that portion of a sovereignty which involves the common interest of all the confederating states, and which cannot be exercised by the states in their individual capacity without endangering the liberty and welfare of the whole, ought to be vested in the general government, reserving such a proportion of sovereignty in the state governments as would enable them to exist alone. . . .

"The Fallacies of the Freeman," 8. This Anti-Federalist, however, would have made provision for states to withdraw from the union. Ibid.

[30]Mancur Olson, "The Principle of 'Fiscal Equivalence': The Division of Responsibilities among Different Levels of Government," *American Economic Review: Proceedings* (May 1969), 479-87.

funded in total or part by the federal government were intended to provide goods such as environmental protection, the benefits of which can be spread broadly over the country. On the other hand, many of the programs, again funded in total or part by the federal government, provided for downtown redevelopment projects, recreational facilities, police equipment, disaster relief, education, and sewer and water facilities, most of which have external benefits that are narrowly confined to communities, states, and regions. In short, the Breton-Olson discussion of fiscal federalism offers conceptual guidance on how government fiscal responsibilities should be divided, not how they will be divided in a democratic environment in which politicians seek to be elected and reelected.

The political-economic problems in establishing a structure for a compound republic should now be evident. Determining which goods should be produced by the national, state, and local governments outside the democratic process, for example by constitutional rule, is highly risky because of the imprecision of the concept of externality. If left completely to the dictates of democracy, however, responsibilities may, because of private interests, be assigned to various levels of government, and such an assignment may have little or nothing to do with attempts to internalize externalities and everything to do with state and local governments passing off their fiscal responsibilities to the federal government, or vice versa. To comprehend additional problems of working out a structured federal republic, rudiments of the modern theory of political economy must be appreciated.

The Political Economy of Fiscal Federalism

Establishing states that are largely independent of one another and the national government has both advantages and drawbacks. As we will see below, fiscal independence can spell fiscal constraints on states. Fiscal independence also can translate into attempts by states to draw income from other states and to externalize the costs of their public goods and services to other states.

In our analysis we assume, as in the past, that states are interested in maximizing their revenues, given the constraints they face. We make this assumption not because we necessarily believe it accurately describes the behavior of states but because we are in search of appropriate constitutional constraints against the states' revenue—maximizing efforts.

Competitive States

The ability of states to tax their residents is severely circumscribed by the fiscal independence of the other states. When making their taxing and spending plans, state and local governments must be concerned with what other state and local governments are doing. In short, states must be aware that they operate within the context of a competitive state market. A state that raises its tax rates without regard to the tax rates levied in surrounding states may find that a significant portion of its base will migrate to lower tax areas, reducing total tax revenues and making a tax rate increase counterproductive.

Many social commentators seem to approve of federal grants on the grounds that the federal government has a larger tax base and can raise more revenue with less pain than states. Fairness dictates, or so the argument is developed, that the federal government share its revenue fortune with the less fortunate states. The problem with this argument is that states collectively have the exact same total tax base as the federal government; the difficulty states confront is that they are less able to exploit their tax bases as effectively as the federal government.

As noted, people can move out of states with greater ease than they can move out of a country. Therefore, people can respond to a tax rate increase at the state level with greater facility than at the federal level. (In the jargon of economics, the demand for living in a given state is more elastic than for living in a given country.) The greater the ability of people to respond at the state level, the less able states are to raise their tax rates on, say, income, without confronting a revenue reduction.

From this perspective, we should expect that the larger and more inclusive a government unit is, the higher the income tax rates. States should be expected, ceteris paribus, to impose higher tax rates on income than local governments, and the federal government should be expected to impose higher tax rates on income than state governments. That is clearly the case. Finally, because of the people's ability to respond to tax prices at the local level, we should expect local governments to concentrate their taxes on tax sources that are relatively immobile—that is, real property that is difficult to move.

Note that voter turnout should vary inversely with voter mobility. Since voter mobility is greater at the local level than at the state level (in the sense that there are more local political units to which the citizen can move than there are states) and greater at the state level than at the federal level, we expect that the voter turnout will, generally speaking, be greater in federal elections than in state elections and greater in state elections than in local elections. This has tended to be the case.[31] At the local level people can move to any number of other jurisdictions if they do not like the tax and spending decisions in their communities, and a move is far more decisive in determining individual welfare than a vote in an election.

Individual votes count for little in most elections. Knowing that their tax base can pick up and move, local politicians must be, comparatively speaking,

---

[31]Richard B. McKenzie, *Voter Apathy: The Economic Dimensions of a Growing Problem* (Palm Beach Gardens, Fla.: Fiscal Policy Council, 1978).

careful about the policies they adopt. State politicians must be less concerned, and federal politicians must be even less concerned. The power of people to vote with their feet imposes a drive for efficiency at the local level that is not felt at the federal level and can be only partially offset by the greater tendency of people to go to the polls in national elections than in local elections.

One of the attractions of a federal republic to the Founding Fathers must have been that it places a break on the power of state and local governments to raise taxes. That is, a federal republic forces states to face continually the prospects that tax rate increases will drive away their tax bases.[32] Equally true is the fact that any movement toward centralized government can be expected to be a movement toward monopoly government—one in which the tax burden of government generally will be increased. Studies have tended to confirm, albeit tentatively, this general proposition: Consolidation of local governments in the production of local government goods, from education to fire protection to water service, has tended to lead to higher cost services.[33]

Federal aid to state and local governments is an indirect means of consolidating or centralizing government fiscal responsibilities. What has been the impact of federal aid on state and local taxes? At present, the question is controversial. The conventional view is that federal aid has led to a reduction in state and local taxes, meaning that state and local expenditures have risen by less than the amount of federal aid received. A number of empirical studies have tentatively shown this to be the case.[34] This view implicitly assumes that members of Congress are unable to construct a federal aid system that overcomes the competition among states. It also assumes, again implicitly, that congressmen will use their political capital to raise federal taxes so that state and local politicians can lower taxes. One must wonder whether members of Congress are that altruistic, especially when such altruism may eventually cost them their jobs (since state and local officials would then be in a more favorable political position to run for the U.S. House and Senate).

The alternative view springs from our maximizing view of the federal government. If the federal government was interested in maximizing its influence, given its own limited resources, then it would generally want to use federal aid to entice or induce state and local governments to raise their own

---

[32]The phrase "must have been" is employed because *The Federalist* papers do not contain an explicit statement of the position described. The Federalists were in full support of market principles, however, and understood from their reading of Adam Smith how competitive markets imposed checks on individual producers. It must have been relatively easy for them to think of competitive governments as an additional check on the fiscal powers of state and local governments.

[33]Thomas E. Borcherding, ed., *Budgets and Bureaucrats: The Sources of Government Growth* (Durham, N.C.: Duke University Press, 1977), especially essays 3, 4, 7, and 8.

[34]For a summary of a number of these studies, see Edward M. Gramlich, "Intergovernmental Grants: A Review of the Empirical Literature," in Wallace E. Oates, ed., *The Political Economy of Fiscal Federalism* (Lexington, Mass.: Lexington Books, 1977), 209-40.

tax rates and assume a part of the financial responsibility for federally established objectives.[35] State and local government officials also may be interested in seeing federal aid being used for such a purpose. If all state and local governments are induced by the federal government to raise their tax rates, then all subordinate governments will be less concerned about an outflow of their tax bases. The view that federal aid has pulled up state and local taxes is supported by several key characteristics of the federal aid system.

First, in a survey of 442 of the more than 500 federal grant programs, the Advisory Commission on Intergovernmental Relations found that 64 percent of the categorical grants based on formulas included matching provisions (which means a portion of the project cost must be covered by state and local taxes) and 61 percent of the project grants required a nonfederal match, which can vary anywhere from virtually nothing to a hefty share of the funding responsibilities.[36]

Second, the competition for federal aid involves, nationwide, eighty thousand subordinate governmental units. This competitive process requires that many state and local governments incur the costs of searching for federal grants and then lobbying the appropriate agencies. As in all competitive processes, competition forces the competitors to raise their bids, which in the case of grants can mean increasing the contribution of state and local governments in the funded projects or expanding the size and the scope of the project for which funding is sought.

Third, many states and communities were hooked on a number of grant programs, such as federal law enforcement assistance, with very little initial matching requirements—deals that elected officials at the time found hard to resist. The matching requirements under a number of grant programs escalated over ensuing years, however, saddling later state and local officials with greater shares of the funding requirements for programs that, by then, had their own local constituencies.

Fourth, according to Professor Catherine Lovell of the University of California-Riverside, ten "typical" communities had to endure nearly thirteen hundred federal mandates and direct orders as conditions of securing federal monies, and nearly two-thirds of the federal mandates required the local governments to initiate or extend their services, all of which tended to impose greater tax burdens on communities.[37]

---

[35]The following arguments are fully developed in Richard B. McKenzie, "Restructuring Fiscal Federalism" (Washington, D.C.: Heritage Foundation, 1982).

[36]*Categorical Grants: Their Role and Design* (Washington, D.C.: Advisory Commission on Intergovernmental Relations, 1978), 106-7. For a delineation of the distribution of the matching requirements by the extent of the nonfederal match, see p. 108, figure IV-1.

[37]Catherine H. Lovell et al., *Federal and State Mandating on Local Governments: An Exploration of Issues and Impacts* (Riverside, Calif.: University of California-Riverside, June 1979).

Fifth, fiscal federalism has made states and communities dependent on their federal nursemaid, and with such dependency has come federal leverage to force subordinate governments to do the bidding of the federal treasury—at, of course, less cost to the federal treasury. And that economic leverage has been exploited to coerce states and communities to tighten their enforcement of consumer protection, environmental, highway, and equal-opportunity regulations. The probable net effect will be greater taxes at the state and local levels.

Sixth, a primary goal of fiscal federalism always has been to offset fiscal inequities at the state and local levels—to aid states that are hard-pressed for funds either because of limited tax bases (as identified by per capita income levels) or because of unusually high tax efforts (as identified by an unusually high percentage of state and community personal income going for state and local taxes). By focusing on such measures of fiscal disparities, state and local governments have been induced to raise their state and local taxes (or to resist reductions in state and local taxes). After all, a dollar increase in state and local taxes would give rise to more federal aid and, therefore, an increase in state and local expenditures of more than a dollar—a bargain from the perspective of the individual state and local governments.[38]

Seventh, the deductibility of state and local taxes from federal income tax has meant that the tax burden of state and local residents goes up by less than a dollar for every dollar of state and local taxes collected. This is because federal taxes go down by some fraction of any increase in state and local taxes. By the very fact that federal aid increases the tax burden that people feel in the form of higher tax rates, the aid system has increased the reluctance of states to lower state taxes. Greater federal tax rates imply a lower improvement in people's after-tax income when state taxes are reduced.

Eighth, the proliferation of grant programs during the 1960s and 1970s may mirror the federal government's attempt to nullify state efforts to match federal dollars with state and local dollars already in the budgets of state and local governments. To explain, a state may meet the federal matching requirement on an education grant by taking money from its police budget, leaving police protection deficient. A federal law enforcement grant may then be devised to correct the budgetary deficiency, which may give rise to a shift of budget dollars from the water and sewer account to the police account. This last shift in budget dollars may then be corrected by a water and sewer grant that requires a state match. The end result of federal efforts to compensate for

---

[38]Empirical studies indicate that taxes per capita and the tax effort factor are important positive determinants of the distribution of federal aid across states. See Richard B. McKenzie and Bruce Yandle, "The Impact of Delegation Size on the Distribution of Federal Aid" (Clemson, S.C.: Economics Department, Clemson University, 1982) and Richard B. McKenzie, "Is there a Regional Bias in the Distribution of Federal Aid?" (Washington, D.C.: Heritage Foundation, 1982).

the natural inclination of states to shift budget dollars (as opposed to raising taxes) can be a growth in the number of grant programs and influence of federal aid on state and local taxes (since states would gradually lose their freedom to shift state dollars in their budget accounts).

All these considerations imply that the federal aid and tax systems have been propping up state and local taxes, a proposition that is strongly supported by a statistical analysis of the history of federal aid across states from 1965 to 1980.[39] Accordingly, a reduction in federal aid may lead to a reduction in state and local taxes, perhaps not immediately but sometime in the future, after state and local governments have had a chance to erase the fixed expenditure obligations developed under the federal aid system. At the very least, this line of analysis suggests that with reductions in federal aid, state and local taxes should rise by less than they otherwise would.

The Redistributive Federal Republic

Public welfare has been justified on grounds of externalities.[40] As the argument is developed, the private grants to the poor that improve their welfare also satisfy a demand for giving felt by the nonpoor and enable the poor to improve the appearances of their neighborhoods, thus increasing property values in adjoining, nonpoor neighborhoods. (This argument will be developed in greater detail in chapter 9.) In the absence of public welfare programs, people will free ride on the gifts of the few, and the poor supposedly will receive less than the optimum level of charity—that is, private aid will be insufficient for the demands of people who wish to help the poor. (See chapter 9.)

The free-rider problem supposedly is compounded by a federal republic. The states that increase welfare benefits will tend to have higher than average tax rates, which will cause some people in the state to move out and discourage some people outside the state from moving in. The higher than average tax rates will encourage a greater percentage of the state population to go on the welfare roles and will tend to attract low-income earners from other states, giving rise to an increase in the state's tax burden. Both consequences supposedly will tend to discourage states from spending the proper amount on public welfare. This line of argument can be rightfully questioned on several grounds.

---

[39]Dolores T. Martin and Richard B. McKenzie, "The Impact of Federal Aid on State and Local Taxes: An Empirical Assessment" (St. Louis: Center for the Study of American Business, Washington University, 1986).

[40]Milton Friedman maintains that private charity may be insufficient because people other than those who make the gifts can benefit from them: "To put it differently, we might all of us be willing to contribute to the relief of poverty, *provided* everyone else does. We might not be willing to contribute the same amount without such assurance." Milton Friedman, *Capitalism and Freedom* (Chicago: University of Chicago Press, 1962), 191.

First, as a statistical matter, although marginal population shifts due to differences in welfare benefits can be observed among states, the effect does not always appear to be very great.

Second, under many government welfare programs, the free-rider problem is replaced by a forced-rider solution, meaning that people in states that do not wish to provide substantial welfare benefits are, through a federal welfare system, forced to pay a portion of the welfare benefits that are desired by others. One must wonder if a shift from free riders to forced riders represents an improvement in social welfare. We can conclude with reasonable certainty, however, that regardless of how one evaluates public redistribution of income, the federalization of the welfare system, either through direct federal programs or by way of federal aid to states, should increase redistributive activity.

Further, we can conclude that to the extent that redistributive programs increase in their prominence in state budgets, there will be a tendency, unless constraints exist, for welfare programs to be federalized. When states differ in their capacity to program welfare benefits, either welfare benefits will vary (giving rise to population shifts in response to welfare benefits) or the tax burdens of people with equal incomes will vary.

Economist James Buchanan made this point more than thirty years ago.[41] He showed that high-income people in generally low-income states would have to pay higher tax rates to achieve the same welfare benefits that existed in higher income states. To equalize tax rates among equal-income earners across the country, the program would have to be federalized. People in low- and high-income states would have an interest in federalizing the programs. It follows that a movement away from federal welfare programs, such as the one contemplated under President Reagan's New Federalism, probably will give rise to greater disparity in welfare benefits and tax rates for given income classes across states.

State Predation

The focus of the foregoing discussion has been on the failure of states to take action. Two general conclusions can be drawn from the above analysis. First, through the federal aid system, the federal government can, from a conceptual perspective, play a productive role by aiding states to overcome the free-rider problem in the provision of public goods. Second, the goal of providing public goods can be corrupted as states attempt to use the power of the federal government to tax and cartelize state and local governments and to extend the scope of government beyond the provision of public goods. The mere existence of external benefits that spill over state boundaries is not a sufficient

---

[41]James M. Buchanan, "Federalism and Fiscal Equity," *American Economic Review* (Fall 1950), 583-99.

argument for developing a federal aid system. The inefficiency of government with a federal aid system may be greater than the inefficiency that exists in the absence of the federal aid system.

State actions, taken independently of one another, also may be destructive of the general welfare of all states. An obvious, commonly acknowledged example is the lax enforcement of environmental laws. Lenient enforcement can mean that costs, reflected in the polluted air and waterways, are imposed on the populations of other states. All states can suffer, as all states rationally allow excessive pollution. As in the case of national defense, each state can reason that its own clean-up efforts can be counterproductive when all other states continue to pollute. When businesses in one state are required to abide by strict environmental laws and businesses in other states are not, the competitive position of the businesses in the states with strictly enforced environmental laws will tend to erode.

Similarly, all states may agree that a free interstate economy will be beneficial for all. As is done with tariffs on international imports, however, each state can logically conclude that its politically powerful residents would be better off with selectively imposed tariffs and quotas on the movement of goods in and out of the state. The breakup of the national economy with interstate trade barriers can be counterproductive for all. In the absence of federal intervention, however, the breakup can occur rationally, as has been done flagrantly in international commerce, given the fact that national economies are separated by extensive tariff and quota systems.

States also may attempt to tax the income of other states through their independently conceived taxation and regulatory policies. States that have extensive coal reserves may, as Montana has, impose heavy taxes, called severance taxes, on the production of coal, knowing that the tax ultimately will be paid mainly by people outside the state who consume the major share of the state's coal production. States whose electric power output is exported largely to other states may attempt to restrict the production of electric power through government regulation, realizing that the production restrictions will mean higher prices for state residents but also recognizing that the higher prices will divert income from other states into the state, enhancing state revenue.[42] Finally, states can impose corporate taxes on the full incomes of corporations chartered in their states, even though a substantial portion of the income may be earned in other states.[43] A negative, counterproductive game of beggar-thy-neighbor can be played as all states attempt to use their state policies to garner their tax revenue.

---

[42]For a discussion of how states have used state utility regulation to garner income in other states, see Robert McCormick and Robert Tollison, *Politicians, Legislation, and the Economy: An Inquiry into the Interest-Group Theory of Government* (New York: Kluwer Academic, 1981).

[43]"State Taxes and Federal Dilemmas," *Regulation,* May/June 1982, 10-12; and "Disputing a State's Tax Reach," *Business Week,* 2 November 1982, 132.

The imposition of costs, whether in the form of pollutants, taxes, or higher prices on goods exported or imported across state boundaries, may be appropriately construed as state economic predation and can justify federal intervention (in the sense that all states may agree to the intervention). Preventing (or at least reducing) state predatory policies was certainly a central concern of the Founding Fathers. They set out to increase the powers of the federal government to override state-imposed obstructions to interstate trade. Because of the economic leverage it provides the central government, federal aid may be used as an auxiliary inducement to states to avoid interstate economic warfare. Grants may be the most efficient means by which the federal government can entice states to institute and enforce environmental legislation consistent across states and to avoid predatory tax and regulatory policies. The avoidance of these bads can be construed as another example of a national public good.

Concluding Comments

In the world of abstract theoretical economics, anything is possible, and solutions for dividing up governmental responsibilities among different levels of government can be readily conceived. In the real world of practical politics, however, considerable disagreement exists over the pervasiveness of externalities and what constitutes a local, state, regional, and national public good and over what government should try to do and can do effectively to rectify problems of externalities. Proposed divisions of responsibilities are almost always arguable.

In the final analysis, the division of government responsibilities can be drawn only on the basis of the weight of conflicting arguments. Clearly, there is an economic role for the federal government in the economy, one of providing national public goods and reducing the effects of externalities either through direct production, as is done in national defense, or through encouraging state and local governments to contribute to the production of public goods by way of federal aid.

Alternatively, except in obvious cases, there are several good reasons for remaining predisposed toward leaving government responsibilities with states. We have noted that states can exploit the federal aid system as they attempt to garner a greater share of the country's purchasing power through higher taxes. States always retain the option of voluntarily cooperating with one another (with the approval of Congress) in the provisions of regional public goods and services. The voluntary nature of these associations can ensure that states are less able to exploit one another by way of the political process.

In addition, a federal aid system may lead to uniformity in the types of goods and services provided. Few states may agree on the types of standardized goods chosen by politicians in Washington. Through the setting of federal standards and elimination of competition among states, improvements in the types of public goods and services may suffer. States will not have to be concerned about the types and qualities of public goods produced in other states, since all will tend to be made uniform through federal subsidies. As a result, we may end up learning less about what people truly want from their government, how the public goods can be produced most efficiently, and how the benefits can be most effectively distributed among state populations.

Granted, in the absence of federal intervention, states may devise policies that obstruct interstate commerce and divert national income. We need federal checks on those kind of policies, but we must reemphasize the risks inherent in the centralization of government powers. The centralization of government also can lead to obstruction in interstate commerce and to attempts by states to redirect income across state and regional boundaries.

The centralization of government power in Washington can mean lower lobbying costs for special interest groups, since the special interest groups do not have to appeal to fifty state legislatures to pass favorable legislation. And the lower lobbying costs can lead to more lobbying at the federal level than occurs collectively at the fifty state levels. These lobbying efforts may be expected to be more effective because the restrictions on commerce achieved at the federal level will be made uniform across states, implying that individual members of the interest groups in different states do not have to fear loss of their relative competitive positions due to the imposition of restrictions in their states. Also, states that impose commercial restrictions do not have to fear as greatly a loss of their tax base as businesses seek to avoid the restrictions.

In short, a federal system imposes severe restrictions on special interest groups by restricting the authority of state governments. A federal system encourages competitive governments. A federal republic is not perfect; no system ever will be. Abuses of state power can be expected. The relevant question is under which system can abuses be minimized? How do we devise a balance of federal and state forces of control?

The Founding Fathers recognized the inherent dangers in an unconstrained democracy. They harbored a fear that has undergirded much of the analysis in this volume: Special interests (or factions) will, wherever possible, exert undue influence over the political process, using the powers of government to pursue their own narrow ends. The founders were, when compared to the Anti-Federalists, nationalists who were intent on creating a unified country that would provide for the common defense of all states and thwart the tendency of individual states to restrain interstate trade. Their enthusiasm for a national government was checked, however, by the realization that an unchecked national government might readily be converted into a monopoly government, with all the ill effects of private monopolies. They saw the compound republic as a reasonable compromise: a central government that has limited taxing authority and state governments that serve to check partially the activities of the national government and that, because they are fiscally independent of each other, serve as competitive checks on the inclinations of each to expand.

Looked at another way, opening the federal treasury to the states and to communities may solve some problems of externality but create others. As noted above, each state can then look upon the tax bases of other states and communities as a form of common access resource, a problem of major concern in environmental studies. A pond is considered to be a common access resource when property rights to it are left undefined. Anyone can use the pond for waste disposal at little or no cost; therefore, the pond will tend to be polluted. Any taxes collected from the national tax pool and garnered by an individual state or community, through the federal grant systems or otherwise, can be treated conceptually as garbage thrown into a pond. Furthermore, each individual state and community can reason that the pressure will have only a minor effect on the tax payment of that state's or community's federal tax payments. The costs of the aid are largely externalized.

Alternatively, the collective pressure of all states and communities (and remember there are eighty thousand of them) can be immense, the aggregate effect of which can be an excessively bloated federal budget. As tends to be the case for all common access resources, the result of a system of fiscal federalism can be that the nation's tax pool will be used, overused, and abused. A central lesson of this chapter is that a compound republic is a constitutional means of assigning rights to the tax base, much as private rights are assigned to property and income, for the purpose of reducing the natural tendency of states to externalize, wherever possible, the costs of their own projects to other states. A compound republic may not provide an optimum distribution of resources, but it is a constitutional device designed in part to contain government influence and to reduce the potential for distortions in the allocation of resources created by government as an institution.

5
The Politicization of Society

> Tolerance is an admirable intellectual gift; but it is of little worth in politics. Politics is a war of causes; a joust of principles. Government is too serious a matter to admit of meaningless courtesies.
> —Woodrow Wilson[1]

Individuals are intent on increasing their wealth for a variety of purposes, a premise at the heart of all we have written. Yet as we also have stressed, available wealth is always and everywhere limited and must be allocated among opposing uses and users. Competition resulting from the scarcity of resources leads inevitably to conflicts and animosities as people see many of their goals and aspirations frustrated, at least partially, by the greed of others.

We have acknowledged that a legitimate function of government is to establish an environment that moderates social discord and directs our energies into efforts more productive than wrath, indignation, and belligerence. The streets of Lebanon and San Salvador have, in recent years, been replete with scenes of destruction brought on by unbounded human passion to possess, to dominate, and to control.

Furthermore, we have emphasized throughout this volume that one obvious way to contain social conflict is for government to establish the rules of the game by which productive, wealth-increasing activities are encouraged. As noted, this requires respect for and enforcement of property rights over productive resources, with the judicial system making it difficult for any person to gain by plundering the wealth of others. Under incentives established by these rules, individuals will engage in those activities that not only serve their personal interests, but, as a serendipity, increase the wealth of the entire community.

Social conflict, however, will continue no matter how much wealth is generated. Concerns over what type of wealth will be produced, and how it will be distributed, will remain as a source of social divisiveness. Pressure will

---

[1]As quoted in Richard Hofstadter, *The American Political Tradition and the Men Who Made It* (New York: Vintage Books, 1973), 309.

exist to bring us together by solving problems through collective action that supposedly will replace the individualism and competition of the market with a spirit of cooperation and community.

Unfortunately, a consequence of these pressures are policies that claim to promote social harmony but, in fact, politicize society and elevate the level of hostility by shifting decisionmaking authority from the market to the political arena. That is to say, the social conflicts that can be imagined in the state of nature devoid of government may be no less intense, no less destructive of the social good with unconstrained government.

Exploring this basic point is the central goal of this chapter. We begin, however, by reemphasizing the incentives of interest groups—including business groups—to enter the political process for the purpose of garnering government powers in pursuit of their own private, as opposed to public, ends. As it has been in the past, the thrust of our argument is that government must be limited—not limited necessarily in size (there are major responsibilities for government under its most restricted conception) but limited in the sense that there are recognized bounds on how decisions are made and how important a role it can play in decisionmaking.

The Control of Business

Many people assume that those who favor limited government are necessarily pawns of business, people who have either been bought off or duped by businesses interested solely in their own narrow self-interest. After all, restrictions on business appear on the surface to be an affront to what it can do and how much profit it can make. Nothing, however, need be further from the truth. Our argument here is that constitutionally imposed restrictions on government are intentionally designed to contain the power and influence of business, or any other private interest group, concerned with pursuing narrowly defined goals.

Like all other groups, business has its private interests. Normally, we think of its interests as being summarized by the bottom line of profit and loss statements. Businesses want to make profits and avoid losses and more or less incidentally, want to provide consumers with goods and services. Admittedly, many businesses take pride in the products they create and produce, but profit is still a key motivating factor. It is the reckless quest for profit from which the public must be protected.

Market competition provides the much needed protection. If the business community at large were solely interested in doing good, as the general public defined doing good (meaning serving the public's interests and not the firms'), we might as well dispense with an acknowledged role of government, establishing the rules for the economic and political games people want to play. From such public-spirited firms, people would get what they want. Much conflict would be avoided and abated in the first instance. We must wonder if government would ever be needed in such a pristine economic world.

The fact is, however, scarcity still exists. Individuals can, as a consequence, find plunder profitable. Many businesses seek to make as much money as they can, and many of these businesses are not particularly concerned with how they make their money, just as long as they make it. When property rights are respected and enforced, this private quest for profits can promote the enhancement of public welfare. In the process of making their money, people get much of what they want. This is because the system of property rights defines the legitimate bounds for people's activity. The competition that emerges among producers who want the same thing, profit, forces prices down and the quality of products up—and, in the long run, restricts the profits that firms actually make.

These have been themes of the book. What we have not stressed at length is that no one likes competition in *his* market. Competition implies that the market will be divided and prices and profits will be lower than they otherwise would be. *It implies restrictions on the control that businesses have over their markets, including the prices they charge.* By the existence of competition—meaning alternative producers—businesses must fear a loss of their customers when they raise their prices or lower the quality of their products. That fear will serve as a check, albeit imperfect, on price increases and the shoddiness of products sold.

As a rule, all market participants may appreciate the benefits of competition. While it may restrict our ability to make a buck in our markets and accordingly may reduce our welfare in that instance, it ensures that we get lower prices and higher quality products from all other markets. The case for a basically market-oriented economy is grounded in one simple proposition: *In the long run and on balance, the vast majority of people will be better off with competition across all markets than without it.*

Still, viewed strictly from our own self-centered, short-term perspective, our individually preferred state is to have complete or perfect competition in all markets aside from ours. This general principle applies to both product and resource markets. Labor also has an interest in restricting entry (competition) into its markets so that it can raise its price (the wage rate).

Government represents an important, legally constituted source of coercive power in society. Indeed, it is the element of coercion that largely distinguishes it from all other legally constituted social institutions. Through its ability to define and enforce rights, it tells people what they can and cannot do. In having that power, Nobel Laureate George Stigler warns, "The State— the machinery and power of the state—is a potential resource or threat to every industry in society. With its power to prohibit or to compel, to take or give money, the state can and does selectively help or hurt a vast number of industries."[2] When government is unbounded, many businesses naturally will view government power as a potential resource and will attempt to thwart competitive pressures in their own markets by turning to government and its coercive power to suppress competition—that is, to restrict entry, divide the market, raise prices, and subsidize production. Examples of how businesses have exploited the powers of government abound:

> Farmers have obtained price supports for their crops (which inevitably means that government must restrict the amount of food consumers will have and buy huge surpluses produced in response to the artificially inflated prices. The federal government continues to help in the cartelization of dairy farmers, lemon growers, tobacco growers, growers of navel oranges, avocado growers, almond growers, and producers of many other agricultural products—all to the detriment of consumers, many of whom have lower incomes than farmers.[3]

> Truckers and airlines in the past have used government regulatory agencies (specifically, the Interstate Commerce Commission and the Federal Aviation Administration) to restrict entry, by way of licensing requirements, into their markets.

> A host of industries, under the guise of fostering domestic employment, have sought and obtained restrictions on imports that invariably reduce foreign competition and enhance the ability of domestic producers to raise their prices and garner more income.

> Electric utilities have sought and obtained exclusive franchises to operate within given market areas, the effect of which has often been to prop up electric bills.

> Medical doctors and those in many other professions and trades (from lawyers to barbers to landscapers) have worked for the establishment of licensing procedures that effectively restrict entry.

> Zoning has been used to restrict entry by reducing the area in communities available for commercial property.

> The power of eminent domain has been employed by businesses to have government condemn private property that is ultimately sold to businesses for less than the government paid for it. To ensure in 1980 that General Motors built its new Cadillac plant within its jurisdiction, the city

---

[2]George J. Stigler, "The Theory of Regulation," *Bell Journal of Economics and Management Science* (Spring 1971), 3.

[3]See Yale Brozen, "The Economic Impact of Government Policy," a paper presented at a symposium titled "Economic Policy in the Market Process: Success or Failure?" (January 29, 1986), Slot Zeist, The Netherlands.

of Detroit condemned a 250-acre section of the city known as Poletown, so named because of its high concentration of Polish people; paid the residents approximately $200 million for their property; and then sold the land to GM for about $8 million. In the interest of acquiring the tax base and jobs, the city had to forcibly evict many of the residents.[4]

Regulation may not always serve the interest of business exclusively. In the mountains of North Carolina and Tennessee, bootleggers have historically provided financial support for religious groups interested in keeping their communities dry, meaning free of beer and liquor. The Baptists may have been concerned with the moral rectitude of the community, but their fight works to the benefit of the bootleggers, who see in local prohibition a means of reducing competition and raising the prices for illegal brew.

Similarly, environmentalists have worked for restrictions on the use of the environment. Established business interests have worked to ensure that new source users of the environment (interpreted, new competitors) must meet higher standards of cleanliness than existing producers. Manufacturers of highly reliable and safe toys have supported safety standards for toys proposed by consumer groups partially because of their interest in promoting safety and partially because of their interest in restricting competition and claiming a larger share of the market.

The list of ways in which the government aids and abets the interest of producers can be greatly extended by a review of the hundreds of pages in the federal government budget. For every government expenditure, some firm sees a profit in it and is, for that reason, willing to invest resources in expanding that expenditure. Defense contractors support an expanded defense budget. The education establishment pushes for increases in aid to education. Downtown businesses are concerned with the dollars allocated to provide grants for redevelopment and beautification programs for downtown business districts. The housing industry keeps a close eye on proposals designed to stimulate housing sales. The political stage is thus set for conflict over the use of the budget.

The less government is bounded in what it can do, the more businesses can do through government to further their self-interests by imposing costs on others. Fewer issues cannot be politicized—that is, settled by the political process. In such a circumstance, business can be expected to divert resources from private market activities to government lobbying. On the margin, such a shift in resources can be quite profitable; how profitable depends on the ease with which government can respond to the wishes of business. From this perspective, restrictions on what government can do and how it decides what it will do can be seen as restrictions on business (as well as any other interest

---

[4]See "The Rope of Poletown," *Inquiry,* 3 August 1981, 11-12.

groups). It is a means of restricting the rights of the people in and out of government to use government for their own narrow ends—and of restricting the potential for political conflict.

The already established, especially large, businesses—not the untried producers of new products—tend to be favored by an open-ended government. Through their workers, stockholders, and suppliers, established firms tend to have unified block votes and because of their market positions, tend to have the financial resources to buy the necessary political support to obtain protection from potential competitors. Constitutional constraints, in other words, contain not just government but also established wealth.

Many businesspeople may appear to be hypocrites in what they say and do. They profess to be interested in free enterprise while working through government for restriction of the enterprise of others. The Poletown case is an example of an acknowledged supporter of free enterprise, GM, which stands ready to use the coercive powers of government to promote its interests. Is there a contradiction in what businesspeople knowingly say and do?

For many businesspeople, the inconsistency between talk and deeds may reflect a moral bankruptcy, a willingness to try to have it both ways—to come off as a defender of a free society and at the same time, benefit by promoting government instrusion into market processes. For others, their free enterprise message may be fully compatible with their willingness to seek government protection from competitors and government handouts. These businesspeople may fully appreciate the case for restrictions on government, which means restrictions on what government can do for people in the pursuit of their private interests.

They understand that they—and others—will be better off in a world in which government is constitutionally restricted from interfering with the private sector. They may lose by not having the benefit of government protection or subsidies themselves, but they will, on balance, gain by being assured that such government benefits are not going to others. They may legitimately fear the consequences of having everyone use the powers of government to tie up markets and restrict production by way of taxes, subsidies, and regulations.

Alternatively, if government is largely unbounded and open to exploitation by interests groups, these same businesspeople may reason that they must, like everyone else, seek government protection and subsidies. Otherwise, they will be the ones who will suffer the burden of government restrictions in other markets and taxes used to subsidize other firms and will get little or nothing in return.

In addition, businesspeople who do not invest resources in profitable government lobbying may be subject to dismissal by their own boards of directors, who, interested in greater profits, will seek to hire someone who is willing to lobby and manipulate government. Many steel and textile executives surely would have been replaced if they had been unwilling to appeal to Washington for protection from foreign imports in the early and mid-1980s.

Recognizing his firm's relatively small size in the overall economy, each executive may conclude that his efforts at lobbying and garnering of government resources will, in and of itself, have an inconsequential effect on the rest of the economy. "There is no harm done" may, with some justice, be the common refrain of individual business leaders.

The moral or correct course for businesspeople to follow may be to follow their words with deeds, but we all must understand the counterpressures that come to bear when use of government powers is defined solely by who has the votes to pass this or that protective measure or this or that subsidy. *Constitutionally contained government is partly a device for economizing on the moral rectitiude of society.* It is a means by which people may be able to live reasonably peacefully within the limits of their own and others' moral imperfections.

Creating Malice by Rewarding Virtue

No matter how much wealth the economy produces, it will never be regarded as enough. There will always be individuals, both rich and poor, who genuinely feel that they have been short changed. Individuals strongly feel that they, or the causes they espouse, deserve more and could effectively use more, and they often see opportunities to get more through political action. Those who have a comparative advantage in exerting political influence will find it personally profitable to engage in the production of political outcomes that favor their interests at the expense of others'. Because of these tendencies, malice and ill will among interest groups can be expected as a by-product of unconstrained political competition.

Of course, political advantages seldom are secured by blatant appeals to self-interest. Effectiveness in the political arena requires that private advantage be disguised behind the rhetoric of social justice and virtue. Political interests that are most adept at depicting as fair those policies that they favor and as unfair those that they oppose will have a major advantage in the competition for political influence.

The result is political competition that pits one view of fairness, justice, and equity against another. Issues tend to become conflicts over principles—philosophic, aesthetic, even theological—that must be decided categorically, with little sentiment for compromise on either side. This tendency for political decisions to become clashes between opposing moral imperatives is strengthened by the desire of political interests to motivate active support for their positions.

The connection between political action and reward is tenuous. People do not become politically exercised over the prospect of a small increase in some commonplace advantage. Noble causes and strong emotions fuel the political process, so the greatest political mileage is achieved by those who minimize the acceptability of compromise.

With little scope for cooperation among competing interests, there is limited opportunity for both sides of a political issue to gain. Typically, the interest that prevails in the political arena does so at the expense of other interests. In fact stripped of the rhetoric that rationalizes political action, one finds that the opportunity to use government power to transfer wealth from one group to another motivates much political activity.

Having perceived that the best way to achieve certain goals is by politicizing the issues, people find their interests furthered by identifying them with a moral imperative, an advantage that greatly strengthens the natural tendency to equal personal advantage with social justice. Emotions are inflamed as opposing sides seek political advantage in exaggerating the benefits associated with the "correct" decision and the dire consequences certain to follow the "wrong" decision. When a decision is made, the losers feel not simply disappointment and frustration, but a righteous indignation that associates evil with those who prevailed and with the process that allowed them to do so.

The process can degenerate easily into a malicious exercise in which the major preoccupation becomes that of inflicting harm and ridicule on the enemy. War, the most blatant example of plunder through government, seldom rewards even the winning combatant with spoils sufficient to pay for the victory. Although the original motivation for war is often conquest and plunder, it is self-righteous hatred that typically prolongs the conflict.

Federal Land Use

Examples of acrimonious political combat are easy to find. One particularly interesting example involves the ongoing political battle between the development interests and the preservation interests over federal land use decisions. At one level, this battle can be described as an attempt by each side to use government for the purpose of plunder—to obtain benefits for which others will in large part pay. Although obtaining permission to explore and exploit public lands can be very profitable for energy companies, it also imposes significant costs on those who value unspoiled landscapes and wilderness preserves. Alternatively, preventing development of vast expanses of federal land provides significant benefits to wilderness enthusiasts, while reduced supplies of energy and minerals result in higher prices for everyone.

Obviously, political rhetoric does not reflect the self-interest motives underlying the public land controversy. Political support depends on appeals to nobler concerns and principles. Those in favor of opening more public lands to development argue that the expansion will increase national security, help alleviate poverty, and promote economic growth. Those opposed to further development of public lands speak of a sacred mission to protect our priceless natural heritage for future generations.

Nevertheless, there is more to these arguments than self-serving rhetoric. The very human ability to believe sincerely in the virtue of those things that serve one's interest guarantees that both sides will view this political contest as something of a crusade against a nefarious enemy. This tendency is reflected in the bellicose statements that have characterized recent exchanges between developers and environmentalists. Those favoring development of federal lands refer to the opposition as unrealistic environmental zealots who should "freeze in the dark." From the other side, an Audubon Society newsletter declared that the Reagan administration "had declared war on our natural heritage," suggesting that the antienvironmental wrecking crew led by former Secretary of the Interior James Watt has begun to wipe out the environmental gains and safeguards won by a generation of active and caring citizens.[5]

There is little hope for the kind of give-and-take compromise that would advance the interests of both sides of this political battle. The lines have been clearly drawn, the issues have been elevated to moral principles, and the gains realized by one side will be viewed as losses by the other. The conflicts engendered by scarcity and associated with political decisions will never be completely eliminated, but much of the divisiveness generated by political decisionmaking is unnecessary and could be replaced by a spirit of mutual accommodation.

The solution lies in a recurring theme of this book: Restrict to the extent feasible government responsibility in areas that would be better handled by the incentive of private property and market exchange. Success in market exchange does not require moral posturing or battling for inviolate principles; it does require broadening the range for compromise and coordination through a willingness to sacrifice incremental quantities of one thing in return for incremental quantities of another. In a market setting, one best furthers his or her aims, no matter what they are, by appealing to the concerns of others and seeking out areas of mutual interests.

The harmony generated by the market process is easily appreciated when the dissension that characterizes public land use decisions is contrasted with the spirit of accommodation and resolution that surrounds similar decisions on the use of privately owned wilderness land. The Audubon Society, a group whose position on the preservation versus development issues is well known, owns large tracts of land that it maintains as wildlife preserves. The largest of these is the 26,800-acre Rainey Wildlife Sanctuary in Vermillion Parish, Louisiana. Like most land, the Rainey Sanctuary can be put to several valuable uses. For one thing, it is the natural habitat of a large variety of birds and other wildlife. Of course, the Audubon Society places a high value on maintaining such habitats, but the Rainey Sanctuary also contains deposits of natural gas that the major energy companies find commercially attractive.[6]

---

[5]As reported by Richard Stroup at a conference for economists and journalists sponsored by the Liberty Fund (June 1981), Bozeman, Mont.

[6]For a more detailed discussion of how the Audubon Society and the oil industry have worked out a mutually acceptable arrangement over the use of the Rainey Sanctuary, see John Baden and Richard Stroup, "Saving the Wilderness: A Radical Proposal," *Reason,* July 1981, 28-36.

If the Rainey Sanctuary were owned by the federal government, this situation would likely find the Audubon Society and the oil industry natural enemies, with each side confronting the other from an unyielding position. The incentives provided by private ownership, however, have enabled the Audubon Society and several oil companies to work out a cooperative agreement, allowing drilling for natural gas to take place in parts of the Rainey Sanctuary.

This cooperative attitude is explained by the simple fact that, under private ownership, each side is best able to advance its interests by accommodating the interests of the other. If the Rainey Sanctuary were publicly owned, restricting its use to a wildlife preserve would cost the Audubon Society nothing; the costs would be imposed on those who value the land for alternative uses. But the situation is far different with the Audubon Society ownership. If alternative uses of the land are prevented, the Audubon Society itself is forgoing the value others place on, and are willing to pay for, these alternative uses. Giving up these potential revenues means fewer opportunities for the Audubon Society to establish wildlife sanctuaries or to further other valued ends. Members of the Audubon Society have a strong incentive to work cooperatively with the oil companies.

Similarly, the oil companies now see their advantage served by taking into consideration the concerns of the Audubon Society. An oil company is more likely to obtain from the Audubon Society the right to recover energy resources from the Rainey Sanctuary on favorable terms by demonstrating a commitment to respect wildlife and other natural features of the sanctuary. The result is a relatively cooperative and harmonious relationship that has served the interests of the Audubon Society, the oil companies, and the energy-consuming public.

This kind of productive cooperation could replace the counterproductive divisiveness that now characterizes federal land use by continuing a national policy of the 1800s, a policy that did much to promote economic growth and social tranquility in this country. That policy was the systematic transfer of land from public to private ownership. More than 33 percent of land is still owned by the federal government. Even if much of this land were simply given away to the private sector, government revenues probably would increase, since taxes paid by private owners productively employing the land would exceed the income that public lands generate.

Also, even if the transferred land were given entirely to preservationist groups such as the Audubon Society, the Sierra Club, Friends of the Earth, and the National Rifle Association, the position of potential developers would be no worse than it is now. An oil or timber company, for example, would almost certainly find economic exchange with the Sierra Club more profitable than political combat.

Giving away federal land certainly would generate acrimonious political competition among different interest groups for their fair share. This reaction is but another example of the type of social strife that always accompanies government allocation. This temporary conflict would be a small price to pay for the elimination of persistent conflict over federal land. The socially disruptive conflict over federal land is just one example of the unnecessary strife caused by the substitution of government control for market exchange.

Gasoline Distribution

Throughout the 1970s, the federal government involved itself in determining the price and distribution of gasoline. Government directives, often politically motivated, replaced market choices as the means of allocating gasoline supplies. The predictable shortages that resulted led to equally predictable political conflicts.

When gas lines began forming in California early in 1979, Governor Jerry Brown argued that the Department of Energy was allocating fuel supplies unfairly. He flew to Washington for an emergency meeting with President Jimmy Carter. The result was that California got more gasoline, while other areas of the country got less. The reaction from those parts of the country adversely affected was predictably angry. Other emergency meetings were held, and the allocation for gasoline became largely a matter of political warfare that pitted one region of the country against another.

Farmers found that they were able to get larger diesel allocations by driving their tractors to Washington, where they created major traffic disruptions and incurred the hostility of commuters. Gas shortages also transformed the friendly service station into a hostile arena where long lines and bitterness were pervasive, fights common, and killings not unheard of.

This strife contrasts sharply with the cooperation that prevails when gasoline is allocated through market exchanges. Ideally, each user of gasoline will be concerned with its value to others and will take this value into consideration when deciding how much to buy. This is what happens when price is free to respond to market forces. The price of gasoline that each consumer pays in an unrestricted market reflects the value of an additional gallon to other consumers. Therefore, each consumer is motivated to consider the demands of others and not to purchase gasoline that is worth less to him than it is to someone else.

Further, the unregulated price always will tend toward that level that equates the quantity suppliers are willing to sell with the quantity consumers want to buy. In other words, when responding to the market-clearing price for gasoline, each consumer will desire a quantity that is comparable with the consumption plans of millions of other consumers and the production plans of all suppliers.

This coordination applies not only to gasoline but to thousands of other products and represents a truly amazing degree of social cooperation. This social coordination and cooperation is possible only because of the ability of hundreds of millions of people around the world to communicate with each other through the universal language of market prices. It is not surprising to find social conflict replacing social cooperation when government jams this communication through market censorship, which is what price controls effectively constitute.

No Consensus on the Census

Increasingly, government programs redistribute wealth among different areas of the country on the basis of population changes, demographic structure, racial mix, and other such considerations. As a result, the U.S. Census Bureau has become embroiled in a growing number of political battles. Despite the fact that the 1980 census is, according to most demographers, the most complete count ever, big city mayors and ethnic leaders bitterly denounced its accuracy almost as soon as the initial reports were released. In a law suit won recently by the city of Detroit, the Census Bureau was ordered to inflate its offical count of blacks and hispanics. Other law suits have been filed, and some judges have even threatened the bureau's director with jail. When the census becomes an instrument of political plunder, it must be expected that it also will become a source of conflict and animosity.

Conflict over the census will never be completely eliminated. Political decisions will always affect wealth positions and will legitimately have to be decided on the basis of census data. But government has generated unnecessary dissension over the census through direct involvement in activities that would be carried out more harmoniously and efficiently by the private sector. Public employment and urban renewal are two examples of programs that have ineffectively substituted government solutions for market solutions while increasing the role of the census in the political transfer of wealth. Not only would reducing (better yet, eliminating) programs of this type increase the likelihood of real solutions to specific problems, but it also would allow the Census Bureau to get on with its important work with a minimum of conflict. Again, there are reasons for containing, perhaps by constitutional devices, the size and scope of government programs.

Conflict over Education

As the federal government has become more involved in financing and controlling public education, government bureaucratic choice has increasingly replaced parental choice in education decisions. Parents are required to send their children to a school (which may or may not be a neighborhood school) decided upon by the government or to pay twice for education by sending their children to a private school.

The public schools have a largely captive clientele and thus have little motivation to respond to the diversity of education preferences represented in a community. Not surprisingly, single interest groups have found public schools to be tempting vehicles for imposing their strongly held views on others. Such groups, of course, encounter hostile reactions from those equally strong but opposing views. With limited choice over where their children attend school, parents who, for example, strongly favor or oppose sex education in school, often find political combat the most effective approach in gaining their objective. Having turned our public schools into battlegrounds for contentious issues such as sex education, racial balance, prayer, creation versus evolution, and censorship of books, it is little wonder that all available evidence indicates that education often is seriously neglected.

Controversy over education would be substantially reduced if individual choice were allowed to replace government choice through a policy of education vouchers, or tax credits. Parents could, under such a policy, select the type of school they think would be best for their children. In response to the incentives that vouchers would provide, schools with diverse approaches and philosophies would become available. Parents could not only exercise a wide variety of legitimate educational preferences, but they could so without conflicting with the preferences of others.

The Old against the Young

As a final example of governmentally inspired conflict, consider the problems with Social Security. The controversy that currently surrounds Social Security, which is sure to intensify in the future, is rooted in political expediency. Soon after the Social Security Act was passed in 1935, the labor force paying into the program was growing rapidly, while the number of retired recipients was small. With the Social Security coffers swelling, the political temptation to expand benefits without increasing taxes was impossible to resist.

It is, accordingly, another grand example of special interest legislation against which restrictions on government are designed to guard. In 1939 benefits were increased as the Social Security Act was amended to become a nonfunded pay-as-we-go program, with current retirement payments being financed by current taxpayers. Instead of a retirement plan in which benefits were tied directly to contributions, Social Security became another transfer program with benefits determined by the political ability of one group to impose costs on another group.

The social conflict inherent in the post-1939 Social Security program lay dormant until recently. For years, economic growth and the demographic mix allowed benefits to be expanded without painful increases in the tax burden. This is no longer the case. Sluggish economic growth in the 1970s, coupled with a rapid increase in the retirement-age population in the 1980s, has placed greater demand on the working-age population and has pitted workers against retirees.

This conflict will intensify as it becomes impossible to save the Social Security System without significant tax increases and/or benefit reductions. A program inspired by concern for the elderly but structured in response to political incentives will pit younger against older persons and create a social division of major significance.

The solvency of the Social Security System could have been ensured, and the divisiveness now surrounding it prevented, if a direct tie between individual benefits and individual contributions had been continued. Whether such a vested retirement program can ever be established and maintained by government is debatable. We do know such programs can be efficiently supplied by private insurance companies; indeed, they are the only type provided by private companies. If individuals had been allowed to provide for their own retirement through private plans, the current and growing conflict between the old and the young never would have arisen. Instead, quite the opposite of conflict would have prevailed.

Under private plans, higher retirement benefits to the old would mean higher take-home for the young, as higher current retirement benefits could have resulted only from higher past savings and investment, which translate into greater current labor productivity. The poverty problem among the elderly could have been handled like all other welfare programs.

The initial justification for the mandatory Social Security program was based on the dubious contention that people will not voluntarily provide for their own retirement. Accepting this judgment, however, still provides no reason for the requirement that individuals purchase their retirement plan from the government. Participation in a social security system could have been required and at the same time have remained private. All that would now be needed to move us quickly toward the privatization of Social Security would be the elimination of the requirement that the obligatory retirement plan be purchased from the government.

Unfortunately, the failure of the existing program, a failure evidenced by the huge indebtedness that has built up, makes this choice politically unrealistic. Given the opportunity, new entrants into the labor force would overwhelmingly opt out of the system because its viability is uncertain. This, of course, would guarantee the demise of Social Security as a self-financing system. As is often the case with flawed government programs, the political viability of the Social Security System is explained by its failure, not its success.

Concluding Comments

When discussing the advantages of market incentives, most economists concentrate on how these incentives promote economic efficiency by directing resources into their most productive employments. This portrayal of market allocation is both accurate and important, but surely the gretest advantage to be derived from reliance on market incentives is the mitigation of social conflict. Economic efficiency can never be realized, and would mean little if it could, in a society that has failed to achieve some minimum level of social cohesion. Rules for government are required to do that.

Maintaining a cohesive social order is not an easy task. Indeed, as long as scarcity exists, social conflict will be a consequence of competition for the limited means of achieving our unlimited ends. Although competition is inevitable, noncooperation and contention are not. Depending on how things of value are rationed among competing uses and users, our persistent desire for more can motivate either cooperative or noncooperative behavior. It is in this regard that we derive the significant advantage from market rationing. Market exchanges establish a positive-sum environment that not only allows mutual gains but regards those who expand the scope of cooperative interaction by increasing the opportunities to realize these gains.

Unfortunately, this source of social cooperation is subject to constant erosion as special interest groups find it to their short-term advantage to replace market allocation with political allocation. The power vested in a government to perform its legitimate functions can be used by politically influential groups to capture gains at the expense of others. When zero-sum political plunder replaces positive-sum market exchange, the stage is set for malice in plunderland. This is a primary reason constitutional restraints on what government can and cannot do are needed.

6

Inflation and the Need for a Monetary Constitution

> The manner in which inflation operates explains why it is so difficult to resist when policy mainly concerns itself with particular situations rather than with general conditions and with short-term rather than long-term problems.
>
> —Frederich A. Hayek[1]

Inflation has become a persistent fact of life. While few people like inflation, we have all, with varied degrees of success, learned how to live with it. From 1967 to 1985 the consumer price index increased by 225 percent.[2] The inflation rate was not constant over this period of time. It ebbed and flowed, running as low as 3.4 percent in 1971 and 1972, as high as 13.3 percent in 1979, and below 4 percent again in the mid-1980s. But ebb or flow, inflation has endured and an entire generation of Americans have come to believe that it is in the natural order of things and there is little they can do to eliminate it.[3]

Fortunately, both these beliefs are erroneous. In U.S. history there have been long periods during which the price level has been relatively stable. Indeed, from the late 1860s until the beginning of the twentieth century, the price level trend was downward. The inflation that has plagued us since the late 1960s is the longest inflation ever experienced in the United States. Furthermore, the cause and cure of inflation has been known by economists for centuries.[4] For a given quantity of goods and services available for purchase, the price level will be determined by the amount of money being spent on them: the more money being spent, the higher prices will be. Therefore, if the supply of money is increasing more rapidly than the supply of goods and

---

[1] *The Constitution of Liberty* (Chicago: University of Chicago Press, 1960), 332.

[2] *Federal Reserve Bulletin,* December 1985, A50.

[3] We have become so used to inflation that people now seem oblivious to any inflation rate below 5 percent. The fact is, however, that an inflation rate of 5 percent will double the price level every fourteen years.

[4] See Milton Friedman, "Empirical Monetary Economics: What Have We Learned in the Last 25 Years?—Discussion" *American Economic Review* (May 1975), 176-79.

services, a persistent increase in the price level is inevitable. If, however, the supply of money is not allowed to increase faster than the supply of goods and services, a persistent increase in the price level is impossible. Since the Federal Reserve System, a governmentally created agency, controls the growth in the money supply, it is entirely possible for federal government policy to eliminate inflation and keep it eliminated.[5]

But if the government can eliminate inflation, why has it not done so? We have heard repeatedly from politicians of all persuasions of their dedication to controlling inflation. A question that naturally arises is Can we be confident that politicians are serious in their anti-inflation rhetoric?

There are compelling reasons to believe that political decisionmakers are less than sincere in their desire to bring inflation under control. Politicians and politically influential interest groups have strong reasons for favoring inflationary expansion of the money supply. Furthermore, once inflation has become an expected feature of the economy, strong political pressures will be exerted against any serious anti-inflationary policy. We will not, of course, hear politicians openly admitting that they favor inflation. Their rhetoric will be consistently anti-inflationary. But the solutions that are favored typically will be little more than attempts to mask the symptoms of inflation or attacks on scapegoats that allow politicians to shift the blame away from their policies, which is where it belongs. Any move to get at the heart of the problem by reducing the growth in the money supply will encounter stout political resistance.

If the supply of money is subject to political influence, we can expect a persistent inflationary bias in the economy. It is our view that political discretion over the money supply all but ensures inflation. The only hope, in the long run, for preventing political decisions from continually reducing the value of the currency is through fundamental reform in the rules governing

---

[5]Supposedly the Federal Reserve System, which has direct control over the money supply, is an independent agency and formulates its policy independently of political considerations. A realistic assessment of the system's independence, however, finds that politics plays an important, possibly overriding, role in its policy. According to Edward Kane,

> The Fed is a political institution designed *by* politicians to *serve* politicians. Its chief officials (i.e., the Board of Governors) are nominated by the President and their appointments are cleared with the Senate. They are forced to defend their performance before Congressional committees several times a month and must be prepared to respond expeditiously to letters and telephone calls from Congressmen and Senators at a moment's notice.

Edward J. Kane, "Politics & Fed Policymaking: The More Things Change the More They Stay the Same," *Journal of Monetary Economics* (April 1980), 199-211.

It also has been argued that bureaucratic incentives provide the best explanation of the Federal Reserve policies quite apart from political pressures. See Mark Toma, "Inflationary Bias of the Federal Reserve System: A Bureaucratic Approach," *Journal of Monetary Economics* (September 1982), 163-90. Also see William F. Shughart II and Robert D. Tollison, "Preliminary Evidence on the Use of Inputs by the Federal Reserve System," *The American Economic Review* (June 1983), 291-304.

control over the money supply. In fact, in the absence of a monetary constitution that insulates monetary control from political influence, it is not at all clear that attempts to bring inflation under control are even desirable. If we, as a nation, are not willing to consider changing the monetary rules of the game, we may well be better off resigning ourselves to the inevitability of inflation and learning to cope with it as best we can. This would, of course, be the second best approach to the problem. No matter how well we arrange our activities and institutions to minimize the cost of inflation, inflation will always reduce the productive capacity of the economy.

Control over the money supply is another example of how we can improve our long-term prospects by imposing restrictions on the options that can be exercised through government. Before expanding on this point, however, it will be useful to consider briefly the important role money plays in a productive economy.

The Productivity of Money

To understand the productivity of money, recall the discussion in chapter 2 on the productivity of specialization. By dividing up the tasks that go into a productive process, skills and capital can be specialized to produce far more than would be possible otherwise. As productive as specialization is, however, it would be completely impractical without exchange. No one could afford to specialize unless it was possible to exchange the output of one's productive effort for items that are being produced by others. If all exchange were impossible, each individual would have to produce everything he or she consumed. Anything that reduces the cost of exchange is productive because it expands our ability to increase wealth through specialization.

The exchange of one particular good for another, or barter, is undoubtedly the oldest form of exchange. Individual A specializes in the production of scarves and is anxious to exchange some of them in return for the hats that individual B has produced. If B happens to want some scarves, then an exchange between A and B is possible. There exists a double coincidence of wants: A has what B wants and wants what B has. A double coincidence of wants does not always exist, however, and barter exchanges will be more difficult to arrange. For example, B may not want any scarves in exchange for his hats. He may want shoes instead. If by chance individual C, who specializes in shoe production, happens to want scarves, then A may be able to trade scarves for hats, but in a roundabout way. A can exchange scarves to C in return for shoes, which can then be traded to B in return for hats. For barter exchanges to take place, the typical situation would require a much more indirect and complicated pattern than a simple example can illustrate.

The difficulties with barter exchange extend beyond the problem of finding a double coincidence of wants. Individual A may want one hat and B may want one scarf. But one of A's scarves may be worth only half as much as one of B's hats. Since B wants only one scarf, he will be willing to give up only one-half of a hat in return for a scarf. This makes no sense, of course, since a half of a hat is not worth half as much as a whole hat. The problem is that hats, scarves, shoes, and most other commodities are not conveniently divisible.

If exchange depended on barter, the cost of arranging exchange (transaction costs) would be extremely high and opportunities for specialization would be unnecessarily limited. It is for this reason that money, which is anything that is widely acceptable in exchange for goods and services, is so productive. Because money is something that everyone wants, the existence of money eliminates the problem of finding a double coincidence of wants and therefore dramatically lowers transaction costs. Why is money widely accepted? The answer, though trivial, is important. Money is widely accepted because it is widely accepted. Each person is willing to accept money, which may not have any intrinsic value, in exchange for valuable goods and services because he knows that everyone else will do the same. It is this confidence in money that gives it its value and makes it so productive.

For money to be fully productive, it not only must be widely accepted as a medium of exchange, but it also must be divisible and durable. For example, live cattle could be used for money and indeed have been known to serve this function. A problem with live cattle as money, however, is that they are not very divisible. An individual with his money in the form of a live cow will face difficulty removing a segment of appropriate size for the purchase of, say, a dozen eggs. It is also desirable that money be durable, since people will find it convenient to hold money in anticipation of future purchases. For example, bananas could serve as money, and divisibility would present no particular problem. The disadvantage here, however, is that your money would likely rot before you wanted to spend it.

Of the many things that have historically served as money in different parts of the world, most have satisfied the divisibility and durability criteria. Feathers, shells, stones, beads, salt, dried fish, and cigarettes are but a few of the wide variety of things that have served in the productive role of money. Historically, the most common materials to serve as money have been metals, especially precious metals such as silver and gold. Metals are finely divisible and extremely durable, and the intrinsic value of the precious metals makes them universally acceptable as a medium of exchange. But the intrinsic value of the material serving as money is really of little consequence, as evidenced by the fact that money in modern economies is nothing more than paper and magnetic computer memory signifying checking account balances. The ability of valueless things such as paper and magnetic memory to become universally accepted as money is testimony to the enormous productivity of money. The advantages of money are sufficiently great that people will latch on to almost anything, no matter how worthless in and of itself, to serve as money.[6] And once people are using a certain form of money, they will continue using it even when the cost of doing so is very large. The tenacity with which people use money will help us understand the advantage governments can realize from inflation.

Why Inflation Is a Problem

To the individual, money represents a personal claim on goods and services, and the more money possessed the greater this claim on wealth. It is natural for each of us then to think that more money is better than less. For the economy at large, however, there is no advantage in having a large money supply over a small one. As long as the monetary unit is finely divisible, a small quantity of money will promote economic productivity by facilitating specialization and exchange just as effectively as a large quantity of money. Having more money in the economy does nothing to increase the availability of goods and services. The only significant difference between an economy with a small quantity of money and the same economy with a large quantity of money is that all prices will be higher in the latter than the former. Higher prices are no disadvantage, since incomes, in money terms, will be correspondingly higher as well. But higher prices are certainly no advantage either.[7]

To say that it makes no difference whether the supply of money is small and prices are low or the supply of money is large and prices are high is not the same as saying that there are no problems with transitions from low to high prices (inflation) or from high to low prices (deflation). Whether prices are low or high, it is preferable to have a stable price level than to switch between one price level and another. The problems associated with deflation will become clear later in this chapter. Our primary concern, however, is with the costs that arise from inflation. But before discussing these costs, it is important to distinguish between changes in the price level and changes in relative prices.

Even if the growth in the money supply and the growth in productivity were the same and thus the price level remained constant over time,[8] we would still expect some prices to increase and others to decrease. As discussed in chapter 2, market prices convey important information on the relative value of different resources and products. Changes in preferences,

---

[6]A common argument is that the less valuable the commodity being used for money, the better. The alternative uses of paper are less valuable than the alternative uses of gold, for example, and according to the argument, since paper money is just as useful as gold money, it is better to use paper. While this argument is correct as far as it goes, we will see that it ignores important political dimensions of the problem of maintaining a sound monetary system.

[7]In saying this we are assuming that the cost of creating extra money is effectively zero; money takes the form of paper rather than gold.

[8]Here we abstract, as we do throughout, from considerations of changes in the velocity of money.

technologies, weather conditions, and so on increase the value of some products relative to that of others. Unless changing relative prices are registering these shifts in relative values, it is impossible for economic decisionmakers to direct resources into their most productive uses.

The importance of relative prices explains one of the costs of inflation. With inflation the price of a product can be increasing in absolute terms even though its relative price is decreasing. The general rise in the price level creates extraneous noise that tends to obscure the important information being conveyed by changes in relative prices. If the inflation rate were perfectly predictable, people would adapt to this inflationary noise and little harm would be done.[9] Historically, however, once inflation has gotten started, it seldom follows a predictable path. Instead, inflation tends to be volatile and erratic with there being little hope of knowing what the price level will be beyond the very short run. This uncertainty not only obscures the information contained in relative price shifts, but it also increases the risk involved in long-term contractual agreements of the type often required in productive investments and thus acts as a barrier to the maintenance and expansion of our productive capacity.

Another problem is that inflation diverts activity and investment away from the creation of new wealth and into measures aimed at protecting existing wealth. For example, inflation erodes the value of cash balances that people keep on hand in order to take advantage, on short notice, of exchange opportunities. The higher the inflation, the more time and effort people will spend arranging their financial affairs to minimize these cash balances. The hyperinflation to post-World War I Germany, when the price level would more than double each day, provides a good example of this problem. The value of money was eroding so rapidly that workers arranged to be paid several times a day, with their wives picking up each paycheck so they could spend it immediately. This example not only points to the waste of potentially productive effort during inflationary times, but it also draws attention to the fact that inflation encourages immediate consumption at the sacrifice of the saving and investment that is essential for productivity growth. Furthermore, inflation invariably interacts with tax laws to discourage investment in business capital. From 1970 through 1977, for example, inflation increased the tax burden on corporate sector capital income by more than $180 billion. In each year 1973 through 1977, inflation increased the taxes paid on corporate capital income by at least 50 percent above what they would have been in the absense of inflation.[10]

---

[9]For a discussion of price level predictabilty as the appropriate objective of the monetary structure, see James M. Buchanan, "Predictability: The Criterion of Monetary Constitutions," in Leland B. Yeager, ed., *In Search of a Monetary Constitution* (Cambridge, Mass.: Harvard University Press, 1962).

[10]Martin Feldstein and Lawrence Summers, "Inflation and the Taxation of Capital Income in the Corporate Sector," *National Tax Journal* (December 1979), 445-70.

It is possible, of course, to index contractual agreements and the tax laws so that obligations are settled in real terms (in terms of constant purchasing power) rather than monetary terms. In severe inflations, indexation can be an improvement and will emerge to some degree from free market exchanges. But indexing is not an easy, or all that effective, solution to the problems of inflation. Some things, such as cash balances, cannot be protected against the eroding effects of inflation. Also, even when a price index can be applied, there are many different price indices (depending on the type of products under consideration, whether the products are being distributed at the wholesale or retail level, and the relevant geographic location), and it is often debatable as to which index is appropriate. Even if all parties to a contract are in agreement on the appropriate index, serious problems with the accuracy of the index chosen remain. No general index is likely to reflect the cost of living changes pertinent to a particular transaction, no matter how carefully it is constructed.[11] Indexing monetary transactions to inflation is, at best, a crude, cumbersome, and costly process. Resorting to price indices and escalator clauses is in effect admitting that inflation has destroyed much of the money's ability to perform its crucial function of lowering the cost of exchange. The best solution to the problem of a suit that does not fit is to retailor it so that it does, not to hunch over and walk bowlegged to accommodate the poor fit. The best solution to the problem of inflation is to control the money supply and eliminate the inflation, not to accommodate it with a host of awkward price index adjustments.

Monetary Policy as a Rudder

For reasons discussed in chapters 2 and 3, the ability of government to solve problems by assuming a detailed role in economic decisionmaking is severely limited. Overly ambitious attempts to employ discretionary government power to promote socially desirable objectives typically do more harm than good. In most cases, the best government can do is to establish a stable setting that is conducive to harmonious and productive interaction between individuals who are intent on promoting their own objectives. In the case of money, the important contribution that government can make is establishing a stable monetary framework that facilitates the specialization and exchange upon which cooperative social interaction depends. Government attempts to accomplish more than this through a discretionary monetary policy designed to smooth out the business cycle are, in fact, likely to undermine the ability of

---

[11]In the indexing of Social Security benefits, the consumer price index is clearly the most appropriate one to use. Yet in the late 1970s, when housing prices were escalating rapidly, a debate erupted over the appropriateness of including the price of houses in the index when figuring Social Security benefits, since most retired persons already own their homes.

money to promote social coordination and in doing so increase, rather than decrease, the disruptiveness of the business cycle.

But the prevailing notion in recent decades that government discretion is a source of social progress has carried over into the sphere of money. The primary impetus for discretionary monetary policy has come from the ascendency of Keynesian economics, which calls for government to manage, or fine-tune, the economy by controlling aggregate demand. One of the implements in the government's kit of Keynesian tools is the supply of money.[12] In anticipation of a decline in aggregate demand and a resulting fall in economic activity, the appropriate monetary policy calls for an increase in the money supply.[13] With an increase in the quantity of money available, consumer spending will expand, and resources that would have been unemployed otherwise will be needed to meet this demand. Also, the increased availability of money is expected to lower the interest rate and thereby encourage investment spending, which will provide employment opportunities. Alternatively, if an increase in aggregate demand is anticipated to exceed productive capacity and exert inflationary pressures on the economy, economic stability can be maintained by reducing the supply of money and thereby moderating aggregate demand. In other words, monetary policy can be used as a rudder to guide the economy along the road of steady growth.

If this discretionary monetary policy is properly implemented, there is no reason, according to the theory, that price level stability could not be maintained while fluctuations in economic activity around its growth trend are eliminated. But in the 1950s economists noticed an empirical relationship between the inflation rate and the unemployment rate. It appeared that unemployment could be reduced by increasing the rate of inflation.[14] The implication of this was appealing to economists, who are used to dealing with trade-offs. Inflation might be undesirable, but so is unemployment. If the inflation rate were zero, the cost of increasing inflation a bit probably would be less than the benefit from having more people employed. Many economists saw the Phillips curve as a constraint on economic policy. The task of the economist was to inform policymakers of the trade-offs required by this

---

[12]While Keynesians consider the money supply to be a tool for controlling aggregate demand, they consider it to be a relatively minor one. The important economic policy tools from the Keynesian perspective are government spending and taxation.

[13]We are not concerned here with the mechanics of increasing the money supply except to point out that Federal Reserve policy exerts important control over the availability of money in the economy.

[14]This graphic representation of the negative relationship between unemployment and inflation is referred to as the Phillips curve after the late British economist A.W. Phillips. It was Phillips's empirical work on the relationship between the rate of change in wage rates and the unemployment rate that sparked economists' interest in the effect of inflation on unemployment. See A.W. Phillips, "The Relationship between Unemployment and the Rate of Change in Money Wages in the United Kingdom, 1861-1957," *Economica* 25 (1958), 283-99.

constraint, and the task of the policymakers was to choose the appropriate combination of inflation and unemployment, a choice that would be implemented with the assistance of policy recommendations from economists.[15] Given the acceptance of this Phillips curve view, deflation was always to be avoided (deflation increased unemployment), but a little inflation could be a good thing. Clearly, this Phillips curve perspective imparts a definite inflationary bias to macroeconomic policy.

Unfortunately, there are serious problems with discretionary monetary policy as a means of achieving stable economic growth. Even if the theory outlined above were entirely correct, economists do not now, and never will, have the necessary prescience to implement countercyclical monetary policy correctly.[16] If the money supply is to be expanded in time, and in sufficient quantity, to counteract a decline in economic activity, for example, the experts would have to know when and how much the economy would turn down in the absence of monetary expansion. No matter how accomplished economists become at understanding the functioning of the economy, predicting the future will remain beyond their, or anyone else's ability.

Even if the timing and magnitude of an economic downturn were known in advance, it would still not be possible to plan effective countercyclical monetary policy with any confidence. There is a lag between the time when growth in the money supply is changed and the time when this change has its impact on economic output. And this lag varies from situation to situation, with no way of accurately predicting how long it will be. Attempting to guide the economy with discretionary control of the money supply is as likely to aggravate as it is to moderate recessionary and inflationary cycles in the economy. Imagine attempting to steer your car down the road with unpredictable lags between turning the steering wheel and changing the direction of the car, and you have an idea of the dangers of attempting to direct the economy with the rudder of money policy. If you do not wind up in a recessionary ditch, it is probably because you have crashed into an inflationary embankment.

We also should point out that the impact monetary policy has on real economic outcomes is, at best, temporary. A good example of the temporary effect of monetary policy is the attempt to reduce interest rates by increasing the rate of growth in the money supply. If money is pumped into the economy at a faster rate, one of the first things that will happen is that the interest rate will decline as competition occurs among banks with more money to lend. This also means that the number of dollars being spent on goods and services will soon be growing at a faster rate, with the consequence being more inflation. Once the inflation rate increases, the demand for money also will increase, as people now need more money to finance the same number of

---

[15]See Arthur M. Okun, *The Political Economy of Prosperity* (New York: Norton, 1970).

[16]The inability to forecast accurately economic conditions is a problem also associated with discretionary fiscal policy.

purchases. Not only will the interest rate increase from its temporarily lower level, but it will increase above its original level. With inflation eroding the value of money more rapidly than before, lenders will require a higher interest rate simply to maintain the same real rate of return. Borrowers will be willing to pay this inflationary premium because they also are aware that the dollars they pay back will have less real purchase power than the dollars they borrowed. If the interest rate increased just enough to cover the additional inflation, then the real rate of interest (the nominal interest rate minus the inflation rate) would return to the level that existed before the increase in monetary growth. Unfortunately, with additional inflation comes additional uncertainty about the future price level. This adds to the risk of lending money and becomes reflected as an increased risk premium in the interest rate. The short-term effect of increasing the monetary growth rate may be to reduce the interest rate and increase investment, but the long-term effect is just the opposite.

Similarly, increasing the rate at which money is pumped into the economy can cause a temporary reduction in unemployment, even though the long-term effect can be to increase unemployment. In other than a completely stagnant economy, some unemployment is not only normal but also healthy. With changing consumer preferences and improved opportunities due to technological advances, shifts occur in the relative values of productive resources, including labor, over different employments. It is clearly desirable that resources respond to the changes in relative values by moving from those employments where they are now worth less to those where they are now worth more. Because information never is complete, time and effort always is required in searching for the more valuable employment opportunities. When workers are entering or returning to the labor force, or when they have been laid off because of shifts in consumer preferences, it makes sense for them to spend time looking for a job that provides the highest return commensurate with their skills.[17] Those who are searching for a job are recorded as unemployed even though they are engaged in the productive task of acquiring valuable information. One can think of a natural unemployment rate that consists of those people who are productively unemployed.[18]

---

[17]Martin Feldstein, "The Economics of the New Unemployment," *The Public Interest* (Fall 1973), 3-42.

[18]Somewhat paradoxically, this natural unemployment rate will tend to increase at the same time the employment rate is increasing and productive employment opportunities are expanding. For example, in recent years the percentage of the working age population that is employed has increased as more spouses have entered the work force to provide the household with a second income. Second income earners, however, tend to change jobs more often than primary income earners, and this increases the measured unemployment rate. Improvements in technology that create new and productive opportunities for workers also will increase unemployment as more employees find it advantageous to search out and train for better jobs.

An increase in the monetary growth rate can temporarily reduce the natural rate of unemployment by temporarily reducing the length of time it takes unemployed workers to find acceptable employment. With money being poured into the economy at a faster pace, consumers will increase their spending and firms will notice that they can sell more of their products at existing prices. The first response of producers will be to expand their output, which requires employing more resources, including labor, at prevailing prices and wages. At first this attempt will be largely successful, as unemployed workers will be willing to cease their job search earlier than otherwise as more employment opportunities become available at acceptable wages.

The decrease in the unemployment rate below the natural rate cannot last for long, however. Eventually employers find that they can no longer hold on to their additional workers at prevailing wages. Workers will discover that employment opportunities have expanded generally and that maybe it was a mistake not to have looked longer for even higher wages. Wages will be bid up as firms compete against each other for workers, and this soon translates into higher prices for goods and services being produced. Workers soon will observe that their higher wages, which were so attractive initially, have been reduced in real terms by rising prices. What constitutes an acceptable wage will be revised upward to compensate for inflation, and the search time required to find acceptable employment will increase. The unemployment rate will head back to its natural level after a temporary dip.

Indeed, it may be the case that unemployment will end up higher because of inflation. When people are deciding how long to continue searching for better employment opportunities, relative prices convey important information, as is the case in all resource allocation decisions. As discussed earlier in this chapter, changes in the general price level can garble the transmission of this information. This is particularly true when price level changes are unpredictable, as they increasingly are when inflation becomes greater. The uncertainty and noise created by inflation can reduce the efficiency with which labor markets work and thus increase the natural rate of unemployment.[19]

So much for the stability of the Phillips curve trade-off between inflation and unemployment. Any policy attempt to reduce unemployment by accepting a higher inflation rate can be successful only in the short run. Once the higher inflation rate becomes incorporated in economic expectations, the natural rate of inflation will again prevail, and at best, the Phillips curve policy has brought increased inflation but no reduction in unemployment.[20] More

---

[19]See David I. Meiselman, "More Inflation: More Unemployment," *Tax Review,* Newsletter of the Tax Foundation, Inc. January 1976. Even if inflation does not increase the natural rate of unemployment, after inflation becomes a persistent feature in the economy, any attempt to reduce inflation will increase the temporary unemployment rate. We discuss this later in this chapter.

[20]Milton Friedman, "Nobel Lecture: Inflation & Unemployment," *Journal of Political Economy* (June 1977), 451-72.

likely the long-term result will be both more inflation and more unemploy-ment. In 1967, when economists were talking about the Phillips curve as a stable constraint on policy, the unemployment rate was 3.8 percent and the inflation rate was 3.0 percent. In 1980, after a decade plus of discretionary policy designed to maneuver the economy toward the best point on the Phillips curve, the unemployment rate was 7.1 percent and the inflation rate was 12.4 percent.

There can be no reasonable doubt that government attempts to improve economic performance by exercising discretionary control over the money supply face serious problems. But even if it were theoretically possible to maintain both a stable price level and full employment growth with discre-tionary monetary policy, and the government had all the knowledge and fore-sight to do so, a fundamental problem would remain. A crucial but implicit assumption behind most proposals to put discretionary power under the control of government is that political decisionmakers are motivated to pursue only those objectives consistent with the broad public interest. Certainly this has been the implicit assumption of those who recommend discretionary monetary policy. The possibility that monetary policy will be put to any pur-pose other than improving economic performance is seldom explored. This ignores the fact that government control over the money supply affords politi-cal decisionmakers opportunities to pursue objectives that are much more compelling politically than is the goal of sound economic performance.

The Temptations Facing a Counterfeiter

Indulge your fantasy for a moment and assume that you, and only you, are granted legal permission to print and spend counterfeit money. Would you refuse this opportunity and continue with your forty-hour-a-week, fifty-week-a-year job, which pays less per year than your printing press could turn out while you were watching the evening news? Probably not. Of course, you would convince yourself that you would not abuse your money-creating privi-lege by being excessively greedy. But why should you not have a few million dollars a year to enjoy some of the nicer things in life? You quit your job to devote full time to the demanding task of printing up stacks of $20, $50, and $100 bills each evening and spending them the next day. Soon you will be enjoying the finest foods, hosting lavish parties in your beautiful home, travel-ing in your private jet, cruising on your luxury yacht, and generally enjoying the good life.

But what effect is your new wealth having on the rest of the economy? You might not have time to think about that question, but if you did give it careful consideration, the answer would be clear. First of all, there has been no increase in the economy's productive capacity or output. Indeed, if any-thing, a little less is being produced because you have quit your job and are producing nothing. You are consuming much more than you were before, so it must be true that there is less for others to consume; they are, in aggregate, worse off. People have more money, of course, as the new money you have printed and spent filters through the economy. With less for others to buy with this extra money, however, prices have increased. You have been able to transfer resources and wealth away from others and to yourself through inflation. Of course, inflation will be reflected in the prices you pay also, and you will find that a few million dollars just do not go as far as they used to. This provides a natural justification for you to increase the rate at which you print money. This will generate yet more inflation, but you are still able to capture additional wealth from others by printing more money because you are the first one to spend the extra money, which does not have its full inflationary impact until after it has passed through many hands and financed many transactions.

Interestingly, while it is your creation of money that is making the rest of the public worse off through inflation, you do not have to worry about being blamed. When prices are increasing, most people blame those who are making the goods and services available. This is analogous to the preacher who blames the congregation for being too small. Those who are in the congregation are keeping it from being smaller than it otherwise would be, and those who are making products available are keeping inflation from being higher than it otherwise would be. You, who by producing nothing while spending millions, are the prime source of the inflation. But you probably will complain about the inflationary policies of retailers, industry, and labor just like everyone else.

Not only will you escape blame for the inflation, but paradoxically enough, your inflationary behavior will be credited with helping people overcome the problems caused by inflation. Those who are poorer because you have been printing money will, in an effort to keep up with inflation, be anxious for you to print yet more money and spend it on their products and services. Furthermore, petitioners can be expected to appeal to your sense of social justice and civic duty and ask you to make more money available for the important causes and programs they espouse. Having spent millions on yourself, you will find it not only easy, but morally compelling, to assume a mantle of benevolence and use your printing press to extend support to a host of worthy projects. By doing so you will simply be taking from some and giving to others, with no clear social gain. But the good you bestow will be focused, highly visible, and clearly the result of your "generosity." The harm that you cause in the form of more inflation will be diluted over everyone in the economy and not blamed on you. You will be able to acquire enormous wealth and a reputation as a caring and compassionate philanthropist while actually damaging the economy and, in the aggregate, making others worse off. All this because you have control over the money supply.

Obviously this story is fanciful. There are laws against counterfeiting because we recognize that few would be able to resist the temptation to abuse the privilege by printing excessive amounts of money for their own use. Yet the assumption behind discretionary monetary policy is that a collection of individuals whose interests are served by increasing the wealth of government can be given control over the supply of money with the confidence that they will ignore their personal interests and be guided only by the public interest. This assumption is naive in the extreme. Political decisionmakers benefit by increasing the money supply in much the same way an individual benefits from counterfeiting. It should surprise no one that political control over the money supply is a sure prescription for inflation.

The ability to finance government programs is important to politicians who want to please their constituents and to those in the bureaucracy whose employment depends on the need to administer these programs. The enthusiasm for expanding support for political programs is tempered to the extent that money has to be taken from the public to do so, with the money being raised either through taxation or borrowing. Obviously the public does not appreciate higher taxes, and borrowing money requires that the government compete against private investors for lendable funds. With the ability to exert influence over the money supply, however, the political liability for increasing government spending is greatly reduced. With it being possible to increase the money supply, politicians can spend more than they raise in taxes with a rather cavalier attitude.[21] A large deficit could be financed entirely through government borrowing, but it is much easier politically to cover much of the deficit simply by increasing the money supply.[22] This can, for a while, give the appearance of the free lunch that is every politician's dream. A new post office building can be constructed, education programs can be expanded, and subsidies can be enlarged—seemingly all at no cost. The government did not have to divert money away from desirable private activity through greater taxes or

---

[21]With the breakdown in the early 1960s of the view that fiscal responsibility required balanced budgets, the federal budget has been in almost continuous deficit. Since 1960 federal spending has exceeded tax revenues in every year, with the exception of 1969. For a discussion of the political forces behind this string of deficits and the role Keynesian economics played in giving rein to these political forces, see James Buchanan and Richard Wagner, *Democracy in Deficit: The Political Legacy of Lord Keynes* (New York: Academic Press, 1977).

[22]Technically, the Federal Reserve System could refuse to monetize the debt by refusing to create the money necessary to do so. This would force the government to finance the entire deficit through borrowing. Unfortunately, with large deficits, this would put enormous pressure on the financial markets, resulting in higher interest rates and the extensive crowding out of private investment. The political cost of this crowding out translates into strong political pressure on the Federal Reserve to help cover the deficit by lending money to the government, money that is created out of thin air. If the Federal Reserve shows reluctance to create the additional money, its tight money policy is quickly blamed for the slowdown in economic activity that results from the reduction in private investment and spending. There can be no doubt that this political pressure is very effective. Recall footnote 5.

borrowing. Indeed, quite the opposite appears to be the case. The government actually made people feel better off, at least initially, by making more money available for everyone to spend.

Unfortunately, the impossible is not possible, and there is no free lunch. Just as the counterfeiter is making people worse off when he creates more money and spends it, so does the government when it finances its spending by creating money. The additional government spending transfers real resources into political use and thus leaves less for people to acquire through private choice. True, consumers have more money to spend, but with less to spend it on, the result is higher prices. People are in effect being taxed as the value of their money holdings diminishes. There is no way of avoiding this inflationary tax short of completely avoiding the use of money. But because of the productivity of money, people are reluctant to abandon it.

It also is true that inflation often will not be blamed on politicians' decisions. The proximate cause of inflation will be the decisions of those who are selling goods and services. And successful politicians are very good at convincing the public that this proximate cause is, in fact, the real cause by arguing that inflation is the result of things such as the profits of big business, the demands of labor unions, and the pricing policy of OPEC. Not only do politicians avoid much of the blame for inflation, but once the ill effects of inflation begin manifesting themselves, individuals will see the answer to their problems in new or expanded government programs, which will be financed largely, of course, by further expanding the money supply.[23] Not surprisingly, politicians find inflation a very convenient means of financing government expenditures.

The Costs of Disinflation

The benefits from the elimination of inflation are significant in terms of long-term economic growth. Unfortunately, there also are significant costs associated with eliminating inflation. Once inflation has become a presistent feature of the economic landscape, any genuine move to reduce inflation will cause temporary, but serious, dislocations in the economy. These dislocations will take the form of reduced economic activity, high unemployment, and high real interest rates, all of which will impose high costs on people.

Earlier we discussed how an increase in the rate at which the money supply is growing will result first in a temporary increase in economic output

---

[23]Speaking both of the harm caused by inflation and the difficulty people have in understanding its real cause, John Maynard Keynes wrote, "There is no subtler, no surer means of overturning the existing basis of society than to debauch the currency. The process engages all the hidden forces of economic law on the side of destruction, and does it in a manner which not one man in a million is able to diagnose." J.M. Keynes, *The Economic Consequences of the Peace* (New York: Harcourt, Brace & Howe, 1920), 236.

and a reduction in unemployment. The reason the impact is only temporary is that the eventual effect is to increase the inflation rate, which informs employers and employees that what appeared to be attractive opportunties to sell more of their products and labor were, in reality, not attractive opportunities at all. The long-term effect of the increased rate of monetary growth is an increased inflation rate with an unemployment rate that is no lower than the natural rate. Once inflation gets started, the only way to bring it down is by reducing the rate at which the money supply is growing. But just as the initial effect of an acceleration in the money supply is to reduce unemployment temporarily, the initial effect of a deceleration in the money supply is a temporary increase in the unemployment rate. Only after a significant lag will the inflation rate be reduced and the unemployment rate drop back to the natural rate.

The problem again has to do with the fact that people learn to expect inflation and adjust their behavior accordingly. Firms and workers expect their costs of production and living to increase continually and accordingly expect the prices they receive for their products and services to increase also. When the growth in the money supply is reduced, there is less money to spend than there otherwise would have been, and thus consumers find that they can buy fewer products at existing prices. Firms will find their sales declining, but since they fully expect their costs to continue increasing, they have little motivation to reduce their prices to recover sales. With declining sales, firms find that they no longer require as many workers as before, and the number of people who are laid off increases. If workers would lower their wage demands in anticipation of lower inflation, many of these layoffs would not occur or laid-off workers would find it easy to acquire new employment. But workers also expect inflation to continue increasing their cost of living, and they are reluctant to adjust their wage demands downward. So the first thing that happens in any serious fight against inflation is that firms reduce their output and unemployment increases. Only after more time elapses do economic decisionmakers begin to lower their expectations and lower (or reduce the rate at which they increase) the prices they charge and wages they will accept. As this happens, inflation begins to decline, and the stage is set for economic activity to pick up and for unemployment to settle back toward its natural rate.

Even as inflation begins declining, however, economic dislocations will persist because inflationary expectations will lag behind the reduction in inflation. It will be observed that the current inflation rate is coming down, but with a history of inflation, people will tend to see this as a temporary phenomenon. Because of this, financial institutions will be reluctant to reduce the inflationary interest premium when making long-term loans. During periods of disinflation, nominal interest rates will decline much more slowly than the inflation rate, the real interest rate will increase, and long-term borrowing commitments that facilitate investment decisions will be discouraged.[24] Much of the problem here arises from the uncertainty over future price levels. If lender and borrowers were in agreement and confident in their expectations of future price levels, the nominal interest rate would adjust accordingly and long-term financial commitments would be unhampered. The higher the inflation rate, however, the more price level uncertainty there is, and this uncertainty is compounded during periods of inflationary transition—for example, when inflation rates are declining.

If the federal government were credible when it announced its determination to fight inflation, the lag between a deceleration in monetary growth and reduced inflation would be shorter, price level uncertainty would be reduced, and the severity and duration of the resulting unemployment would be less. Because people believed that inflation really was going to decrease permanently, firms and workers would be willing to reduce prices and wages, which would allow output and employment to remain at high levels. Unfortunately, few people take the government seriously when it announces another fight against inflation. Most fights against inflation have been little more than cosmetic attempts to disguise the symptoms of inflation (such as wage and price controls and political exhortations and guidelines), which fail to address the fundamental cause of inflation. When policy does come to grips with the fundamental problem and the growth in the money supply is reduced, the temporary costs of recession and unemployment tend to weaken the political resolve necessary if control over the money supply is to be continued long enough to complete the job and eliminate inflation. Several times in recent years a serious fight against inflation was begun, but the political pressure to do something about unemployment soon resulted in a reversal in monetary policy, a rapid expansion in the money supply, and a new wave of inflation. Each time this happens the federal government deservedly loses yet more of its credibility, and the unemployment cost of a genuine fight against inflation in the future becomes that much greater.[25]

The most recent fight against inflation will seem to some to be an exception to this pessimistic assessment of government's ability to control inflation. As this is being written, the inflation rate has been reduced to below 4 percent, and the view is spreading that inflation is a problem of the past. Do not count on it. It is precisely when the public begins assuming that the price level will be stable, and begins making decisions and commitments based on

---

[24]When inflation declined during the early 1980s, interest rate declines lagged behind the decline in the inflation rate, and the real interest rate reached record high levels during this period.

[25]Government credibility is not the only factor that increases the time and unemployment costs of reducing inflation. Mancur Olson has argued that the more powerful and entrenched political interest groups are, the greater the unemployment that will result from a serious anti-inflationary policy. See chapter 7 of his book *The Rise & Decline of Nations* (New Haven, Conn.: Yale University Press, 1982).

that expectation, that government has the most to gain from another round of inflation. When inflation is unexpected, it does the most to stimulate the temporary expansion in economic activity that does so much to enhance the election prospects of incumbent politicians. A reduction in inflationary expectations also means falling interest rates, including those the government has to pay on its borrowing, and therefore greater opportunity for government to profit by an inflationary repudiation of much of its debt obligation. When government has discretionary control over the money supply, the time to be worried about the threat of inflation is when people quit worrying about the threat of inflation.

The problem here is one of political myopia. The employment and output benefits from accelerating the money supply are immediate, while the inflationary costs are delayed. Once inflation gets going, however, the costs of eliminating it are immediate, while the benefits come only after a long lag. Quite apart from the previously discussed direct benefits that government receives from inflation, the structure of these cost-benefit lags arising from inflation and disinflation establishes a clear political bias toward inflation. If the government has discretionary control over the money supply, the only hope for a stable price level is that political decisionmakers will resist the opportunity to capture immediate gains for themselves by imposing future costs on the public at large. This hope is sure to be disappointed in the long run. When the money supply is made subject to political manipulation, an inflationary bias is created that only occasionally and temporarily will be overcome.

Toward a Noninflationary Monetary Constitution

If inflation is to be eliminated, and eliminated permanently, there must be a restructuring of the monetary rules of the game. Without a rule with the force of a constitutional restriction (one not subject to the whims of ordinary politics) that prevents short-term political considerations from influencing the money supply, the long-term prognosis is for a continuation of inflation. There surely will be recurring episodes during which a serious attempt is made to reduce inflation, and these attempts will meet with some success. But we can expect this success to be only temporary, as political resolve will wither under the transitional but high cost of reducing inflation and the temptation of short-term political gain from a resurgence of inflation.

Indeed, without a constitutional restriction that insulates monetary control from the political process, serious attempts to bring inflation under control may well be ill advised. The temporary cost of recession and unemployment would be a small price to pay in the fight against inflation if the fight were successfully completed and the objective of price level stability, once obtained, would not be relinquished. But to put the economy through the wringer, so to speak, to reduce inflation partially and temporarily is to incur a heavy cost in return for little benefit. Why incur tremendous costs now in the hope of long-term benefits that can, and almost surely will, be quickly swept away by shortsighted political decisions? The cost of inflation is high, but if inflation is going to continue anyway, we only add to its cost by increasing the volatility and uncertainty of inflation through sporadic halfhearted attempts to bring it under control. And sporadic halfhearted fights against inflation are exactly what we will continue to get as long as the money supply is left to political discretion.

Giving up, however, and simply letting inflation erode the value of our currency and undermine the long-term productivity of the economy is not an attractive option. Years of inflation have offered convincing evidence as to just how unattractive this option is. It is not suprising then that there has been much recent discussion of the possibility of returning to the gold standard. The overriding advantage seen in the gold standard is that it removes money supply decisions from political influence and offers hope for the elimination of a persistent inflationary bias. Under a domestic gold standard (we will not be concerned with the workings of an international standard), the government is obligated to buy or sell gold at a specific price. For example, the federal government would be required to buy or sell gold at $300 per ounce. Further, the government is required to destroy the money it receives when it sells gold.[26] If, under these rules, the general price begins to rise, the price of gold included, people will find attractive the government offer to sell gold for $300 per ounce. As money flows into the government and is destroyed, the money supply declines and the general price level begins declining toward its initial level. If, however, there is a general fall in prices, including the price of gold, the opportunity to sell gold to the government for $300 will be attractive and new money will flow into the economy as government purchases of gold are made. With the money supply increasing, prices will increase until there is no longer any advantage in selling gold to the government. As described, the money supply is independent of political discretion, and the operation of standard market forces prevent long-term biases in the direction of either inflation or deflation.

We quickly acknowledge, however, that in actuality the gold standard is unlikely to function as effectively as was just outlined. A major problem is that the market price of gold will not, in general, move in step with the general price level. For example, the unsupported market price of gold could decline

---

[26]Note that under the gold standard as described, the government cannot create extra money to finance its general expenditures. It can create money only for the purpose of buying gold at the specified price. Either taxation or borrowing is necessary for the government to finance its general operation.

below $300 per ounce if new gold deposits were discovered at the same time the general price level was increasing. This situation would find an increase in the money supply and a further increase in the price level as people sold gold to the governnment. Or new commercial uses for gold could increase the demand for gold even though the general price level was decreasing. In this case, the money supply would be reduced as gold was purchased from the government, and the price level would decline further.

There is, therefore, no guarantee that imposing a gold standard would stabilize the general price level, but it would surely be an improvement over the politically sensitive arrangement we now have for monetary control. Historically, when a nation's money supply has been limited by adherence to the gold standard, long-term inflationary trends have been eliminated and the general price level has been relatively stable. Great Britain was on the gold standard for the two hundred years prior to 1914, and as best as can be measured, the price level was approximately the same at the end of this period as it was at the beginning. There was price level fluctuation over this extended period, but except during the Napoleonic wars, when the gold standard was suspended, the price level rarely deviated from its initial position by more than 33 percent.[27]

It is our strong belief that a genuine commitment returning us to the gold standard would, by depoliticizing monetary policy, establish a monetary framework more consistent with productive and orderly economic activity than is the existing framework. This is not the same, however, as recommending a return to the gold standard.[28] Other changes in the monetary rules of the game could accomplish the same purpose as the gold standard, possibly more effectively or at less cost. One proposal has been to back the value of the currency with a commodity bundle reserve. Instead of pegging the price of gold, the government would be required to buy or sell a particular bundle of commodities at a specified price. This commodity bundle standard would work in principle just like the gold standard: If the price of the commodity bundle began to rise or fall, the money supply would decrease or increase accordingly. The advantage this arrangement has over the gold standard is that by being able to contain a large number of diverse commodities, the market price of the bundle is more likely to move with the general price level than is the price of any one particular item such as gold.[29]

---

[27]This compares with the fact that from 1967 to 1985, the U.S. price level, as measured by the consumer price index, increased by 225 percent. The evidence on price level stability in Great Britain comes from Friedrich A. Hayek, *The Constitution of Liberty* (Chicago: University of Chicago Press, 1960), 329. Hayek also mentions the absence of any significant upward trend in the U.S. price level during the long interval during which the United States was on the gold standard.

[28]For a spirited argument in favor of returning unequivocally to the gold standard, see Murray N. Rothbard, "The Case for a 100 Per Cent Gold Dollar," in Yeager, *In Search of a Monetary Constitution.*

[29]For an extensive discussion in support of a commodity bundle standard, see Benjamin Graham, "The Commodity-Reserve Currency Proposal Reconsidered" in Yeager, ibid.

An important disadvantage of backing the currency with any commodity, gold or otherwise, arises from the requirement that commodities with valuable alternative uses must be stored rather than used. Does it make sense, for example, to go to the trouble of digging gold out of the ground to put it back in the ground at Fort Knox, especially when the gold has alternative uses? The answer depends in large measure on whether there is a cheaper and just as effective way of insulating the money supply against political manipulation. Does such a way exist? Many economists believe it does.

It has long been argued by monetarists that the Federal Reserve System should be bound by a monetary rule to increase the money supply at some specified annual rate between 3 and 5 percent.[30] Without going into the detailed argument favoring this monetary rule, it is enough for our purposes to point out that the big advantage it offers is the same one offered by a commodity standard: It erects a barrier against the proclivity of politicians to debase the currency.

The purpose here is not to decide whether a commodity standard or a monetary rule is the best alternative to our current monetary structure. The important concern is getting the political process to accept a reasonable variation of either rule and to allow it to be faithfully implemented without political interference. We cannot expect that this will be done in response to the incentives provided by ordinary politics. Indeed, it is precisely because of these incentives that political discretion cannot be trusted in managing the money supply and a nonpolitical monetary structure is needed. This is clearly the type of situation that calls for a rule at the constitutional level. When harmful long-term consequences will be the result of decisions that are sure to be made if discretion is allowed in the face of short-term temptations, the advantage is with a commitment to a rule that restricts available options and cannot be easily abandoned. In few areas are the advantages that can be realized from such a constitutional commitment greater than in the case of our monetary system. The importance of a sound and stable currency to the maintenance of a productive social order cannot be overemphasized. There is no surer way of undermining such a social order than by leaving unfettered political influence over the money supply.

Concluding Comments

One of the more persistent facts in political history is that governments have tried to obtain a monopoly of the country's money supply, and having done so, they have proceeded to tax the public with inflation. In ancient days, when the money supply consisted of coins made from the alloy of a precious metal, the monarch constantly looked for excuses to inflate by debasing the value of the

---

[30]The case for a monetary rule has been most persistently and forcefully made by Milton Friedman. See especially Milton Friedman, *A Program for Monetary Stability* (New York: Fordham University Press, 1959), 77-79.

currency. The king would call in the coin of the realm, for example, to have it recoined to commemorate some joyous national occasion such as the birth of a male heir to the throne, a military victory, or the beheading of the queen. Once the coins were melted down, the king would conveniently reduce their precious metal content before returning them to the public and use the precious metal to produce additional coins for his royal use. With this additional money, the king would increase his purchases of the goods and services being produced, which, of course, meant less was available for the public to consume. The king would have returned the same nominal amount of money to the public, after it had been recoined, as he collected. But with less to spend this money on, the result would be higher prices. The king was able to make himself better off at the expense of his subjects by, in effect, taxing them through inflation.

The only thing that has changed over the years is that governments have discovered more indirect and subtle ways to debase the currency. Instead of just reducing the precious metal content of the coinage or increasing the rate at which paper money is printed (both of which the government still does), the government now reduces the value of money as a consequence of financial transactions by the Federal Reserve System. Although the means are more subtle, the result is the same. Those whose interests are tied to government wealth receive short-term benefits at the cost of an inflationary erosion of long-term productivity growth in the economy.

The only effective way to protect ourselves against the consequences of persistent inflation is to impose clear constitutional limits on the federal government's ability to create money. The first thing this requires is discarding the widespread but incredibly naive view that the collection of individuals who comprise the government will, if given enough power and authority, use it to promote the general welfare. Unless this view is seen for the wishful thinking it really is and government discretion is significantly reduced, we can be confident that the federal government will continue with inflationary policies that expand its wealth at the further expense of the productive private sector. There is room for debate over the form restraint on government's monetary powers should take. But the time has long since come for jettisoning the belief that an unrestrained government can be trusted to restrain itself in monetary matters.

7

Supply-Side Economics in a Constitutional Perspective

I'm just not going to spend a lot of political capital solving some other guy's problem in 2010.

—David Stockman[1]

The 1970s will not be remembered in the United States as a period of economic growth. Of all the major industrial countries in the free world, the United States experienced one of the lowest growth rates in worker productivity during the 1970s. The annual growth in Gross National Product (GNP) per employed worker was only 0.1 percent from 1973 to 1979. This compares with a labor productivity growth rate of almost 2.5 percent from 1948 to 1965 and 1.6 percent from 1965 to 1973.[2] There are, no doubt, many factors that lie behind this decline, but of major importance has been the slowdown in the rate of capital formation and expenditures in research and development. Total spending on research and development as a percentage of GNP, for example, has declined from 3.0 percent in 1964 to 2.2 percent in 1979.[3] The amount of capital per U.S. worker barely increased during the second half of the 1970s, which resulted in the almost invisible growth in worker productivity.[4] The effect of these trends can be masked for a time by straining existing productive capacity and bringing an increasing

---

[1]Quoted in William Greider, *The Education of David Stockman and Other Americans* (New York: E.P. Dutton, Inc. 1982), 41.

[2]See the *Economic Report of the President: 1980* (Washington, D.C.: U.S. Government Printing Office, 1980), 85.

[3]Ibid., 87.

[4]See Martin Feldstein, "The Retreat from Keynesian Economics," *The Public Interest* (Summer 1981).

percentage of the working age population into the labor force.[5] In the long run, however, there is no way to escape the negative impact of declining investment in capital and basic research on our economic well-being.

An important response to the slowdown in economic growth during the 1970s was a renewed emphasis on the supply side of the economy. The old adage "you cannot consume what has not been produced" was forced back into our consciousness. Those economists who have been most concerned with the effect public policy has on the long-term productive capacity of the economy have become known as supply-side economists, and their analysis had been dubbed supply-side economics. One can easily get the impression from the popular press and some political pundits that supply-side economics is little more than a passing fad that emerged from the rhetoric of President Ronald Reagan's 1980 presidential campaign. This is not the case. Supply-side economics is solidly based on a body of theoretical economics that has been developing for more than two hundred years.[6] Stripped to basics, supply-side economics is simply a restatement of the most fundamental of all economic principles: If you increase the relative return on engaging in an activity, there will be an increase in that activity. Of particular relevance to the concerns of supply-side economics is the return to leisure and consumption relative to the return to production and investing. If the relative return to leisure and consumption is increased, people will produce less and attempt to consume more, an attempt that can be successful only in the short run. If, however, the relative return to productive activities is increased, people will substitute productive pursuits for consumption. This substitution will lead to more consumption in the long run.

All government economic activities, whether spending money or raising taxes, affect the relative returns on different activities. For example, by reducing the cost of searching for new employment, unemployment compensation will increse the unemployment rate.[7] Although concerned with the entire spectrum of public policy and its effect on incentives, supply-side economics has concentrated attention primarily on the impact of taxation. To supply-side economists, the importance of a change in taxes comes from the change that

---

[5]One response to lagging productivity has been an increase in the percentage of women who have taken jobs outside the home. In 1954 only 32.7 percent of the white female population over 20 participated in the labor force. In 1980 this percentage had increased to 50.8 percent. See the *Economic Report of the President: 1981* (Washington, D.C.: U.S. Government Printing Office, 1981), 268. This response to the decline in productivity growth further reduces the growth rate in worker productivity by adding to the size and subtracting from the average experience of the work force.

[6]See David G. Raboy, "The Theoretical Heritage of Supply Side Economics," in David G. Raboy, ed., *Essays in Supply Side Economics* (Washington, D.C.: The Institute for Research on the Economics of Taxation, 1982), 29–61.

[7]See Martin Feldstein, "The Economics of the New Unemployment," *The Public Interest* (Fall 1973), 3–42.

results in the relative returns from different activities.[8] The advantage a supply-sider would see in reducing the marginal tax rate applied to interest income is that this would increase the incentive to save and thereby increase the potential for investment and long-term economic growth. Similar advantages are seen for reductions in the marginal tax rate on income (the return to labor) and capital gains (the return to investment). In each case the tax reduction may immediately increase take home income and motivate taxpayers to spend more.[9] But this short-term spending effect is not of primary interest to supply-side economists. The focus of supply-side economics is on productivity increases that necessarily require a long interval before they are fully realized.

Keynesian economics, which has dominated the macroeconomic policy perspective for several decades, also has been concerned with the effects of government spending and taxing policy. As opposed to supply-side economics, however, the pivotal feature of government policy from the Keynesian view comes from its influence on the demand side of the economy. Keynesians focus a great deal of attention on the gap between potential GNP (the value of output the economy is capable of producing) and actual GNP (the value of output that is actually being produced). When this gap is positive, the problem is seen as one of inadequate demand, and the appropriate Keynesian response is for government to cut taxes and increase spending in order to increase the current rate of spending in the economy. Through a multiplier effect, a relatively small initial increase in spending can, in the Keynesian view, stimulate a large increase in demand and restore a depressed economy to its full productive protential. If demand exceeds the full employment potential of the economy, however, the result will be inflation, and the appropriate response is some combination of tax increases and spending cuts to reduce demand.

The objective of Keynesian government policy is to fine-tune aggregate demand in order to stabilize the economy and keep actual GNP as close as possible to potential GNP.[10] The orientation of Keynesian policy is relatively short term, emphasizing the short-term consequences of changes in spending and taxing decisions. The long-term effect of these decisons on the productive

---

[8]In this regard it is the change in marginal tax rates that is important. For more on this see Robert E. Keleher, "Supply-Side Tax Policy: Reviewing the Evidence," in Thomas J. Hailstones, ed., *Viewpoints on Supply-Side Economics* (Richmond, Va.: Robert F. Dame, Inc., 1982), 105-114.

[9]Note that a marginal tax rate can be reduced without lowering the average tax rate, so a marginal tax rate reduction may have no effect on spendable income. Also, even if a tax cut reduces total tax payments, it does not follow that there will be a positive income effect (an increase in real income) once the value of publicly provided services are taken into consideration. On this point see James D. Gwartney and Richard Stroup, "Labor Supply and Tax Rates: A Correction of the Record," *American Economic Review* (June 1983), 446-51.

[10]Contrary to the claims (or hopes) of the Keynesians, it has been argued that the federal budget has, on balance, probably been a source of instability in the economy. See Milton Friedman, *Capitalism and Freedom* (Chicago: Phoenix Books, 1962), 77.

capacity of the economy has received little attention by Keynesian economists. In contrast, supply-side economists emphasize that the real economic problem is not encouraging consumption but pushing back the limits on our ability to produce. There will be short-term fluctuations in demand, but if we are able to increase the goods and services that are produced, we can be sure that over the long run, demand will keep pace.

The success of supply-side economics is dependent on the ability of the political process to take a long-term perspective. Unfortunately, the incentives generated by ordinary politics place the overriding emphasis on the short-term consequences of public policy. When political decisionmaking is restrained only by the sentiments of the moment, long-term consequences will be ignored. Only through a constitutional perspective can we see the advantages of restricting our ability to respond to opportunities that are tempting in the short run but harmful in the long run. In this chapter, we argue that, in the absence of genuine constitutional limits on government discretion, political policy will concentrate on short-term objectives, thus reducing the prospects for implementing a genuine policy of supply-side economics and realizing the full potential of long-term economic growth.

Our Supply-Side Forefathers

In the broad sense of the term, the Founding Fathers were supply-siders. They were not interested in govenrment policy designed to maintain strong demand. They were quite confident that if goods and services were produced, there would be a demand for them. As framers of the Constitution, the Founding Fathers were interested in establishing a political structure that, among other things, would be conducive to the emergence of a wealthy nation. In this they were guided by a view that broke sharply with that of the mercantilists, whose views were dominant at the time of the American Revolution and whose policies were a significant factor leading to the Revolution.

To mercantilists the wealth of a nation was increased by selling more to foreign countries than was bought from them and by amassing hoards of gold and silver. An important role of government, in this view, was to encourage exports and discourage imports. Enacting high tariffs and generous subsidies to accomplish this purpose was considered a means to national prosperity. Colonies were considered important because they provided largely captive consumers for a country's export of expensive manufactured goods and a source of inexpensive raw materials. Much of the burden England imposed on the American colonies in the form of taxes and commercial restrictions was motivated by the desire to realize maximum advantage from the colonies both as customers and as suppliers. To mercantilists, economic activity was primarily a zero-sum game, and extensive government regulation of economic affairs was seen as necessary to increase the wealth of the home country by transferring as much wealth as possible from other countries or colonies.

By the time of the American Revolution, however, the mercantilist notions were under serious assault. Locke, Trenchard and Gordon, Montesquieu, and Hume all had developed influential arguments critical of the appropriateness and effectiveness of promoting wealth with high taxation and detailed regulation. The American revolutionaries were aware of these arguments and made full use of them in their resistance to British rule.

The most influential antimercantilistic work was Adam Smith's *An Inquiry Into the Nature and Causes of the Wealth of Nations,* which was published in March 1776, just a few months before the signing of the Declaration of Independence. As the title of Smith's book indicates, he was concerned with the question of what contributes to a nation's wealth, and his answer, in brief, was productivity. Smith begins his book by considering "the causes of improvement in the productive powers of labor," and emphasizes the importance of specialization and exchange (considerations we discussed in chapter 2) and the return to labor. According to Smith, "the liberal reward of labor . . . increases the industry of the common people. . . . Where wages are high, accordingly, we shall always find the workmen more active, diligent and expeditious, than when they are low. . . . ."[11] In a similar vein Smith pointed out that, "It is not from the benevolence of the butcher, the brewer, or the baker, that we expect our dinner, but from their regard to their own interest. We address ourselves, not to their humanity but to their self love, and never talk to them of our own necessities but of their advantages."[12]

In the second book of *The Wealth of Nations*, Smith emphasizes the importance of capital stock to productivity. There are strict limits on how much productivity can be increased through hard work. An increase in the captial accumulation that is available to complement human effort is essential if there is to be a sustained increase in a country's wealth. Again quoting Smith,

> [T]he annual produce of the land and labour of any nation can be increased in its value by no other means . . . but in consequence of an increase in capital. . . . When we compare, therefore, the state of a nation at two different periods, and find that the annual produce of its land and labour is evidently greater at the latter than at the former, that its lands are better cultivated, it manufactures more numerous and more flourishing, and its trade more extensive, we may be assured that its capital must have increased during the interval between those two periods. . . . [13]

As with labor, Smith knew that capital accumulation would not take place without the assurance of an adequate return, in this case to saving and investment.

---

[11]Adam Smith, *The Wealth of Nations* (New York: The Modern Library, 1937), 81.

[12]Ibid., 14.

[13]Ibid., 326.

Taxation was an important concern to Smith because it had the effect of lowering the return to productive effort and investment. Obviously, some money must be raised through taxation if the government is to carry out its limited role in providing the setting necessary for the productive system of specialization and exchange to function. But Smith emphasized the importance of keeping the disincentive effects of taxation as low as possible:

> Every tax ought to be so contrived as both to take out and keep out of the pockets of the people as little as possible, over and above what it brings into the public treasury of the state. A tax may either take out or keep out of the pockets of the people a great deal more than it brings into the treasury . . . [I]t may obstruct the industry of the people, and discourage them from applying to certain branches of business which might give maintenance and employment to great multitudes.[14]

In other words, unless government is moderate in the use of its taxing powers, productive effort and investment will be discouraged and real wealth sacrificed. Adam Smith was a supply-side economist more than two hundred years ago.

There can be no doubt that Smith's supply-side perspective had a strong influence on the intellectual climate that existed when our Constitution was being drafted and debated.[15] While an important motivation for replacing the Articles of Confederation with the Constitution was to give the national government more power to raise revenue, a fear of the burden that taxation could impose on the economy remained. Alexander Hamilton, who was one of the leading proponents of a strong national government with effective taxing powers, argued, "It might be demonstrated that the most productive system of finance will always be the least burdensome."[16] Hamilton anticipated modern supply-side arguments by pointing out that increasing the tax rate could reduce productive activity so much that, even at the higher rate, tax revenues would be reduced.[17]

In drafting and ratifying the Constitution, the Founding Fathers in effect set up an experiment for testing the effectiveness of supply-side

---

[14]Ibid., 779.

[15]For a discussion of the influence Smith had on the Founding Fathers, see William D. Grampp, "Adam Smith and the American Revolutionists," *History of Political Economy* 2, no. 2 (1979): 179-191. Other early writers with a supply-side orientation also exerted strong influence on the perspective of the founders. See James Ring Adams, "Supply-Side Roots of the Founding Fathers," *Wall Street Journal,* 17 November 1982, 26.

[16]Alexander Hamilton, *Federalist Papers,* no. 35, (New York: New American Library, Mentor Books, 1961), 217.

[17]Alexander Hamilton, *Federalist Papers,* no. 21, 142-43. Hamilton anticipated the tax rate-revenue relationship that is currently known as the Laffer curve, named for its contemporary popularizer Arthur Laffer. The Laffer curve and the implications it has for constitutional limits on government will be discussed in some detail later in this chapter.

economics. Government was restricted in its ability to insert wedges, through taxation and regulation, between the value generated by an individual's effort and investment and the return the individual received. There also were constitutional restrictions on the ability of government to transfer income to those who did not earn it from those who did. In short, the return on productive activity was high relative to the return on nonproductive activity. This supply-side experiment worked wonderfully. It did not, of course, produce overnight miracles, as supply-side economics is not a short-term policy. It did, however, motivate people to pursue their objectives through hard work and investment, and this resulted in a steady accumulation of human and physical capital that, over the long run, transformed the United States from a poor, undeveloped country into the most productive country on earth.

Can supply-side economics work again? From a strictly economic perspective, the answer is of course. There can be no doubt that people will respond to supply-side incentives today much as they did in the past. The important question is not whether supply-side economics will work if given a chance, but instead whether the political environment is such that supply-side economics will, in fact, be give a chance. The problem here is that a genuine supply-side economic policy is a long-term policy, and the political process within which all policy is implemented is guided predominantly by short-term considerations. The objective of supply-side policy is not that of making short-term adjustments to stabilize demand but of maintaining a permanent structure of incentives to encourage long-term growth in our productive capacity. Giving this policy an honest chance requires a time perspective that extends beyond that normally associated with the political process.

The Short-Term Political Perspective

Democratic political processes are inherently myopic. In designing an economic policy, it is important to recognize this myopia. If an economic policy is to be successful, it is just as important to be aware of the implications of political incentives as it is of economic incentives. The political success of Keynesian economics, for example, surely had less to do with theoretical soundness than with the fact that it appealed to the shortsighted proclivities of the political process.[18]

It is impossible to eradicate completely the problem of political myopia in a democratic political order. Some short-term political expediency is simply one of the prices that must be paid for the major advantages that political

---

[18]This political shortsightedness provides an explanation for the failure, as well as the success, of Keynesian economics. Even if Keynesian economics had been completely sound as an economic theory, its success as an economic policy would have been undermined by the shortsightedness of political decisionmaking. See James M. Buchanan and Richard Wagner, *Democracy in Deficit: The Political Legacy of Lord Keynes* (New York: Academic Press, 1977).

democracy offers over its alternatives. But realizing the ideals of democracy is not dependent on embracing any particular institutional arrangement, and some arrangements can be expected to perform better than others.[19] Before returning to the challenge political myopia poses for supply-side economics and considering possibilities for mitigating this myopia, a discussion of why political decisionmakers tend to concentrate on the short run while ignoring the long run will be useful.

The first thing to remember is that politicans are not inherently short-sighted. As individuals, politicians are much the same as anyone else. They will take a long-term perspective if it is to their advantage to do so; otherwise, they will concentrate on the more immediate effects of their decisions. Politicians tend to be shortsighted because of the political incentive structure within which they operate. The most obvious inducement for politicians to focus on short-term consequences is provided by the desire to survive the periodic elections they must face. Not surprisingly, when considering alternative policy proposals, there is a tendency to exaggerate the importance of those policy impacts that will occur before the next election and to put less weight on postelection consequences. The politician whose policy recommendations provide long-term benefits far in excess of the costs is unlikely to receive credit for his foresight if, because the cost came first, he is defeated at the polls. Alternatively, a policy that provides immediate benefits will be attractive to a politician facing an election, even if the long-term costs (which may be hard to trace back to the policies and politicians responsible) are far greater than the benefits.

It is not difficult to find examples that strongly suggest political sensitivity to preelection outcomes. From 1950 (when the first major increase in Social Security benefits was legislated) through 1974 (after which Social Security benefits were indexed in inflation), Congress increased Social Security benefits eleven times. Eight of these increases occurred during election years. Furthermore, in seven cases out of eight, the increase in Social Security taxes necessary to pay for the augmented benefits was postponed until the following year—after the election. After Social Security payments, veterans benefits make up the largest component of government transfers. The most likely time to observe a surge in these benefits is shortly before elections. According to Edward Tufte, "Since 1962, [veterans] benefits have increased an average of $660 million (at annual rates) between the third and fourth quarters of election years, but only $220 million in years without elections."[20]

Recurring elections would not provide much of an explanation for myopic political decisions if voters were motivated to be informed on the long-term

---

[19]See, for example, F.A. Hayek, *The Political Order of a Free People* vol. 3 of *Law, Legislation, and Liberty* (Chicago: University of Chicago Press, 1979).

[20]Edward R. Tufte, *Political Control of the Economy* (Princeton, N.J.: Princeton University Press, 1978), 38. This example, along with the Social Security example, is documented in chapter 2.

consequences of the decisions made by their elected representatives and to hold them accountable. Indeed, giving voters the power periodically to vote politicians in or out of office is based on the hope that this will make them responsive to the concerns of the public, concerns that surely include long-term considerations. But the fact is that individuals have little motivation to acquire the information necessary to determine before the fact, or recognize after the fact, the long-term impact of political decisions. As is evident from the discussion in chapter 2, informed public decisions can usefully be thought of as public goods.[21] Being informed on broad political issues provides no claim on the advantages of good public policy that are not equally available to the uninformed. For this reason it is quite rational for people to remain politically ignorant and concentrate on becoming informed in those areas where additional knowledge provides differential advantages. (This not not to ignore, however, the fact that some people realize personal satisfaction simply from being informed on a broad range of political issues.) Our well-being is surely much more influenced by political decisions on major economic policy than, for example, by our choice of shoes. Yet most people will be more informed on shoe fashions and what shoes go with what outfit than they will be on the intricacies of economic policy.

The immediate consequences of a policy often can be associated with that policy without detailed information or knowledge. But even the most informed citizen generally will find it difficult to anticipate the long-term effects of a policy or make the connection between these effects and the policy responsible for them. The politician is fully aware of this problem and recognizes that he is much more likely to be held accountable for the short-term results of his decisions than the long-term results, and he focuses his time perspective accordingly.[22]

A pertinent example was discussed in the last chapter. Expanding the money supply allows politicians to provide highly visible and immediate benefits for which it is easy to take credit politically. Public projects can be financed, services provided, subsidies given, interest rates temporarily reduced, and

---

[21]See Gordon Tullock, "Public Decisions as Public Goods," *Journal of Political Economy* (July/August 1971), 913-18.

[22]A political machine is one way of mitigating this problem. Long-term political consequences are easier to connect to a dominant political machine than to particular policies or politicians. Machine politicians, whose political fortunes are closely tied to the viability of the machine, will find it to their advantage to give more weight to the long-term impact of their decisions than they would if they had no property right in an enduring political institution. In a like manner, political parties also provide incentives that extend, to some extent, political time horizons.

Support for this view comes from contrasting the policies of Mayor John Lindsay of New York City and Mayor Richard Daley of Chicago. Lindsay, who was elected to his second term as an independent and was untainted by machine politics, opted for solutions to political problems that bankrupted the city during his successors' terms of office. During the same time, Daley, the last of the machine politicians, ran Chicago in such a way that future solvency was not sacrificed for short-term expediency.

employment temporarily increased by the simple expedient of expanding the money supply. Only after some lag will these benefits be paid for through the cost of higher inflation. And politicians have been remarkably successful at shifting blame by convincing a rationally ignorant public that inflation is the fault of things such as labor unions, business profits, bad harvests, OPEC, and irresponsible consumer spending.[23]

Another approach to explaining political myopia concerns a flaw in political communication. As noted in chapter 3, it is easier for relatively small groups with narrowly focused concerns to communicate through the political process than it is for large groups with diverse concerns. With the breakdown of constitutional restraint on government, this bias in political communication has allowed single issue groups to use political influence to capture preferential benefits at the expense of the general public. The end result of this process is a pattern of government expenditure and involvement that no one probably would choose if it was judged as a complete package. Each special interest group likely would see an advantage in moderating and deferring its political demands if, in return, similar moderation and patience would be exercised by all other special interest groups. Unfortunately, since it is hard to arrange for well-defined private property rights in politically controlled resources, the information and incentives that come from market exchange are absent.[24] As opposed to the market process, in the political process individuals are unable to communicate their preferences to each other in such a way as to motivate honesty and reciprocity.

Each politically influential group, when in a position to exploit the political process for immediate gain, realizes that refraining from this exploitation will establish no preferential claim on future benefits in exchange. The political

---

[23]It probably is true that most people still accept nonmonetary explanations for inflation. But increasingly the public is making the connection, at least vaguely, between political decisions and inflation. As this happens, there are reasons to believe that the lag between the benefits from monetary expansion and the onset of increased inflation will shorten. If this is indeed occurring, the political advantages from pursuing shortsighted monetary policy will be reduced. It also is true that the shorter the lag between changes in the rate of monetary growth and adjustments in prices, the smaller the short-term political cost (in the form of unemployment and reduced economic activity) when a serious fight against inflation is made. This provides a plausible explanation for the apparent fact that hyperinflations have been easier to stop than moderate inflations. See Leland Yeager and Associates, *Experiences With Stopping Inflations* (Washington, D.C.: American Enterprise Institute, 1981). The strength of special interest coalitions also can be relevant here, with the cost of combating inflation being greater the stronger and more entrenched these coalitions are. See Mancur Olson, *The Rise and Decline of Nations* (New Haven, Conn.: Yale University Press, 1982), chapter 7.

[24]Politically controlled resources are usefully characterized as common property resources with control determined by the rule of capture. The problem that arises when resources are commonly owned is discussed in a general context by Garrett Hardin, "The Tragedy of the Commons," *Science* 162 (1968), 1243-48. For a discussion that deals specifically with the problem of politically controlled resources as common property, see John Baden and Rodney D. Fort, "Natural Resources and Bureaucratic Predators," *Policy Review* (Winter 1980), 69-81.

capital that would be generated by responsible fiscal decisions is nonmarketable because it is not owned as private property. The politician who exercises the restraint necessary to maximize the long-term value of his contribution cannot realize this value at the termination of his political career by selling his political capital. Similarly, constituents who contribute to the value of political capital by moderating their current demands are unable to benefit from their individual contributions. Politicians, and the special interest groups that support them, are in much the same position as the buffalo hunters of the 1870s. Each knew that all would be better off in the long run if everyone reduced his slaughter of the buffalo. But in the absense of private ownership, each also knew that the buffalo he did not shoot today would be shot by someone else tomorrow. Individual buffalo hunters found themselves in a situation in which there was little to gain, but much to lose, from taking a long-term perspective and exercising restraint in the extermination of the buffalo.[25] Political decision-makers find themselves in a situation in which there is little to gain, but much to lose, by refraining from placing short-term demands on the economy that will, in the long run, exterminate much of our productive capacity.

The Destructive Tax Trap

Given the shortsighted proclivities of unrestrained political action, it is possible to understand the obstacles to implementing a genuine supply-side economic policy. To appreciate fully what is in fact a political dilemma facing the supply-side approach, we must examine the shortsighted dynamics that have led us to the destructive tax burdens that supply-side policy hopes to alleviate. Once this dynamic is spelled out, it will be found that excessive tax burdens will tend to persist even after they are widely recognized to be destructive.

To present a convincing story that the democratic process tends toward excessive tax burdens, we must establish a criterion for judging the appropriateness of the tax burden. Such a criterion is straighforward conceptually, even though it is difficult to apply in practice. As with everything else, increasing taxes generates costs and benefits. In the case of taxes, the costs are measured by the value of the private production that is sacrificed, and the benefits are measured by the value of the public service provided. Ideally, taxes should be increased until the value of the additional private production sacrificed is equal to the value of the additional public service provided. It is difficult to know exactly where this point is reached, but some things can be said about the range within which the ideal tax burden is found. It is helpful to consider what has become popularly know as the Laffer curve, which charts the relationship between tax rate and tax revenues.

---

[25]For many interesting details of the buffalo slaughter, see John Hanner, "Government Response to the Buffalo Hide Trade," *The Journal of Law and Economics* (October 1981), 239-71.

Although there are many different taxes and tax rates, little harm is done at the conceptual level by talking as if there is but one relevant rate. The Laffer curve depicts the long-run relationship between this tax rate and the tax revenue that is raised. If the tax rate is zero, it is obvious that no tax revenue will be raised. If the tax rate is increased above zero, tax revenue will become positive. Over some initial range of tax rates, there are two reasons why increasing the tax rate will increase tax revenue. First, increasing the percentage of a given tax base that is taken through taxation increases tax revenue. Second, up to some point, the tax revenue allows government to protect private property rights and provide important public goods, which creates a favorable environment for productive economic activity and thus generates an extension in the tax base. At some point, however, the productive disincentives caused by an increase in the tax rate more than offset any positive effect from government activity, and the higher tax rate causes a reduction in the tax base.[26] Tax revenue will continue to increase with an increasing tax rate, however, as long as the percentage reduction in the tax base is not as large as the percentage increase in the tax rate. A point will be reached, however, where the tax base will decline enough in response to a higher rate that increasing the rate will have no effect on tax revenue. It is at this point that the government maximizes the revenue it receives from taxes. If the tax rate is increased above this point, revenue will decline as the reduction in the tax base more than offsets the effects of the higher tax rate. At some sufficiently high tax rate, tax revenue will fall to zero, as the tax burden has destroyed all incentive to remain productive, except possibly in the underground economy.

The controversy that surrounds the Laffer curve is not over the existence of the rate-revenue relationship just described, but over the question of where we are on the Laffer curve. Some of the more enthusiastic supply-siders have argued that we are on the upper half of the curve. In the view of these Lafferites, a reduction in the tax rate would motivate such an increase in productive activity that tax revenue would increase. Others have argued that taxes have never reached the destructive levels claimed by the Lafferites. Much of the popular discussion of supply-side economics has centered on this controversy and has left the impression that the case for supply-side economics depends on tax rates having been increased beyond revenue-maximizing

[26]The reduction in the tax base will occur because some production that would have taken place at a lower tax rate will not take place at the higher rate and also because some production will be hidden from the tax authorities—that is, they will go underground. Although underground production is better than no production at all, because of the resources and effort devoted to avoiding detection, economic activity carried on underground is generally less productive than if it were performed above ground. For a discussion of the literature on the underground economy, see Carl P. Simon and Ann D. Witte, "The Underground Economy: Estimate of Size, Structure and Trends," *Special Study on Economic Change,* vol. 5 of *Government Regulation: Achieving Social and Economic Balance* (Washington, D.C.: U.S. Government Printing Office, December 8, 1980), 70-120.

limits. This is emphatically not the case. The case for supply-side economics is that the tax burden has become excessive—that is, that tax rates have increased beyond the point where the value the government can provide by an additional increase in taxes is equal to the resulting sacrifice in private production.

As stated earlier, we may never be able to pinpoint the ideal tax burden, but clearly it is reached well below the point where tax revenue is maximized. As the tax rate approaches the revenue-maximizing level, an increase in the rate will reduce private productivity (and therefore the tax base) to such an extent that little if any additional tax revenue is raised. This large sacrifice of private sector output to realize little additional public sector output indicates that the tax rate has increased above the ideal level.[27] There are strong reasons for believing that the democratic process exerts pressure toward excessive tax burdens. Indeed, we will see that it is quite possible for politicians, responding to the incentives of ordinary politics, to increase the tax rate to levels that are destructive of both private output and tax revenues—that is, rates on the upper half of the Laffer curve.

Politicians obviously place a positive value on additional tax revenue. The more tax revenue available, the easier it is for politicians to satisfy the urgent demands being put on them by politically influential interest groups. Of course, special interest groups do not have a completely free hand when it comes to acquiring government favors. There are political costs associated with raising taxes, and politicians are sensitive to these costs.[28] But tax increases are widely spread over a politically unorganized public and can be made to appear largely independent of political decisions (for example, inflation-induced bracket creep), while the tax proceeds can be rather pre-cisely directed to those coalitions and constituencies with the greatest politi-cal influence. Therefore, the costs of tax increases will be heavily discounted relative to the political gains from the additional tax revenue. This bias alone exerts tremendous pressure in the direction of an excessive tax burden. In an ideal world the political benefit-cost ratio would mirror the social benefit-cost ratio, and politicians could gain from raising taxes only when the social bene-fits from doing so exceeded the social costs. But given the opportunities for

---

[27]Somewhat surprisingly, some Lafferites have argued that the appropriate tax rate maximizes tax revenues. According to Jude Wanniski, for example, "This [the revenue-maximizing rate] is the rate at which the electorate desire to be taxed." Jude Wanniski, "Taxes, Revenues, and the Laffer Curve," *The Public Interest* (Winter 1978), 8. Since the marginal cost of tax revenue, in terms of sacrificed productivity, is infinite when tax revenues are being maximized, Wanniski is in effect saying that the electorate is willing to sacrifice any finite amount of privately produced goods and services in order to transfer one more dollar to government. This is clearly not the case.

[28]Here we are talking about raising taxes in the narrow sense of transferring money from the private sector to the public sector. Of course, politicians can respond to many special interest demands by imposing regulations that often seem innocuous but in fact destroy wealth. These regulations certainly are part of the tax burden, broadly defined, and taking them into considera-tion would strengthen the argument that the tax burden is excessive. Although the discussion will proceed as if taxes were being considered only in the narrow sense of transferring money, it would not be materially altered by including regulatory taxes.

maximizing political gains by concentrating benefits while minimizing political losses by spreading costs, the political benefit-cost ratio is distorted in favor of taxing and spending.

This tendency toward excessive tax burdens is accentuated by a political myopia that causes politicians to see tax rate increases as more potent sources of revenue than they really are. To understand the problem, we must reconize that long lags exist between the time a change in the tax rate occurs and the time when the effect of this change is fully realized. The existing stock of capital, whether physical or human, does not immediately diminish when the tax on the return they generate is increased. Decisions to replace and expand these capital assets will be discouraged, but the productivity of those already in existence will depreciate only through time. Similarly, decisions to expand investment will be encouraged by a tax cut, but the resulting increase in productivity and the tax base cannot be fully achieved immediately. Realizing the full impact of a tax cut requires time for investments in physical and human capital to be planned and implemented. Often only after a significant period of time do the cuts affect the production of new wealth.

Political attempts to disguise as much of the tax burden as possible—to create a fiscal illusion—further lengthens the time required for full adjustment to a tax increase. Also, the supply-side objective of minimizing the economic distortions, or deadweight loss, imposed by taxes serves to increase the lag between the short-term and long-term impact of a change in tax rates. The conventional recommendation for achieving this supply-side objective is to choose tax bases that are price inelastic—that is, for which the amount demanded supplied in not very sensitive to changes in price because there are no close substitutes.[29] Just because a tax base does not currently have a close substitute, however, does not mean that, given sufficient time, close substitutes will not be found in response to a tax increase. It means only that complete adjustment to the tax increase will take longer than otherwise. As the result of unavoidable rigidities in the economy and deliberate public policy, a change in tax rates will generate effects that will not be fully realized for years, and in many cases decades.

The result of these lagged fiscal effects is a temporal asymmetry between increasing taxes and reducing them. Increasing tax rates will increase tax revenues more in the politically relevant short run than in the eventually

---

[29]For example, the demand for liquor does not seem to be very sensitive to price, and liquor has always been a popular item for government to tax. Traditional public finance theorists do not seem to recognize that the recommendation to tax inelastically demanded items puts government in the same position as a monopolist facing an inelastic demand curve. The implicit assumption behind the suggestion that government tax inelastically demanded bases is that political decisionmakers, unlike their private sector counterparts, will not take advantage of their monopoly power and will be concerned only with promoting the public interest. For a critical look at this assumption and traditional public finance theory, see Geoffrey Brennan and James M. Buchanan, *The Power to Tax: Analytical Foundations of a Fiscal Constitution* (New York: Cambridge University Press, 1980).

revelant long run. Similarly, a tax rate decrease will decrease tax revenues more in the short run than in the long run. The political bias this creates in favor of tax increases is obvious. Although much of the revenue gain derived from increasing taxes is temporary, temporary gains fuel the political process. Tax increases that are obviously too high (even from the politician's perspective) once their long-term consequences have been entirely realized still will be enticing to myopic politicians. Even when the long run arrives, those politicians who inherit the unfortunate legacy of high taxes will have little incentive to reduce them. Even if a tax rate reduction increased revenue in the long run, it could result in a significant revenue decrease in the short run, and this latter consideration would be politically controlling.

The Lafferites, in their enthusiastic claims of immediate benefits to be realized from a tax cut, have ignored the importance of the short-term long-term distinction in the impact of taxation. Ironically, it is this distinction that provides the theoretical support for the central claim of the Lafferites—that reducing tax rates will increase tax revenues. If the impact of tax changes were as immediate as some of the Lafferites seem to indicate, it would be extremely difficult to argue that any government would increase taxes to the point of actually reducing revenues. If the government operated as a benevolent despot, concerned only with promoting the broad public interest, it certainly would not increase tax rates to the point of reducing tax revenues. To do so would impose unnecessary costs on private production while reducing the ability of government to provide useful goods and services. At the other extreme, if the government operated as a revenue-maximizing Leviathan, concerned only with promoting the narrow interests of those with political power, it would find no advantage in increasing tax rates above revenue-maximizing limits.

What would make no sense in the absence of fiscal lags, however, may be quite understandable once those lags are taken into consideration. The possibility that tax rates will be increased to a level that actually reduces revenues becomes plausible once the time dimension of fiscal effects is recognized. Politicians, tempted by the transitional revenue gains from successive tax increases, may well continue pushing up tax rates even when the long-term effect is to reduce revenues.[30] It seems quite likely that this is exactly what has

---

[30]This possibility has been explored in some detail in James M. Buchanan and Dwight R. Lee, "Politics, Time, and the Laffer Curve," *Journal of Political Economy* 90, no. 4 (August 1982), 816-19; and by the same authors, "Tax Rates and Tax Revenues in Political Equilibrium: Some Simple Analytics," *Economic Inquiry* 20, no. 3 (July 1982), 344-54. In the first paper it is shown, assuming political myopia, that a strictly revenue-maximizing government will always move toward a political equilibrium where the tax is above that which maximizes long-term revenue. In the second paper, the objective of government is to maximize a generalized utility function in which tax revenue enters as a good and tax rate enters as a bad. Staying with the assumption of political myopia, it is shown that political equilibrium still may call for a tax rate above its long-term revenue-maximizing level.

happened in the United States and other Western democratic countries in recent years. Effective tax rates have increased steadily over the years, commonly with the help of inflation, even though the long-term consequences have been to impede economic productivity and possibly reduce tax revenue below what they would have been with more modest tax burdens.

The point here is not that economically destructive tax burdens have ever reached the point of reducing tax revenues. Rather, the argument is that this possibility cannot be dismissed out of hand. The dynamics of short-term political expediency are capable of driving tax rates up to the point where cutting taxes actually would generate a long-term increase in tax revenue. And whether tax rates have been increased into the upper half of the Laffer curve or not, there can be no reasonable doubt that the myopia of ordinary politics has imposed an excessive tax burden on the economy. Who can honestly believe that the long-term gains in productivity that would be motivated by a permanent reduction in the tax burden would not exceed the long-term losses that might result from underfunding government programs?

In the case of the tax burden, as in many other situations, how we got to where we are has important implications for the prospect of improvement. In traveling the shortsighted political path to excessive tax rates, expectations are formed that will make it difficult to reverse direction. The reason for this goes beyond the obvious point that short-term revenue loss from reducing taxes will, in the minds of shortsighted politicians, outweigh the long-term economic benefits. Even genuinely farsighted politicians will find it difficult to reduce taxes once they have reached excessive levels.

The tax-paying public increasingly becomes aware that taxes increase to destructive levels because of the short-term incentives that guide political decisions. As long as the public realizes that there has been no permanent restructuring of the political incentive structure or no additional restraints imposed on the politician's ability to respond to short-term pressures, they quite rationally expect that any tax cut will be temporary. Investors will see an immediate and full investment response to a tax cut as locking their wealth into a position that makes it vulnerable to the next tax increase.[31] The supply-side stimulus provided by a tax cut, which takes a long time under even the most favorable circumstances, takes even longer in the expectative environment created by a history of shortsighted government policy.

In this expectative setting, even if a farsighted political administration arrived on the scene, it would have difficulty implementing a permanent tax

---

[31]An example of the fickle nature of tax cuts that supposedly are motivated by the desire to prompt long-term commitments of investment funds is seen in congressional repeal, within a year of its enactment, of the law permitting companies to buy and sell tax benefits that arise from depreciation on capital investment. For a discussion of the pending repeal and the effect on investment, see "Uncertainty Cripples Tax Leasing as Law Makers Consider Change," *Wall Street Journal,* 5 April 1982, 25.

cut. There would be a reluctance to respond quickly and fully to tax cuts put into effect by such an administration, even if investors had complete confidence in that administration's ability to maintain the cuts. Given the short-term incentives facing politicians, the farsighted action of such an administration will be seen as an anomaly that soon will be reversed by politicians with more conventional time horizons. This investor reluctance can undermine the resolve of the most resolute political tax cutters. The delayed and timid supply-side response to tax cuts will create temporary shortfalls in tax revenues and activate strong political pressure against maintaining the cuts. The 1981 Reagan tax cuts provide an example of this problem. We should point out that in the case of income taxes, the Reagan cuts really were not cuts at all. They amounted to nothing more than a partial offset of inflationary bracket creep and increases in Social Security taxes.[32] Despite this fact, politicians in both political parties were expressing concern that the Reagan cuts were not working even before they went into effect, and there arose significant political pressure to reverse them. As a result, in 1982 Reagan backed away from his pledge not to raise taxes and supported a successful move to offset the 1981 tax reductions with tax increases that were euphemistically referred to as revenue-enhancing measures. Obviously, political pressures and reversals of this type do little to generate the investor confidence needed for a genuine supply-side response to tax cuts.

Even if tax rates do reach the destructive levels represented by the upper half of the Laffer curve, it will be extremely difficult to reduce them. The transactional gains that activate the political process can lead us into a destructive tax trap, and the hope of supply-side economics can find itself frustrated by a catch-22 situation. A supply-side response to tax cuts will not be forthcoming unless they are known to be permanent, and tax cuts will not be permanent unless they motivate a prompt supply-side response.

The Prospects for Flat Rate Tax Reform

The seriousness with which flat rate, or modified flat rate, tax proposals were being considered by Congress in the mid-1980s may suggest that politicians can be motivated by long-term supply-side considerations. If one takes a closer look, however, there are reasons to be skeptical.

The argument for replacing the large number of graduated income tax rates with one relatively low rate (or a small number of slightly graduated rates) along with eliminating many of the loopholes that permeate the existing tax code, is basically a supply-side argument. The lower marginal tax rates

---

[32]See Steven A. Meyer and Robert J. Rossana, "Did the Tax Cut Really Cut Taxes?" *Business Review*, Federal Reserve Bank of Philadelphia (November/December 1981), 3-12.

would increase the return to productive activity, and fewer tax rates and tax loopholes would reduce the tax-induced distortions in economic decisions. Effort and investment would increase and be channeled into those activities that created the most valued output, not the biggest tax break. But even the politics of flat rate tax reform probably have more to do with considerations of short-term political advantages than with considerations of long-term economic productivity.

To understand why politicians may find modified flat rate tax reform an attractive option, it is useful to consider the political advantage of a highly progressive tax structure. By imposing high marginal tax rates on those with high incomes, politicians are able to accomplish two things that they consider desirable. First, they are able to obtain more revenue from the few without imposing any additional cost on the many. Second, they are able to give the appearance of shifting the tax burden to the wealthy, a shift the majority of taxpayers will appreciate. It is interesting to note that in the early 1960s the U.S. income tax was steeply progressive on paper, but in fact almost everyone faced the lowest marginal rates. More precisely, in 1962 the highest marginal income tax rate was 91 percent, but approximately 89 percent of all households paid either no income tax or faced marginal rates of between 20 and 22 percent.[33]

If politicians had desired a flat rate tax in 1962, without the need to close many loopholes or sacrifice much revenue, they could simply have reduced all income tax rates to 22 percent. This is not what politicians desired, and it is easy to understand why. The largely unused portion of the progressive tax structure provided politicians the opportunity to increase tax revenues while taking credit for reducing taxes. With the help of inflation, politicians took full advantage of this opportunity as taxpayers were propelled into higher tax brackets whether their real incomes were increasing or not. During the late 1960s, throughout the 1970s, and into the 1980s, this bracket creep swelled the federal coffers even though politicians provided tax "relief" several times by reducing taxes rates.[34]

As more and more taxpayers moved into high marginal tax brackets, another opportunity arose that was too tempting for politicians to resist. Higher tax rates increased the amount taxpayers were willing to pay for tax

---

[33]See James Gwartney and James Long, "Is the Flat Rate Tax a Radical Idea?" *The CATO Journal* (Fall 1985), 407-32.

[34]In 1965 only 2.9 percent of U.S. taxpayers faced marginal federal income tax rates of 28 percent or more. This percentage rose steadily during the late 1960s and the 1970s, and by 1979 35.5 percent of U.S. taxpayers were facing a marginal federal income tax rate of 28 percent or more. See James Gwartney and James Long, "Tax Rates, Tax Shelters, and the Efficiency of Capital Formation," in Dwight Lee, ed., *Taxation and the Deficit Economy* (San Francisco, Calif.: Pacific Institute, 1986). Over the period 1965-1979, federal tax revenues increased to $463.3 billion from $116.8 billion. See the *Economic Report of the President: 1982* (Washington, D.C.: U.S. Government Printing Office, 1982), 318.

preferences and loopholes. Politicians found that organized interests were more sympathetic to their need for campaign contributions and other forms of support when they were sympathetic to the organized interest's special need for tax relief. The sale of tax loopholes became very profitable politically, and politicians entered into the loophole business with genuine gusto.

Unfortunately for politicians, the profits from selling exemptions to high marginal tax rates tend to erode over time. First, the organized interests that have yet to purchase their tax loopholes become smaller in number. Second, over time taxpayers become increasingly successful at organizing their financial affairs to take advantage of loopholes for which others have paid. Eventually, few loopholes are left to sell, and the high marginal tax rates on the books cease to be effective revenue producers. Further, the progressive rate structure loses its value as a symbol of equity as the average taxpayer becomes increasingly aware that the wealthy are not really paying the higher rates.

We can expect that, as the political advantages of a highly progressive tax structure erode, politicians will begin seeing advantage in moving toward a flat rate tax. Despite the talk of revenue neutral tax reform, the elimination of tax loopholes in return for lowering high but largely useless tax rates appeals to the revenue-enhancing impulses of Congress. But how likely is it that anything like a flat rate income tax structure will come out of the political process, and how long could such a tax structure last even if it were enacted?

In any attempt at flat rate tax reform, the politicians will be torn between two objectives: lowering tax rates as much as possible without sacrificing tax revenues and maintaining the favor of special interests that benefit from the loopholes that will have to be eliminated if the first objective is to be realized. In facing the trade-off between these two objectives, it is safe to predict that politicians will not choose all of one objective at the complete sacrifice of the other. Any tax reform is sure to retain many loopholes at the expense of tax rates that are higher than they could otherwise be. Also, always anxious to give the impression that tax reform will protect the poor while making the rich pay their fair share, politicians will be reluctant to go all the way with flat rate tax reform. One can confidently predict that more than one tax rate will be retained in a modified flat rate scheme rather than having only a single tax rate as required by a genuine flat rate tax.

If tax reform results in lower tax rates consolidated in a few tax brackets, with the number of tax loopholes reduced but not eliminated altogether, can we expect this tax reform to endure? Surely not. With multiple tax brackets accepted as consistent with reform, it will be relatively easy for politicians to yield to the persistent temptation to raise more revenue in the short run. Taxes on a few can be raised without imposing costs on the many by increasing the rate in the highest tax bracket or adding another bracket with a higher rate. And once tax rates begin increasing, so will the political profits of adding new tax breaks. Soon tax reform will be undone, as the reformed tax system becomes as progressive and riddled with loopholes as it was originally. Just as before, the revenue raised over this long run will be less than myopic politicians anticipated and eventually there no doubt will be new calls for tax reform.[35]

The problem is obvious once we recognize that constant tax reform is costly. Enormous amounts of otherwise productive time and resources are channeled into efforts to promote and oppose tax changes when they are proposed and to understand and devise new ways around them once they are enacted. Further, an erratic tax system is a bad tax system. The inability to estimate with any confidence the future tax costs associated with long-term investment commitments reduces the advantage seen in such commitments. Even if an otherwise ideal flat rate tax were enacted, it would do little to motivate a supply-side response if taxes were seen to be subject to constant charges.

There always will be short-term political advantages to be realized from reforming taxes. Unless shortsighted politicians are restrained from pursuing these advantages by constantly churning the tax system, there is little hope of realizing a tax system that is consistent with the long-term objectives of supply-side economics.

Constitutional Reform and the Long View

Supply-side economic policy will never be given a genuine chance unless politicians give serious consideration to the long-term consequences of their decisions. Yet unless real constraints are imposed on the ability of politicians to respond to special interest demand, political decisionmaking will continue to be dominated by short-term considerations. There is really no basis for blaming politicians for behaving in a shortsighted way. Given the situation in which they find themselves, their behavior is perfectly predictable. As long as the only criterion for determining the legitimacy of a government action is the approval it receives from politically influential interest groups, politicians will be compelled to focus on short-term expediencies if they are to survive.

When unrestrained political power has made politicians the lackeys for organized special interests and special interests have become the victims of the productivity-destroying excesses of their own short-term demands, the potential exists for all to benefit by accepting some self-denying limits on government. If politicians could honestly say to politically organized groups,

---

[35]See Dwight R. Lee "Real Flat Rate is the Only Desirable Tax Reform," *Wall Street Journal,* 22 August 1985, 22.

"My hands are tied—I cannot provide any more benefits to special interest groups by imposing additional costs on the public at large," the scope for shortsighted political exploitation of one group by another would be reduced. A government that can, with credibility, tell people that there are clear limits on how much of their productive efforts can be taken from them will be in a better position to encourage productive investment than will a government that cannot commit itself to such limits. The best, maybe the only, hope for motivating a move away from parasitic transfer activities and into productive wealth-creating activities that will, in the long run, make everyone better off, is by placing constitutional limits on the scope of government.

The destructive tax trap discussed earlier provides a good example of the need for constitutional limits if there is to be hope that government will extend its sights beyond the short run. Once the tax burden has reached destructive levels, there is little hope that permanent tax cuts can be achieved through the workings of ordinary politics. Even if the long-term effect of a tax cut would motivate an expansion in investment and productivity sufficient to increase tax revenues, politicians would be reluctant to cut taxes if the short-term effect was to reduce revenues. Because investors have learned to model the political process as shortsighted, they will be reluctant to make productive, long-term investments in response to any tax cut because they will see the tax cut as only temporary. This is a self-fulfilling expectation, as their reluctance to respond to a tax cut in ways that expand the tax base makes it politically impossible to maintain such a cut. Without some escape from this dilemma, we continue in a situation where everyone is worse off in the long run: Government has less revenue than it could have, and the private sector suffers from a higher tax burden and lower productivity than it needs to.

Escape from the destructive tax trap requires that government somehow convince the public that it is not only cutting taxes but cutting them permanently. This means that the public must first be convinced that current politicians will persist with a tax cut and further that the cut will not be rescinded by future politicians. It is here that the advantage of a constitutional constraint on the fiscal powers of government can be seen. Constitutional limits are a means by which we can reach forward in time and control the behavior of future decisionmakers in a way that allows current decisionmakers to behave in a more responsible manner. Constitutional restrictions that prevent future politicians from gaining short-term advantages by increasing taxes creates a setting in which current politicians can look beyond short-term concerns and focus on the long-term advantages of lower taxes. Durable limits on the ability of politicians to cater to the demands of organized interests by increasing the tax burden is essential if the political process is to lengthen its vision and provide supply-side economic policy a real opportunity to revitalize the productivity of the economy.

Concluding Comments

In the eighteenth century the French political philosopher Montesquieu asked the question, "Will the state begin by impoverishing the subjects to enrich itself? Or will it wait for the subjects to enrich it by their own prosperity?"[36] In most countries during most of human history, the answer to Montesquieu's first question has been yes, and the answer to his second question has been no. Those of us in the United States have been fortunate in that U.S. government has, until recent decades, been restrained against the temptations to enrich itself by exploiting the productivity of its citizens. The result of this restraint has been years of savings, investment, and productive effort that created a prosperous population and a prosperous government. There can be no doubt that the U.S. government today has the wealth to do much more than it otherwise would have because it did not from the beginning attempt to enrich itself at the expense of the people. The constitutional limits on government made the policy of supply-side incentives the de facto economic policy of the country, and the long-term effects of this policy have been unmistakably successful.

We in the United States have inherited an enormously productive economy from the efforts and vision of those who came before us. It is clearly possible to do quite well in the short run, given this inheritance, by consuming the benefits from our productive capacity while doing little to maintain it. And in recent years that is exactly what we have been doing. Economic productivity was relatively stagnant throughout the 1970s and into the 1980s, yet Americans lived very well. We lived in bigger houses; spent more on vacations, jewelry, and clothing; enjoyed shorter workweeks; and rapidly increased the amount we spent on government services, subsidies, bailouts, and regulations. But the effects of policies that encourage consumption while naively assuming that productivity will take care of itself cannot be ignored indefinitely.

The current interest in supply-side economics is a predictable response to the problems that have arisen because we have, for too long, given too little attention to the long-term importance of maintaining our productive capacity. But unfortunately, no matter how well grounded supply-side policy is in sound economic theory, supply-side economics will not be able, by itself, to return the economy to the path of productivity and growth. Capital projects and technological advances do not spring up overnight and immediately begin paying dividends in terms of increased productivity. The payoff to supply-side policy is necessarily long term. With the breakdown in constitutional restraints on government, however, the political process has become

---

[36]Quoted in Adams, "Supply-Side Roots of the Founding Fathers," 26.

increasingly myopic. The success of supply-side economics depends as much on the restructuring of political incentives as it does on the restructuring of economic incentives.

It is no accident that stagnating economic performance has prompted both the supply-side economic movement and a movement to limit the taxing and spending powers of government through constitutional amendment. As long as politicians have wide-ranging freedom to respond to organized and narrowly focused interests, there will be little hope that they will be able to take the long-term view that a serious supply-side economic policy requires. One may debate the particulars of the different tax limitation, spending limitation, and balanced budget amendments to the Constitution that have been proposed. None of these proposed amendments is without fault, and none will solve all our economic problems. But the support and discussion that has accompanied these proposals are healthy signs. People are recognizing that we have to look carefully at the fundamental rules that define and shape our political order if we are to address intelligently many of our current economic problems. This constitutional attitude is probably just as important as the details of the constitutional amendments that are being considered. The recognition that constitutional reform is needed is an essential first step if such reform is to be successful.

8

The Deficits of Democracy

> There is simply no rational basis for an individual to support, to "vote for," fiscal prudence in the operation of ordinary democratic politics. Public debt will tend to be overextended relative to any plausible long-term arguments for the use of this fiscal instrument.
>
> —Geoffrey Brennan
> James M. Buchanan[1]

There is widespread agreement that the federal budget is out of control. In spite of President Ronald Reagan's three-year, highly praised tax rate cut passed in 1981, government revenues continue to rise in real terms and as a percentage of the GNP. Government expenditures continue, however, to rise at a faster clip, resulting in federal budget deficits.[2] Since 1960 the federal budget has been in surplus only once, and then the surplus was only $3.2 billion (see figure 8-1).

Not only are we experiencing chronic deficits, but these deficits have been escalating at an alarming rate. During the 1960s, the average federal budget deficit was a mere $6.1 billion. Over the five-year period 1971-1975, the average federal deficit was $22.2 billion. Over the next five years, the average federal deficit was $52.1 billion. The first half of the 1980s has seen this escalation continue, with the average annual deficit over the period 1981-1985 equal to $145.6 billion. In 1986 the expected deficit for the last

---

[1] *The Reason of Rules: Constitutional Political Economy* (Cambridge, Mass.: Cambridge University Press, 1985), 94.

[2] Many believe that President Reagan actually cut spending during his first term in office, but the federal government spent 18 percent more real dollars in fiscal 1985 than in fiscal 1981. Indeed, it spent a scant 0.1 percent less during the 1982-1985 period than would have been spent if the short-term expenditure trend chartered under the Carter administration had continued through 1985. Although total federal tax collections fell in 1982 due to the recession and Reagan tax rate cuts, total federal tax collections in 1985 were virtually the same as would have been projected for 1985 under the long-term (1967-1981) trend. All the Reagan administration accomplished was to reduce the rate of growth in tax collections from the short-term trend to the long-term trend. For a detailed discussion of federal taxes and expenditures during the Reagan years as compared with long-term (1967-1981) trends and short-term (1978-1981) trends, see Richard B. McKenzie, *Taking Stock of the Federal Budget* (St. Louis: Center for the Study of American Business, Washington University, 1986).

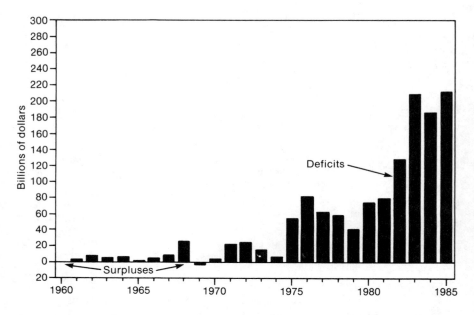

Source: *Economic Report of the President: 1986* (Washington, D.C.: U.S. Government Printing Office, 1986), 339.

Figure 8-1. The History of U.S. Deficits: 1960-1985

half of the 1980s appeared to be up for grabs, dependent somewhat on how the politics of the moment influence budget estimate assumptions about future economic growth, inflation, and employment.[3] Interest payments on the debt have taken and will continue to take a growing share of federal tax revenues, which in turn will represent a growing share of national income.[4]

---

[3]In 1985 the average federal deficit for 1986 through 1990 was projected to be $253 billion, estimates that have been pared back substantially, perhaps by as much as half. The deficits estimated in 1985 would mean that by 1990 the total federal debt held by the public would reach $2.8 trillion and account for almost 50 percent of the GNP. Congressional Budget Office, *The Economic and Budget Outlook: Fiscal Years 1986–1990*, a report to the Senate and House Committees on the Budget (August 15, 1985), xxi and chapter 2. The federal funds deficit, which accounts for all federal taxes and revenues exclusive of trusts (Social Security, for example), was projected in 1985 to reach in 1990 nearly $100 billion more than the total federal deficit. The surpluses in the trust funds account for the difference in the federal funds and total federal deficits. See Congressional Budget Office, *The Economic and Budget Outlook: Fiscal Years 1986–1990*, a report to the Senate and House Committees on the Budget, part I (February 6, 1985), 63. For the much lower deficit estimates developed in 1986, see Congressional Budget Office, *The Economic and Budget Outlook: Fiscal 1987–1991*, a report to the Senate and House Committees on the budget, part 1 (February 18, 1986), xv.

[4]In 1985 net estimated federal interest payments ($129 billion) had risen to 61 percent of the estimated federal deficit ($210 billion).

Only the naive fully expect politicians to live up to their frequent but faint promises to balance the budget, especially when they say at the same time that they can hold taxes down. When federal income and Social Security taxes are combined, most Americans will be paying higher tax rates in the last half of the 1980s than they did at the start of the decade,[5] and their tax rates in 1980 were higher than they were in 1970. If raising tax rates was a cure for federal deficits, red ink would have been expunged from federal budgetary records long ago.

The economic harm of routine federal deficits is commonly acknowledged. Government deficits crowd out private borrowers from capital markets in the process of driving up interest rates. Employment in the housing, durable, and investment goods industries is especially depressed by high interest rates, and the cost of resulting idle labor includes sluggish economic growth and tens of billions of dollars of goods and services never produced.

Deficits can, albeit indirectly, contribute to inflationary pressures. High interests rates put pressure on the Federal Reserve to increase the rate of growth in the money stock, which as experience has taught leads inextricably to a higher inflation rate. Higher rates of inflation, in turn, can result in even higher interest rates, which further distort the economy's use of resources. More resources are directed into the public sector and are used by private citizens in trying to avoid the adverse consequences of inflation, which may be measured in part by the reduced value of people's monetary wealth and by higher tax rates on income caused by the forces of bracket creep.

In the final analysis, federal deficits act like a tax on people's incomes. The deficit tax, however, is indirect in its effects and obscured from full public scrutiny. Because of its obscurity, the deficit tax allows Congress to impose a heavier government burden on the citizenry than it could impose if Congress had to legislate overt tax increases to cover the deficits.

President Reagan entered office dedicated to supply-side economic principles, through which he believed a universally held goal—higher economic growth with lower unemployment and inflation rates—could be achieved. The failure of the supply-side policies have been attributed to federal deficits and to the higher interest rates they have spawned. Such a conclusion is much like blaming inflation on higher prices: It describes what has happened but offers little insight for developing politically palatable remedies.

The purpose of this chapter, in general, is to continue the application of principles developed in earlier chapters and, in particular, to explain why budget deficits occur and how they can be corrected. An important point of the discussion is that to achieve a balanced budget, policymakers, specifically

---

[5]See Richard B. McKenzie, "Supply-Side Economics and the Vanishing Tax Cut," Atlanta Federal Reserve *Economic Review* (May 1982), 20-24; and U.S. Department of the Treasury, Summary of Staff Papers on Scheduled Tax Changes (June 15, 1982).

members of Congress, must be given incentives to seek a balance between government outlays and revenues.

Attention is focused on the problem of inducing Congress to balance its budget. We conclude that regardless of whether any one of several proposed balanced budget amendments first seriously considered in Congress in 1982 is ever passed by Congress and signed into law by the president, members of Congress must be given pay incentives to restore a balanced budget. The same general solution developed can be applied, with adjustment in the pay objective, to the president and the board of governors of the Federal Reserve System. While suggestive of what must be done to achieve balanced budgets, the proposal put forth here reexposes an ever-present catch 22 in democracy: How can we get those who govern to regulate themselves?

We start with a statement of the political problems inherent in the budget process. In developing our arguments, we draw a parallel between the incentives polluters have to overuse environmental resources in the absence of property rights and the incentives representatives have to overuse the budget process by way of expanded government programs. The argument here will be familiar to those who have worked through the preceding chapters. We add that a correction in the use of environmental and budgetary resources can be achieved by a marginal realignment in incentives people have to produce public and private goods. In the case of environmental economics, the public good is served by cleaner, but not necessarily perfectly clean, air and water. In the case of the government budget, the public good is served by a movement toward, but not necessarily to, a balanced budget.

The Political Bias toward Deficits

The tendency of the federal government to incur additional debt emanates from three primary sources. First, deficits tend to obscure the cost of government programs. Second, individual members of Congress can blame budget deficits on federal programs promoted by their colleagues. Third, democracy tends to shorten people's time horizons (or tends to increase their discount rates). Overall, members of Congress have an inadequate incentive to avoid deficits, meaning that deficits of a certain magnitude, while destructive to the economy generally, possess elements of political rationality.

Maximizing Reelection Chances

Members of Congress, interested in being reelected, have a built-in incentive to vote for federal programs that benefit their constituencies and to vote against tax increases imposed on those same constituencies. This has been a premise fundamental to much of the political theory in this volume. Special interests have undue political power because the benefits of the programs designed with their welfare in mind are concentrated on a relatively small number of people who have a strong interest in enlisting congressional support. Federal programs in a representative's district tend to earn him supporters, whereas federal taxes tend to lose him votes. The politician interested in maximizing his changes of being reelected will, in the absence of budget deficits, vote for additional government expenditures as long as the additional dollars spent earn more votes than are lost by the accompanying additional taxes.

For several reasons, voters will perceive a $1 million government expenditure financed by overt taxes as being more costly than the same expenditure financed by a debt.[6] Clearly, workers can directly observe legislated taxes in terms of reduced take home pay. When explicit taxes are used to finance government projects, the personal cost of the additional government expenditures can be measured by the worker in terms of the fewer personal goods and services he can buy.

Furthermore, many Americans have little conception of the deficit's relative magnitude. (Many may not even know what is meant by a deficit.) Others have never thought through the complicated logical sequence by which deficits impinge on the use of the nation's resources—and are tantamount to legislated taxes. For these Americans, the costs of reduced goods and services indirectly brought about by deficits may not be fully attributed to the deficits but to, for example, the profit-maximizing efforts of firms that actually raise their prices.

Many Americans, steeped in Keynesian economic theory, actually believe that deficits are good for the economy: "After all, they help balance the economy and maintain employment," or so the argument has been developed. Keynesian economics has led (or, rather misled) a whole generation of economics students to believe that in times of economic distress, federal deficits are the only way to acquire the fabled economic free lunch—that is, greater production at zero or almost zero cost. The result of the power of special interests in politics combined with the demise in what James Buchanan and Richard Wagner call the "balanced budget norm" caused by Keynesian economics has been a form of "budgetary anarchy" in which almost every conceivable special interest seeks to gain from some government program, with a result that the budget appears virtually out of control.[7]

---

[6]For a comparative analysis of the relative fiscal deception of taxes and debt, see James M. Buchanan and Richard E. Wagner, *Democracy in Deficit: The Political Legacy of Lord Keynes* (New York: Basic Books, 1978); and James M. Buchanan, "Debt, Demos, and the Welfare State," a paper presented at the 1982 annual meeting of the Western Economic Association (July 19, 1982).

[7]Buchanan and Wagner, *Democracy in Deficit*. The balanced budget norm was the commonly held view among politicians through the 1950s that the federal budget must be balanced.

Granted, many people do understand the economic consequences of federal deficits and may fully equate them with taxes. For these people, deficits do not understate the cost of government. The people who induce politicians to employ deficits are those who can see clearly the economic consequences of taxes but cannot see with equal clarity the economic impacts of deficits. They shift the distribution of votes toward those politicians who offer to expand government programs without raising explicit taxes. To the extent that federal deficits obscure the tax cost of government expenditures, deficits should lead to an expenditure level greater than would otherwise occur—greater than the polity would choose in the light of full information concerning the personal cost of government outlays, regardless of how the outlays are financed. This is because on the margin, when the prospect of a deficit is first introduced, the votes gained from an additional $1 million government expenditure, unaccompanied by offsetting taxes, will then be greater than the votes lost. The perceived tax cost will be understated, something less than $1 million. How much the cost will be understated and to what extent a deficit is politically practical we cannot know in the abstract, outside the political process.

We do know, however, that under current political constraints, members of Congress can be rewarded by running deficits up to a certain point. By spending more than they collect in taxes, they can secure additional votes at the public's expense, and they can secure additional votes with fewer expenditures from their own campaign accounts (or more votes with the same campaign expenditures). Beyond some point, the cost of deficit spending can become so readily apparent that deficits, like taxes, begin to lose votes. The central point still holds: Because of the relative fiscal illusion of deficits, there is some politically optimum budgetary deficit, established largely independent of economic conditions in the country.

Pollution and Public Outlays

Economists have a relatively straightforward explanation for the existence of a polluted waterway. Property rights to the waterway are nonexistent (or have been, in some respects, attenuated). Because no one has property rights to the waterway, no one can be excluded from its use. All can use the waterway at no cost (or at an understated cost) to themselves. Each can reason that the wastewater he dumps into the waterway can be carried away to become someone else's problem; the cost of the pollution is thereby externalized, to employ a bit of economic jargon. Aside from the very large users of the waterway, each polluter also can reason that the small amount of waste he dumps in the stream has little or inconsequential effect on the overall water quality. Hence, for all practical purposes, the individual imposes no cost on himself or others.

The individual polluter can conclude that his own clean-up efforts will result in little or no improvement in the overall water quality. Besides, additional clean-up costs, incurred by one producer but not by others, will reduce a firm's competitiveness and decrease its share of market sales. The reduction in the firm's contribution to pollution can be offset by additional pollution from other firms, enabling the polluters to reduce their costs and expand their share of the market. The rational position of each polluter is to use the waterway to the greatest extent necessary. The collective result of rational behavior of all water users is, however, perverse: The waterway is used, abused, and overused and can become an environmental mess. At the extreme, the waterway can become the practical equivalent of a cesspool, with no one pleased with the result, not even those who are responsible for the pollution.

The general solution economists offer to solve problems of environmental deterioration is to provide individuals with incentives to do that which is in their collective interest—that is, cut back on their individual pollution levels. Such incentives can be achieved through the following:

1. Assignment of property rights (which allow the owners to charge for the use of the assigned property rights);

2. Imposition of government fees for the use of the waterways (which implies that the government has assumed ownership of the environmental resource);

3. Government regulation by way of the establishment of pollution standards with fines for nonobservance (which can translate into fees for the use of the environmental resource).

Our purpose here is not to debate the relative merits of the alternative solutions; that task has been handled admirably elsewhere.[8] Rather, our purpose is simply to note the general nature of the solution: the institutionalization of private incentives to realign the allocation of resources.

Environmental pollution is another way of saying that too few environmental goods and too many other goods and services have been produced. One way the problem can be corrected is to change, and thereby discourage, the inefficient use of the environment. A proper balance between the production of environmental and other goods can be achieved, theoretically speaking, by adjusting the charges. If a given schedule results in too much attention being given to cleaning up the environment, then fees can be lowered.

The federal government's treasury is much the same to individual members of Congress as the environmental resource is to the individual polluter: Both

---

[8]For a discussion of the pollution problem as seen from the perspective of a property rights paradigm, see Hugh H. Macaulay and T. Bruce Yandle, *Environmental Economics and the Market* (Lexington, Mass.: Lexington Books, 1974).

can be exploited fully in the absence of constraints and incentives to do otherwise. Each member of Congress can, for the most part, reason that any bill he offers in support of this constituency will have an imperceptible impact on the overall budget total, the level of taxes, and the magnitude of the budget deficits. The bills supported by individual members of Congress are likely to contribute little to the costs the taxpayers in their districts bear in the form of either higher explicit, legislated taxes or higher implicit, deficit-induced taxes. Most of the costs of a government program, like the costs of pollution, are externalized to the rest of the citizenry through the federal tax system. As in the case of the polluter, the politician also can reason that any restraint on his part in supporting expensive programs for his constituency is likely to provide representatives from other districts in his state and in other states with an opportunity to expand programs favored by their constituencies.

The rational course of behavior of each individual member of Congress is to pollute Congress with proposed government expenditures that benefit differentially and preferentially his constituencies. Just as in the case of the polluted waterway, the collective outcome can be perverse: a federal treasury that is used, abused, and overused—bloated beyond rational boundaries. In short, the federal treasury may become the fiscal equivalent of an inverted cesspool. As opposed to throwing too much waste into the pool, which is the outcome of environmental pollution, politicians throw in too many bills and extract too much in the way of resources from the national income pool.

The individual member of Congress typically may be unmoved to do anything about the budget deficits, even if the general public is upset by the prevalence of deficits. Just as the individual polluter of the waterway can claim, with some justification, that the pollution is due to the waste of all the other polluters, the individual member of Congress can claim that the bloated budget is due to the fiscal irresponsibility of most of the other 534 members of Congress. Further, each member of Congress can, at the same time he is introducing expansive legislation, creating what may be dubbed bill pollution, call for fiscal restraint and fiscal responsibility through reduced deficit spending, blaming all other members for the deficits that emerge. The conventional wisdom that "when responsibility is shared by all, it is assumed by no one" is fully applicable to the way Congress is inclined to view the budget.

As in the case of waterway pollution, the solution to the inverted treasury cesspool must lie in imposing restrictions on the budgetary process, such as requiring a balanced budget, or in providing members of Congress with private incentives to do what should, on the margin, be in their acknowledged collective interest—that is, to reduce the deficit. Each member of Congress must be held accountable (in the sense that he incurs a cost) for deficits before we can realistically expect them to be eliminated from budgets.

The Shortened Political Time Horizon

In their private dealings people understand that their current decisions will directly affect their long-term decisions and welfare. An individual private citizen may willingly (and eagerly) forgo consumption today in the anticipation that, for example, his investments will increase his future income. Given two options today over which he must exercise private choices today, the private citizen may choose the one that yields less satisfaction today in the anticipation that his future satisfaction will increase by more than what is currently lost. He does this in the knowledge that he has a great deal of control over choices made today and in the future.

In the political process, however, the individual is only one among many who has the right to participate in decisions. The individual voter understands that his control over future outcomes is impaired by the simple fact that he has less control over collective decisions, especially those made by very large and changing groups of voters. Each voter can legitimately reason that any restraint made today can be undone easily in the future. Hence, restraint on consumption is of less value in public affairs than in private affairs. Accordingly, each individual voter has a rational reason to trade, on the margin, deficits (that can directly reduce current investment and future income) for taxes (that can, to a greater degree than deficits, directly reduce current consumption).[9]

Similarly, politicians must acknowledge the pressure from their short-sighted constituents. In addition, they also can reason that they may not be around after their terms of office are up. As discussed in chapters 6 and 7 in greater detail, they can reasonably conclude that the benefits of any restraint on their part can accrue to the politicians who follow them.

Fiscal Constraints on the Legislative Process

Concerned about mounting deficits, Congress in 1985 appended what was called the Gramm-Rudman-Hollings amendment to a bill that would raise the national debt ceiling to $2 trillion. The bill, which was quickly signed by President Reagan, sets deficit limits for fiscal years 1986 through 1991 in an attempt to eliminate gradually the deficit by 1991. If Congress and the president do not approve sufficient expenditure cuts or tax increases to meet the deficit targets, defense and certain nondefense expenditures (excluding Social Security and a number of programs affecting the poor) will be cut automatically

---

[9]This line of argument is more fully developed in Brennan and Buchanan, *The Reason of Rules,* chapter 5.

more or less across the board.[10] The bill will, for example, require that if taxes are not raised, expenditures must be cut by around $12 billion in fiscal year 1986 and $55 billion in 1987.

The Gramm-Rudman-Hollings legislation has much to recommend it. Its intention—to correct the deficit problem by setting a plan that Congress should follow—is admirable. In addition, by making deficit reductions automatic if congressional discretionary changes are not enacted, Gramm-Rudman-Hollings can make congressional inaction painful and politically costly to members of Congress. It encourages decisive action. Its major flaw, however, is that it is just legislation, adopted by a political body that can repeal it with no more difficulty than it was passed. As a consequence, Gramm-Rudman-Hollings may very well prove to be a soft congressional commitment to balance the budget.

If Congress is unable to balance the budget when confronted with the political pressures of each fiscal year, we can only wonder if it can stand the test of those same pressures in future years when expenditure cuts are required. As Speaker of the House Thomas O'Neill, Jr., told reporters immediately following the passage of Gramm-Rudman-Hollings, "Wait until you get to 1987 and have to cut $55 billion. Wait until you hear what American people say about that. The only way you salvage it at that time would be for the President to come out with a tax bill. If he doesn't, it will be the last law of the land. They will be up here waiving points of order to change Gramm-Rudman."[11] True fiscal cynics fear that the Gramm-Rudman-Hollings amendment amounts to little more than a short-term political cop-out, a form of Washington doublethink that allows politicians to vote for deficit spending (through a hike in the debt ceiling) and, at the same time, to vote against deficit spending (through the Gramm-Rudman-Hollings fiscal restrictions). Indeed, as this book was going to press, the Supreme Court ruled the provision mandating automatic cuts to be unconstitutional.

The single most promising long-term solution for the political bias toward excessive government spending and deficits is an amendment to the Constitution (the balanced budget/tax limitation amendment).[12] This amendment was

---

[10]Actually, the cuts would be split between defense expenditures and the limited number of nondefense expenditures that are not specifically excluded from coverage by Gramm-Rudman-Hollings. Several health programs, including Medicare, cannot be cut by more than 1 percent in 1986 and 2 percent in subsequent years.

[11]As reported in Jonathan Fuerbringer, "Plan to Balance Federal Budget Passes in Senate," *New York Times,* 12 December 1985, 17.

[12]For a more extensive treatment of the legal and economic issues concerning the balanced budget/tax limitation amendment, see Alvin Rabushka, *A Compelling Case for a Constitutional Amendment to Balance The Budget and Limit Taxes* (Washington, D.C.: Taxpayers' Foundation, 1982); U.S. Senate, 96th Congress, 2nd Session, Committee on the Judiciary, *Hearings on S.J. 58* (January 14 and February 22, 1980), and *Report on S.J. 58* (July 10, 1981); and W.S. Moore and Rudolph G. Penner, *The Constitution and the Budget: Are Constitutional Limits on Tax, Spending, and Budget Powers Desirable at the Federal Level?* (Washington, D.C.: American Enterprise Institute, 1980).

first actively considered by Congress and fully supported by the Reagan administration in 1982. The following is the text of the amendment as passed by the Senate in 1985:

Joint resolution proposing an amendment to the Constitution altering federal budget procedures.

Resolved by the Senate and House of Representatives of the United States of America in Congress Assembled (two-thirds of each House concurring therein), First: That the following article is proposed as an amendment to the Constitution of the United States, which shall be valid to all intents and purposes as part of the Constitution if ratified by the legislatures of three-fourths of the several states within seven years after its submission to the states for ratification:

Article:

Section 1. Prior to each fiscal year, the Congress shall adopt a statement of receipts and outlays for that year in which total outlays are no greater than total receipts. The Congress may amend such statement provided revised outlays are no greater than revised receipts. Whenever three-fifths of the whole number of both Houses shall deem it necessary, Congress in such statement may provide for a specific excess of outlays over receipts by a vote directed solely to that subject. The Congress and the President shall pursuant to legislation or through exercise of their powers under the first and second articles ensure that actual outlays do not exceed the outlays set forth in such statement.

Section 2. Total receipts for any fiscal year set forth in the statement adopted pursuant to this article shall not increase by a rate greater than the rate of increase in national income in the last calendar year ending before such fiscal year, unless a majority of the whole number of both Houses of Congress shall have passed a bill directed solely to approving specific additional receipts and such bill has become law.

Section 3. The Congress may waive the provisions of this article for any fiscal year in which a declaration of war is in effect.

Section 4. Total receipts shall include all receipts of the United States except those derived from borrowing and total outlays shall include all outlays of the United States except those for repayment of debt principal.

Section 5. The Congress shall enforce and implement this article by appropriate legislation.

Section 6. On and after the date this article takes effect, the amount of federal public debt limit as of such date shall become permanent and there shall be no increase in such amount unless three-fifths of the whole number of both houses of Congress shall have passed a bill approving such increase and such bill has become law.

Section 7. This article shall take effect for the second fiscal year beginning after its ratification.[13]

There are two requirements central to the amendment. First, Congress must plan for a balanced budget (section 1), meaning that government outlays (fully inclusive of all expenditures) must match anticipated government revenue in any budget approved by Congress. Money received from debt issues are specifically excluded from the definition of revenues. Even if the amendment is adopted by two-thirds of the membership of both houses and three-fourths of all states (which is the test any amendment must hurdle), a balanced budget requirement would not be an absolute, unvarying standard for the federal government. The amendment explicitly allows for deficits in years when the country is involved in a declared war (section 3). A deficit budget also may be incurred if 60 percent of both the Senate and the House vote for a deficit of a specified amount. Further, if the economy enters a recession and the government's tax collections fall short of outlays because the nation's income falls, the resulting deficit is acceptable under the amendment. Alternatively, Congress may not incur a deficit during a recession due to an increase in outlays, such as greater than planned unemployment payments, due in turn to a faltering economy. The amendment obligates Congress and the president to hold outlays to the budgeted outlays unless revisions in the budget are expressly adopted.

Second, the amendment restricts the growth in government by tying the growth in tax revenues to the growth in the nation's income (section 2). Specifically, this provision means that Congress may not allow government revenue to increase by more than the percentage increase in the national income level of the previous year. A 4 percent increase in national income during the previous calendar year, for example, means that federal government revenue for the forthcoming fiscal year cannot increase by more than 4 percent. Assuming a balanced budget to begin with, the cap on the growth in revenue also places a cap on the growth in government expenditures. Government may continue to grow in absolute terms under the amendment; it just cannot, without an explicit vote to the contrary, take a growing share of the nation's income.

If the amendment is ever passed, should we expect Congress to abide by the Constitution, balance its budget and hold the growth in tax receipts to the growth in the last year's income? Unfortunately, we cannot be confident in the outcome. Legal opinion differs over whether the federal government's budget

---

[13]Ibid.

can be and will be reviewed by the court.[14] In other words, there may be no legal recourse for people who believe that Congress and the president have acted unconstitutionally by intentionally adopting an unbalanced budget or by fabricating forecasts for national income and taxes that give the impression that planned outlays and revenues are in balance. After considering various ways of adding an enforcement clause to the amendment and deliberately omitting one, the Senate Judiciary Committee concluded that judicial review of the amendment would be sharply limited by both the Constitution and past judicial practices. The supporting members of the committee believed that few people would be able to meet the conventional tests for court review of complaints—standing, political question, and justiciability:

> (a) there would only rarely, if ever, be "standing" in any individual or group of individuals to challenge alleged breaches of the amendment [meaning the complaining party or parties would have to be able to show they had actually been affected by a congressional violation of the amendment and legal remedy could conceivably be devised]; (b) even if such "standing" were conferred, the courts would normally treat issues raised under the amendment as "political questions" to be decided in the discretion of other branches of government; and (c) it is most questionable that the courts would find most issues arising under the amendment to be "justiciable" in the sense of presenting the kind of "case" to which the judicial powers attaches under Article III of the Constitution.[15]

Supporters of the amendment believe, however, that the ratification of a balanced budget/tax limitation amendment will impose a moral obligation on our representatives to be more open about their support for deficit spending. This greater openness—stemming from the explicit votes that must be taken to run a deficit and to raise tax revenues by more than the growth in national income—should lead to greater political information and increased political pressure for members of Congress to abide by the dictates of the Constitution. Realistically, we should expect the adoption of the amendment to result only in marginally lower deficits, not necessarily a balanced budget. More direct incentives must be imposed to lower the deficit further or even balance the budget.

The Solution: The Deficit-Pay Schedule

Much economic policy—from welfare to defense policy—is grounded on one simple but general proposition: People respond to incentives and disincentives.

---

[14]See U.S. Senate Committee on the Judiciary, *Report of S.J. Res. 58*, chapter 12.

[15]Ibid, 62.

The deficit problem has emerged in part because that simple principle has not been applied to the development and achievement of fiscal goals. Let us explain the internal contradiction in policy formulation, the correction of which would require a radical change in the way policymakers are paid.

Members of Congress receive the same annual pay, about $75,000 year, no matter whether the deficit is $50 billion, $100 billion, or $200 billion. Similarly, the president is paid $250,000 annually, regardless of the state of the economy. Members of the board of governors and the Open Market Committee of the Federal Reserve System are paid a fixed amount without regard to the rate of the growth in the money stock directly under their control or the rate of inflation indirectly related to their control of the money stock.

While attributing blame for excessive government spending to others, members of Congress claim that achieving a balanced budget is impossible or impractical. The Federal Reserve argues that it does not know how to keep the growth in the money stock within the bounds of its own self-imposed growth targets. The circularity of blame is complete: The president blames Congress and the Federal Reserve for excessive spending and money growth. Congress blames the president for lack of effective leadership and for following "voodoo economics" by drastically cutting taxes, and the president blames the Federal Reserve for high interest rates that deter growth. The Federal Reserve chairman blames Congress and the president for the deficits that push up interest rates, while they pressure the Federal Reserve to expand the money stock. The blame is fully diffused, therefore, and nowhere accepted.[16]

Of course, the claims of Congress, the president, and the Federal Reserve have an element of truth. The lack of blame is indigenous to the incentive system that has been constructed. If IBM executives and workers were paid the same way as members of Congress, the president, and the Federal Reserve's board of governors, one could accurately forecast that IBM executives would hum a similar chorus: "Computers, especially reliable ones with sophisticated capabilities, are impossible or too costly to produce. We do not know how to produce microcomputers with extensive RAM capacity that are adaptable to a variety of programming languages."

Given the magnitude of the lost output linked to federal deficits, it is time that we seriously rethink the way in which policymakers are paid, recognizing that they are not much different from the rest of us: They too respond to regulation and incentives. We can start by providing representatives and senators with monetary incentives to eliminate deficit spending.

While outright prohibition of deficit spending has definite merit (consider the balanced budget/tax limitation amendment currently before Congress), it also has, as noted above, several definite drawbacks. First, the balanced

---

[16]Apparently, members of Congress have been reasonably successful in dispersing blame for government deficits. A mid-1982 Gallup Poll found that the public's disapproval rating for Congress as a whole was substantially greater than constituents' disapproval rating of their representatives. *Washington Post,* (1 August 1982), 13.

budget/tax limitation amendment may never be passed. Second, even if passed, it probably will take years for the amendment to pass in the necessary number of state legislatures. Third, even if adopted as constitutional law, it lacks flexibility, which Congress needs to pursue national objectives not fully captured by a requirement to balance the budget. Fourth, it lacks the incentives that would induce members of Congress to abide by the then amended constitution—that is, to limit taxes and balance its budget. Finally, serious questions remain whether the courts will be willing and able to review the constitutionality of proposed budgets.[17]

A new incentive pay system for Congress could be inaugurated as part of a quasi-constitutional effort to control Congress in the formulation of the budget. This incentive system could involve the development of what could rightfully be called a deficit-pay schedule because it relates the pay of members of Congress to the actual budget deficit of the preceding year.[18] We suggest that once and for all the country should recognize the honor and responsibility of being an elected U.S. representative by establishing the annual pay at, for example, $300.000. The members' pay could be scaled downward for, say, every $50 billion of additional budgetary deficit.[19] The minimum pay could be held at its current level of $75,000 a year.[20] Realizing that each $20 billion reduction in the deficit is more difficult to achieve and each increment in congressional pay may be worth less to the members, especially after progressive income taxes are applied, each successive marginal reduction in the deficit should be accompanied by a progressively greater marginal increase in pay. Using these principles, the hypothetical pay schedule in table 8-1 could apply.

We need not make the members worse off, even at very high deficits, than they currently are. We need only provide them with an incentive to do their job, much as they might provide incentives for welfare recipients to move off public relief or to investors to expand their expenditures on new plants and equipment.

Problems with the Solution

Admittedly, the proposed pay system for Congress is not perfect. Problems abound, several of which can be resolved with additional rules for the structure

---

[17]The vote on the balanced budget/tax limitation amendment may be construed as a vote on the optimum deficit that must be achieved by an appropriate incentive structure.

[18]The pay of members is related to the deficit of the preceding year to avoid misleading forecasts that would be present if pay were related to projected estimated deficits.

[19]The pay schedule could, of course, be more detailed than the one suggested, providing for adjustments in congressional pay for every $1 billion or $5 billion change in the budget deficit.

[20]We need not penalize representatives by reducing their pay below what it is now. We need only provide them with an incentive to balance the budget.

Table 8-1
A Hypothetical Deficit-Pay Schedule
for Congress

Budget Deficit (billions)	Congressional Pay
$0	$300,000
50	225,000
100	150,000
150 or above	75,000

of congressional pay. For example, such a pay schedule provides no incentive for members of Congress to control inflation and tax rates. The budget could be balanced by legislated tax increases or inflation-induced tax increases. The latter problem could be guarded against in two ways. First, we could over-compensate members of Congress in the sense that their congressional pay would exceed their viable alternative pay in the private sector. A reduction in purchasing power of the members' pay, brought about by inflation, would then mean a true economic loss to the members. Second, we could disconnect, to the extent possible, the pay of Congress from the inflation rate. The members' pay could be adjusted at the same time congressional seats were reapportioned, meaning that the real purchasing power of congressional pay could erode with the forces of inflation for as many as ten years. Granted, at the end of the decade just before the pay schedule was adjusted, members would lose much of their pay incentive to work toward the control of inflation. Although defective in this regard, the proposed system would be an improvement over the current system, which allows members of Congress to adjust their pay for inflation automatically or whenever they think it is politically expedient to do so.

The problem of the budget being balanced via tax increases could be partially, but not completely, resolved by imposing a rule that the tax rate increases imposed on the general public will translate into a more severe penalty on representatives and senators. Currently, the contrary is true. Members of Congress have exempted themselves from Social Security taxes and have provided themselves with many nontaxable perquisites of office and deductions for living and working in Washington. Special tax privileges for members could be prohibited. How general tax rate increases were converted into more severe penalties on Congress would be largely arbitrary. The important point is that considerable incentive must remain in the deficit-pay schedule after taxes to balance the budget, and a definite mathematical link must be established and maintained between the tax rates imposed on the public and the tax rates imposed on Congress.

One possible rule (and the possibilities are numerous) would be to adjust the deficit-pay schedule inversely to the percentage of the nation's income going to taxes. An increase in tax rates imposed on the general public would then mean a downward shift in the deficit-pay schedule. The details of the pay schedule could be so constructed that members retained a strong incentive to balance the budget by controlling expenditures rather than by raising taxes. Again, the important point is that a mathematical link must be established between the tax rates imposed on the public and the burden imposed on members of Congress.

Inherent in any pay schedule that provides incentives for congressmen to balance the federal budget is the risk of too severely tunneling the social vision of our policymakers whose goals are necessarily varied. The deficit-pay system can be so constructed that members of Congress allow other social and defense goals to go unattended. The proposal being tendered here is intended not to unbalance the political incentives members of Congress have to spend and the lack of political incentives those same members have to raise revenue and balance the budget. The task facing those who actually construct the deficit-pay schedule is to tilt the incentive system *toward,* but not necessarily *to,* a balanced budget. With the pay system installed, members of Congress can still express their devotion to the principles of social welfare and national defense; they can still use the budgetary process to pursue purely political objectives; they can still run budgetary deficits. *They will, however, have to bear a personal cost to do those things.* To that extent, lower deficits can be expected. As in the environmental economics example, resulting budget deficits can be adjusted by marginal changes in the incentives built into the deficit-pay schedule.

A pay schedule like the example in table 8-1 is expensive. If the annual projected deficit of the United States were reduced from more than $200 billion to zero, the pay of members of Congress would skyrocket. The total additional pay for the 535 senators and representatives, however, would only be slightly more than $120 million a year. The achievement of a balanced budget at that expense should be a bargain. If the economic harm of government deficit spending is not greater than an eighth of a billion dollars, all the concern about federal deficits has surely been misplaced.

The deficit-pay schedule does not fully correct the problem of budgetary pollution—that is, the tendency of individual members of Congress to propose new government programs. Even with the deficit-pay system in force, individual congressmen may continue to propose new expenditure programs, hoping that the deficit is reduced by the defeat of all the other bills introduced by other members. While a tax on the introduction of bills by individual members would deal more directly with the problem, such a corrective device would likely be viewed as an undue intrusion on congressional activities. While imperfect, the deficit-pay system has one redeeming quality: It increases the attention members are likely to give to the costs of legislation introduced by others and increases resistance to an expansion of expenditures. To that extent, the deficit-pay system will act as a brake on the growth of the government. An increase in the use of taxes and a decrease in the use of deficits to finance government outlays should fortify voter resistance to politicians who favor new and expansive government programs.

Finally, with pay tied to computed deficits, Congress will have an incentive to shift government support of social goals from outright expenditures to off-budget programs, loan guarantees, and regulations that distort market prices and effectively impose taxes on the public. These forms of government intrusions in the private sector have become so important that the concept of the government budget will, sooner or later, have to be broadened to include them. The installation of the deficit-pay system must be predicated on a more inclusive concept of the federal budget.

Concluding Comments

This chapter has focused on the economic foundations of the current budget crisis and the ways in which economic principles can be used to control politicians' behavior by outright regulation and by improving the incentive policymakers have to achieve commonly acknowledged goals. The emphasis has been on the necessity of external fiscal constraints on Congress and on the realignment of incentives, which have in the past been distorted in favor of deficit spending. The same general pay principles can be applied to other government officials such as the president and members of the board of governors of the Federal Reserve System.[21]

Such pay schedules do not have to be so narrowly constructed that the affected officials would choose to do nothing other than, say, hold the money growth rate to the target rate or that the president would seek no other objective than to minimize the inflation rate. As noted in our discussion of congressional pay, the schedules need only to tilt the incentive structure toward, but not necessarily to, achievement of those specified national goals deemed worthy of special attention.

This chapter has been, as others have been, concerned with the failures of public policy and has offered a solution for discussion. The particulars of the tendered solution (whether the top pay for a congressman is $500,000 or $200,000) are not, at this point, important. The important concern should be the underlying principle, which is illustrated in the deficit-pay schedule of table 8-1. Above all, in every sphere of human endeavor, we need a way of converting the public interests into private interests. In our private dealings,

---

[21]The pay of the board could start at $750,000 annually and decline with some measure of the growth in the money stock (above or below target growth rates). The president's annual pay could start at $1 million and be reduced with increases in a composite economic indicator such as the misery index (which is the sum of the inflation and unemployment rates). See Morgan Reynolds, "Incentive vs. Bad Money: Let's Try Indexing Salaries of the Board of Governors," *Pathfinder* (July/August 1981), 2.

the market makes that conversion tolerably well. In seeking private profits, entrepreneurs tend to produce what members of the general public want at competitive prices. The general good that is created is not, for the most part, done out of love of country or a sense of duty to higher public objectives but out of self-interest.

In our public dealings, we need similar devices to convert policymakers' public interests into private interests. Competitive politics helps to hold our representatives accountable for what they do. The modern history of escalating government deficits, however, accompanied by rising unemployment and inflation rates, is ample testimony to the need for other devices. The balanced budget/tax limitation amendment to the Constitution will help; it will put pressure on Congress to balance its budgets, and marginally lower deficits (not a balanced budget) can be expected. Even if that amendment is adopted, however, one must wonder how persuasive an amendment by itself will be. We suspect that members of Congress will still need some additional incentive to abide by the Constitution. Patriotism, sense of duty to country, and public opinion have proven too weak for the task of making public and private interests compatible.

The good news is that mechanisms for altering the congressional incentive system can be conceptualized. The catch lies in convincing members of Congress and the general public that they should set up an incentive system that will result in a lower deficit than they would otherwise choose.

9

The Redistributive Society

The political decisions of the redistributive state, taken in disregard of the indispensable functions of the price system, must be unsystematic themselves. A pretense was kept up that they flowed from informed and disinterested thought devoted at the top levels of government to promoting the public interest—that even a decision to help a particular group resulted from a conscientious consideration of the interests of us all.

—Jan Tumlir[1]

The United States has become to a considerable extent a redistributive society. Such a statement is a matter of fact, not polemics. The taxing power of the state continues to be used to transfer massive amounts of purchasing power from those who earn their keep to those relatively few who are truly in need and to those relatively many who are skillful in finding ways to remain on the receiving end of government handouts.

Many people now believe, and act as if, everyone can live at the expense of everyone else. Consider the extent to which current Washington politics is concerned with Social Security, veterans' benefits, aid to education, agricultural support programs, federal aid to states, and Aid to Families with Dependent Children. As government welfare programs have expanded—or perhaps because of the expansion in those programs—democracy has tended to be converted to a great extent into a competitive struggle over slices of the government welfare pie. The numerous groups who have an interest in the maintenance and expansion of the welfare system must now scramble for money in the political arena, fearful that their budgets will be allotted to someone else more skillful in securing political favors.

Unfortunately, large redistribution programs can be a negative-sum, not simply a zero-sum, game. This is because redistributive efforts on the part of government can reduce the incentive people have to work and to generate real output and income. Furthermore, the resources used in the redistributive

---

[1]*Economic Policy as a Constitutional Problem* (London: Institute of Economic Affairs for the Wincott Foundation, November 1984), 11.

political scramble are diverted from other productive uses. Given the considerable increase in welfare expenditures in the past forty years, however, it takes a lot of imagination on the part of those playing the redistributive game to see that redistribution is, or even can be, ultimately destructive of the social product. At present, they must see only the positive correlation between their redistributive political efforts and the expansion of the welfare system. Indeed, to argue successfully that political efforts to redistribute income are illogical simply because redistribution, on balance, reduces the national income, is extremely difficult.

A fundamental cause of the gross expansion in redistribution programs is relatively obvious: Government has become so open-ended that virtually nothing is necessarily outside its purview. Stated differently, there are practically no constitutional restrictions on what government can do—for good or bad.[2] It should surprise no one that people seek to employ the power of the state in the pursuit of their own narrowly conceived ends. As a result, we have become something of a constitutional anarchy.

In this chapter, we attempt to focus greater attention on government as a redistributive force in society. We begin by briefly presenting data on the distribution of income and the effects that government programs have had on the distribution. We then critically evaluate traditional and not-so-traditional arguments for redistribution that presume to justify redistributing income from one sector, particularly the rich, to another sector, particularly the poor. Our discussion concludes with a discussion of social remedies for the redistributive trap in which the American—and British and French and German and any number of other—people find themselves.

Social Welfare Expenditures

The facts relating to governmental efforts to redistribute the nation's income reveal the stark dimensions of the modern welfare state and its limited ability to relieve what are perceived to be problems of absolute poverty and maldistribution of income. In 1985 the federal government alone spent $439 billion (46 percent of the budget) on so-called "entitlements," which are welfare expenditures that appear to be largely untouchable in political attempts to control federal spending. This level of spending represented a dramatic increase over 1955, a year in which social welfare outlays were only $15 billion. By 1990 entitlement spending is expected to reach nearly $600 billion.[3]

We should keep in mind, however, that these figures actually understate the federal government's welfare efforts. A complete accounting of federal

---

[2]This theme has been developed for the United Kingdom in ibid.

[3]See Congressional Budget Office, *The Economic and Budget Outlook: An Update* (Washington, D.C.: U.S. Government Printing Office, August 1985), 77.

welfare expenditures would include social programs embedded in the budgets for agriculture, housing, and community and regional development, among others.

From the figures that have been presented, one might get the impression that the welfare state has heaped benefits on the poor. Such an impression is grossly distorted. Billions of dollars have been spent to help the poor, but federal outlays benefiting the poor remain a small portion of the total. Poverty relief totaled a mere $107 billion in 1983, less than 25 percent of total federal welfare expenditures. (These poverty expenditures cover, but are not limited to, Aid to Families with Dependent Children, general assistance, Medicaid, food stamps, and housing assistance.) Even the *Washington Post,* whose editorials tend to favor expansion of the welfare state, acknowledges that in the 1981 federal budget, officially classified transfers were sufficient to provide every person in the lower 20 percent of income earners with $6,000 (or every family with $24,000), whereas a family of four with no source of support is provided about $6,500 in cash and food stamps.[4]

Clearly, the welfare state is not intended, in the main, to help the poor. Most of the welfare expenditures, perhaps 75 percent of welfare budgets, are passed around among income groups above the officially defined poverty level. As the number of poor has erratically declined, rather significantly from almost 40 million in 1960 to 34 million in 1984,[5] and as welfare budgets have increased, rather substantially, the growth in the welfare state has meant a dramatic increase in the number of people who are effectively on the welfare rolls.

Even if we could believe, and we cannot, that most welfare programs are intended to move purchasing power from the higher income groups to the lower income groups, the magnitude of the increase in social welfare expenditures indicates that, over time, higher and higher income groups, in absolute and relative terms, have become recipients of social welfare programs. Of course, not all social welfare outlays are intended to benefit the lower income groups. Some outlays—such as higher education, some forms of medical outlays, Social Security, veterans' programs, and housing—are intended to benefit the higher income groups at the expense, in part, of the poor.

Note that even the small portion of the welfare budget that is expended on the poor is enough to raise the average income of all poor people above the official poverty level. The total poverty budget was enough in 1983 to give each poor person $3,048. But even though one of every five American citizens (42 million people) received some form of poverty relief in 1983, 40 percent of those defined as poor received no government aid at all. The nation not

---

[4]*Washington Post,* 23 June 1982, 16.

[5]The number of officially defined poor actually declined from 40 million in 1960 to 26 million in 1975, rose to 35 million in 1983, and declined again to 34 million in 1984. The number of poor people as a percent of the U.S. population declined from 22 percent in 1960 and was 14 percent in 1984.

only has a poverty problem, but it also has a problem in providing poverty relief.

Sadly, as noted above, the dollars spent on social welfare programs do not cover—nor are they intended to cover—the full extent of government efforts to engage in redistribution (that is, helping one group at the expense of another). The government intervenes in the market in a variety of ways, with the net effect usually being to help one particular group. Minimum wage laws effectively increase the incomes of some workers—those who retain their jobs in the affected market—at the expense of people who lose their jobs and are forced to take work at lower wages. Tariffs blot out foreign competition, giving the protected industries opportunities to raise their prices and make more money. In their impact, the higher prices have much the same effect on consumer purchasing power as a direct tax increase on personal income. The greater incomes received by workers, owners, and suppliers of the protected industries are categorically the same as welfare transfers such as checks distributed to low-income mothers with children. Incomes in the protected industries are greater than what could have been earned in a free market; they are the consequence of forced shifts in purchasing power.

Finally, we must remember the variety of regulatory agencies and commissions—such as the ICC, FPC, FCC, SEC, and a host of licensing boards at the state and federal levels—whose basic function has been or remains to be the protection of regulated industries from competition. Although they often offset one another, the function of such agencies and commissions is to alter the flow of income in the country toward their regulated industries. Given the tariffs in effect in a wide variety of markets, the many regulatory agencies and commissions, and the number of people directly or indirectly dependent on government expenditures, it is safe to say that there are relatively few Americans who are not, in one way or another and to one extent or another, on the welfare dole.

The Impact of Government on the Distribution of Income

Before discussing the implication of a government with an open-ended capacity (from a constitutional perspective) to redistribute the nation's income, the impact of past government efforts must be assessed. During the first half of this century, there was a marked trend toward greater equality in the distribution of earned and spendable income. This move toward equality was fostered in part, but not entirely, by the new social welfare programs of the 1930s.[6] Since 1950 (when, it might be added, government efforts to change the distribution

[6]Morgan Reynolds and Eugene Smolensky, "The Fading Effects of Government on Inequality," *Challenge,* July/August 1978, 32–37.

of income began to mushroom), the distribution of income has barely changed. The data in table 9-1 on the shares of the nation's income going to the lowest and highest quintiles of the population tend to bear this out.

The most widely reported figures on the distribution of income come from the Current Population Survey (CPS) undertaken by the Census Bureau. The CPS income measure includes salaries and wages, net income from self-employment, Social Security income, interest and dividends, net rental income, government cash transfers, private pensions, alimony, and regular gifts. Table 9-1 reveals that the share of income going to those families in the lowest quintile of the surveyed families changed from 4.9 percent in 1952 to 4.7 percent in 1984. The actual magnitude of the shifts in relative shares of income for the various groups depends critically on the years chosen for comparison. Still, the trend movements in the income shares of the highest and lowest (as well as all other) quintiles have been relatively minor.

Other measures of income and calculated distributions of income tell basically the same story: The distribution of earned income has not changed very much in the past two to three decades. In a study of the distribution of family personal income, Daniel Radner and John Hinrich found that the lowest quintile of the population received just about the same share from 1950 through 1971.[7] Morgan Reynolds and Eugene Smolensky, after making a number of adjustments to the CPS income measure, found that the lowest quintile of households had 6.4 percent of net income in 1950 and virtually the same share, 6.7 percent, in 1970. They concluded that the data showed that

> when the benefits of all government expenditures were added to the labor and capital income of U.S. households and the burden of taxes subtracted, the overall distribution of income had not changed significantly between 1950 and 1970. To be sure, the distribution of income that included the effects of

Table 9-1

Percentage of National Income Received by Each Fifth of U.S. Families, Selected Years 1952-1984

	Lowest Fifth	Second Fifth	Middle Fifth	Fourth Fifth	Highest Fifth
1952	4.9	12.9	17.1	23.5	42.0
1962	5.0	12.1	17.6	24.0	41.3
1972	5.0	11.9	17.5	23.9	41.4
1982	4.7	11.2	17.1	24.3	42.7
1984	4.7	11.0	17.0	24.4	42.9

Source: U.S. Bureau of the Census, *Statistical Abstract of the United States* (1972, 1982, 1984 data); *Current Population Reports,* no. 149 (Washington, D.C.: U.S. Government Printing Office, March 1985, advance data), 11.

---

[7] Daniel Radner and John Hinrich, "Size Distribution of Income in 1964, 1970 and 1971," *Survey of Current Business* 50, no. 10 (October 1974), 47, table 10.

government budgets was significantly closer to equality than the distribution made up of just labor and capital income, but we could not detect any significant trend in the degree of inequality.[8]

Only one major study of the distribution of income in recent years contradicts the data that have been presented. It was done by Edgar Browning at the University of Virginia.[9] Browning made five major adjustments to the CPS income measure for families. First, he included in the distribution of income an imputed value for in-kind government transfers. Second, he added an estimate of the potential earnings of all adults in the labor force. Third, he included an estimate of the costs of the education provided by all levels of government. Fourth, he computed the distribution of family income on a per capita basis, thereby adjusting for the observed reduction in the number of people in families, especially among the poor. Fifth, he deducted an estimate for the personal income and Social Security taxes people pay. After making these additions and subtractions, Browning found that the lowest quintile received 8.1 percent of net income in 1952 and 11.7 percent in 1972, a 44 percent improvement in relative income share, which is a rather startling assessment given the findings of all the other studies.

Has the distribution of income moved toward greater equality or has it not? This question has no simple answer. All measures of income are defective in one way or another. Adjustments that are made to measured incomes are often more or less arbitrary and rather crude. For example, when the goods and services given under welfare programs are not bought by their recipients in the market, it is difficult to place a dollar value on in-kind transfers. Also, it is difficult to say whether the reduction in the size of the family has lowered the standard of living of the poor or whether it is a consequence of an improvement in their standard of living. Finally, when people are unemployed, it is extremely arbitrary to specify a market value for their so-called leisure time. A detailed accounting of the pros and cons of particular adjustments to income made in individual studies would take this chapter far afield.[10] Suffice it to say that at a conference of researchers working in the area of income distribution, the trend in the distribution of income, as revealed by Reynolds and Smolensky and by Browning, was critically evaluated, and "the consensus

---

[8]Morgan Reynolds and Eugene Smolensky, "The Fading Effects of Government on Inequality," 32. See also Morgan Reynolds and Eugene Smolensky, *Public Expenditures, Taxes, and the Distribution of Income: The United States, 1950, 1961, 1970* (New York: Academic Press, 1977), especially chapter 5.

[9]E.K. Browning, "The Trend Toward Equality in the Distribution of Net Income," *Southern Economic Journal* 43 (July 1976), 912-23.

[10]For an in-depth critique of these studies as well as of others, see Michael K. Taussig, "Trends in Inequality of Well-Offness in the United States since World War II," a review paper presented at the Conference on the Trend in Income Inequality in the United States held at the Institute for Research on Poverty, University of Wisconsin-Madison, October 29-30, 1976.

at the conference placed the 'true' trend between these two positions, but somewhat closer to Reynolds and Smolensky; although many biases have a large impact on the level of inequality [as measured by the CPS income], the net results of these biases on the trend were judged to be small."[11]

Over the past twenty-five years governments at all levels have inaugurated innumerable social welfare programs and have spent literally hundreds of billions of dollars in their quest for income redistribution. The record reveals, however, that nothing much seems to have happened. *Standard techniques for measuring income tend to show that the distribution of income has changed very little from what it would have been in the absence of government programs.* This conclusion is drawn without accounting for many government redistribution efforts (such as tariffs and regulation) that work through the market, that adversely affect the poor's purchasing power, and that are of necessity not included in most of these studies. Why? Is the answer simply that government is ineffectual, incompetent, impotent—unable to accomplish efficiently what it has set out to do? Is it that government never really had its heart in the pursuit of its professed objective, helping the poor? Is the answer that social welfare programs have ended up benefiting those who run them more than the poor themselves? Very possibly all the answers implied in the questions have more than a grain of truth in them. Other speculative answers can, however, be offered. As Reynolds and Smolensky have pointed out, attempts to redistribute income initially met with some success, but over the past two decades several discernible changes have occurred.

First, the expansion of welfare programs, especially Social Security, has meant that the programs' coverage has expanded. Although welfare programs may have begun with well-defined low-income groups in mind, they have ended with coverage for virtually the entire population. Consequently, the redistributional effect of the programs has eroded.

Second, workers, who must ultimately fund the welfare programs through taxation of their incomes, have learned over time to alter the form of their earnings from taxable income, such as wages and salaries, to nontaxable income, such as fringe benefits and leisure.

Third, recipients of the welfare programs have adjusted their own behavior. In light of the very high marginal tax rates implicit in social welfare programs,[12] they have decided quite rationally to work less in order to secure

---

[11]Sheldon Danziger, "Conference Overview: Conceptual Issues, Data Issues, and Policy Implications," summary statement of the Conference on the Trend in Income Inequality in the United States held at the Institute for Research on Poverty, University of Wisconsin-Madison, October 29-30, 1976, 98-99.

[12]See Martin Anderson's discussion of the poverty wall in *Welfare: The Political Economy of Welfare Reform in the United States* (Stanford, Calif.: Hoover Institution Press, 1978); and Arthur B. Laffer's discussion of marginal tax rates in Los Angeles, "The Tightening Grip of the Poverty Trap," *Policy Analysis* (Washington, D.C.: Cato Institute, 1984).

more welfare benefits. On balance, their incomes may have risen by only a fraction of the dollar value of the welfare benefits.

Fourth, the welfare system has progressively reduced the efficiency of the U.S. economy. The result may have been that the improvement in the earned income share of the lower income groups has been impaired.

Fifth, over the past fifty years the tax code has been gradually broadened to include lower and lower income groups. The first federal income tax in 1913 applied to the incomes of only the very high income groups. Now the tax code applies to just about everyone aside from the very low income groups. The result has been a reduction in the equalizing effects of the tax system. The Social Security tax on employer and employee income has been progressively raised, with a disproportionately strong effect on the lower income groups.

Sixth, in the past twenty years state and local government taxes and expenditures have risen relative to federal taxes and expenditures. Aside from education, social welfare programs make up a relatively small part of the expenditures of state and local governments. Hence, growth in government at the state and local levels has tended to offset the redistributional effects of federal welfare programs designed specifically to help the poor.

Mancur Olson in an important book concerned with the ultimate stagnation of an open-ended political process indirectly suggests an alternative explanation for the evaporation of net benefits that initially may be channeled through the political process to the poor.[13] Olson starts with a basic premise developed in considerable detail in his earlier work.[14] Small groups of people with identified interests can effectively coalesce and politically promote their mutual objectives. This is because of their small number. Each individual in the group receives, by definition, a significant portion of the benefits from the government program (or from any other objective pursued privately). Each is, therefore, willing to bear a significant cost in pursuit of the common objective because each's contribution would be missed by all relevant parties within the group. This fact discourages shirking or, as economists say, free riding on the contributions of others.

Large groups are inclined to be latent power centers in the political process because each person's contribution to the common objective is more or less insignificant or difficult to detect. Each person within a large group has little incentive to make his contribution to the attainment of the group's commonly acknowledged objective. Although all may lose by the failure of all group members to make their contributions, each individual must reason that his contribution by itself will have no detectable effect on what the group

---

[13]Mancur Olson, *The Rise and Decline of Nations* (New Haven, Conn.: Yale University Press, 1983).

[14]Mancur Olson, *The Logic of Collective Action: Public Goods and the Theory of Groups* (Cambridge, Mass.: Harvard University Press, 1965).

does or fails to do. Olson concludes, as we have done in earlier pages, that to provide public goods and services desired generally by a large community, coercive taxation is mandatory.

The Olson premise reduces to an argument that it is more costly to form politically effective large groups than it is to form small groups. Alternatively, the larger the group, the greater the cost that must be incurred to transform the group from a politically latent to a politically kinetic status. Nevertheless, the transformation of most interest groups of varying sizes from passive to active status can be devised.

Once the political process is opened to redistribution, the poor may benefit initially on balance from the transfers that are then made. Other interest groups may not then be operational in the sense that they have developed the cohesion necessary to overcome the tendency of group members to free ride. With time, however, they may see the benefits to be gained from a political process open to transfers. As time passes, more and more groups will form to lobby for their interests. As time passes, more and more groups will be successful in having legislation that benefits themselves at, of course, the expense of everyone else. And as time passes, larger and larger groups will be able to overcome the costs of achieving political cohesion, all of which will tend to negate the initial efforts of, perhaps, well-meaning people to redistribute income from the nonpoor to the poor. Indeed, when the political process becomes crowded with interest groups, there is no reason to believe that the poor will on balance benefit from the transfer society that was started for their betterment. Indeed it is then that the poor may even question the ethics and desirability of the welfare state.

Theories of Income Redistribution

Proponents of income redistribution have developed a number of theories intended to justify governmentally induced shifts in the nation's income. Several of the more prominent theories are evaluated in this section. The general conclusion drawn is that income redistribution by government has a very spongy, if not nonexistent, theoretical foundation.

Redistribution as Social Welfare Maximization

One of the oldest arguments used to rationalize income redistribution relates to a misunderstanding and misapplication of the principle of diminishing marginal utility in consumption. Stated properly, that principle says that as a person consumes additional units of a good, there is some point beyond which the relative marginal utility of each additional unit consumed will begin to diminish. In the nineteenth and early twentieth centuries the principle was taken to mean that beyond some point in consumption, the absolute marginal utility of consuming additional units of a good begins to diminish. Indeed, it was readily but incorrectly assumed by many economists that marginal utility in consumption diminishes from the very first unit.

Social reformers concluded that aggregate social welfare could be enhanced by redistributing the nation's income from the rich to the poor. It was thought that the marginal utility of the last units of goods consumed by the rich was, by the very fact that the rich consumed more, lower than the marginal utility of the last units consumed by the poor. Hence, redistribution increased the total "utils" of satisfaction in society.

This justification for redistribution has been severely criticized on most grounds. First, it is conceptually impossible to make interpersonal utility comparisons. (We would not know a unit of satisfaction if we saw it, much less be able to say how different people value different goods!) Second, there is no real reason to believe that the marginal utility in consumption actually does diminish within the relevant range of consumption (that is, within realistic budget limitations).

Third, the principle of diminishing marginal utility applies to the allocation of a given budget among a list of specified goods and services, not to the impact of changes in the budget level. For all we know, from a conceptual point of view the marginal utility of additional units of goods increases in absolute terms when more of all goods are consumed. If the principle of diminishing marginal utility has any use at all in consumption theory, it must relate to the change in the individual's relative marginal evaluation of goods when allocation decisions are made. There is no necessary reason, therefore, to believe that the rich's relative evaluation of goods on the margin is any lower or higher than the poor's relative evaluation of those same goods, that the rich's marginal evaluation of income is any lower or higher than the poor's marginal evaluation of income, or that a shift in the distribution of income from the rich to the poor will necessarily increase social welfare.[15]

The Rawlsian Theory of Justice

Through the centuries philosophers have grappled with the question of whether there is a logical basis for ethical values. A primary concern of their struggle has been with developing principles that will enable people to decide whether a community's distribution of basic rights (such as the rights of free speech and voting), wealth, and income are socially just or unjust. In other words, philosophers—economists included—have been in search of the broad

---

[15]In addition, as Gordon Tullock stresses, the argument suggests that social welfare can be enhanced by increasing population and that it leads to the conclusion that we (those of us in relatively high-income countries) should consent to giving up most of our income to the rest of the world in the interests of maximizing social (world) welfare. Gordon Tullock, *The Economics of Income Redistribution* (Boston: Kluwer-Nijhoff Publishing, Inc., 1982), chapter 1.

theoretical outlines of the just society. During the 1970s and 1980s Harvard philosopher John Rawls has organized what he calls "a theory of justice" that he believes incorporates the guiding principles people seek.[16] His theory is particularly relevant to this volume because in developing it, he assumes a constitutional rules-making perspective. Extra attention to his theory of justice is warranted.

Rawls's theory is founded on several intuitively plausible postulates.

1. In some endeavors people are better off acting cooperatively than they are acting alone.

2. There are a number of ways of organizing human interaction.

3. People must have some means or set of principles for judging and choosing from among the various potential social arrangements which arrangement is best. "These principles," according to Rawls, "are the principles of social justice: they provide a way of assigning rights and duties in the basic institution of society and they define the appropriate distribution of the benefits and burdens of social cooperation."[17] (Examples of basic social institutions are legal protections of freedom of thought and liberty of conscience, competitive markets, private ownership of the means of production, and the monogamous family.)

4. People are moral in the sense that they understand the need for and are prepared to affirm a conception of justice by which all social institutions can be judged.

In developing his theory of justice, Rawls is not interested in seeking and defining principles of justice that flow solely from the dictates of reason or science or that are derived from the teachings of a religion, although religious views may be part of the process by which the guiding principles are derived. Rather, Rawls is interested in developing those principles that "free and rational persons concerned to further their own interests would accept in an initial position of equality as defining the fundamental terms of their association."[18] The acceptance of the principles of social justice by all people, however different their motives, is the essential element of the Rawlsian theory. In taking this position Rawls recognizes, as James Buchanan has suggested, that "unless we are to be rescued by a 'savior' or 'saviors' who will enslave us all, modern men and women must reform their own institutions. Rules can be

---

[16]John Rawls, *A Theory of Justice* (Cambridge, Mass.: Harvard University Press, 1971). For an excellent summary of this book, see John Rawls, "A Kantian Conception of Equality," *Cambridge Review* (February 1975), 94-99.

[17]Rawls, *A Theory of Justice*, 4.

[18]Ibid., 11.

changed while the game continues to be played, but few players are willing to delegate decisions on such changes to the self-anointed witch doctors."[19]

With respect to changes in the distribution of income, Rawls seeks guiding principles that are not imposed upon, but rather emerge from, a social setting of people who recognize the need for general agreement: "The scheme of social cooperation must be stable: it must be more or less regularly complied with and its basic rules willingly acted upon; and when infractions occur, stabilizing forces should exist that prevent further isolations and tend to restore the arrangement."[20] In short, as suggested several times before in this book, without general agreement on basic rules, society may perpetually exist in a Hobbesian jungle, a state of noncooperation in which all can be worse off.

What are the basic principles of social justice on which people in general can agree? Rawls argues that these principles will emerge from a setting in which people jointly choose a social contract that incorporates the principles of justice. For the principles to be fair, the social contract setting, according to Rawls, must be fair in the sense that no participant has an advantage in determining what those generally accepted principles of justice will be. If anyone has an advantage, the principles will be devised to correspond to the private interests of that individual and will lack the necessary general agreement that is so important in the Rawlsian theory for social stability.

A fair contract setting is one into which all those who engage in social cooperation enter as equals. Further, they are all behind what Rawls calls "a veil of ignorance." Behind this veil "no one knows his place in society, his class position or social status, nor does any one know his fortune in the distribution of natural assets and abilities, his intelligence, strength, and the like, . . . [his] conception of the good or . . . [his] psychological propensities."[21] Without any knowledge of what their positions in society will be, the participants are asked to devise rules for distributing basic rights in society and for distributing society's benefits—the distribution of income. Rawls argues that two fundamental principles will emerge. First, each person is to have an equal right to the most extensive basic liberty compatible with a similar liberty for others. Second, social and economic inequalities are to be arranged so that they are reasonably expected to be to everyone's advantage and are attached to positions and offices open to all.[22]

---

[19]James M. Buchanan, "Notes on Justice in Contract" (Working Paper CE 76-6-4, Center for the Study of Public Choice, Virginia Polytechnic Institute and State University, Blacksburg, Virginia, 1976), 25.

[20]Rawls, *A Theory of Justice,* 6.

[21]Ibid., 12.

[22]Ibid., 60.

In the Rawlsian system of justice, inequalities in the distribution of wealth and income are just only when they are advantageous to everyone, especially the lower income groups. Inequalities in the distribution are unjust when they are to the disadvantage of anyone, particularly to someone in the lower income groups. Rawls concludes that justice—a concept developed when people are in the initial contract state behind the veil of ignorance—requires that the income of the lower income people in society be maximized. This is called the difference principle.

Many people who have read Rawls have concluded that the difference principle justifies a massive transfer of income from the rich to the poor because that is a redistribution scheme that even the rich would have accepted in the initial social contract setting behind the veil of ignorance. The difference principle, therefore, justifies present government poverty programs and expansions of them.

On the surface, a redistribution from the rich to the poor does appear to be consistent with the difference principle; the income of the poor apparently is raised by the design of the program. The transfers can, however, be inconsistent with the goal of maximizing the income of the poor. Massive government programs to redistribute income can reduce the incentive of the relatively rich to work and invest in productive assets. To the extent that the productive efforts of the rich are beneficial to the poor—to the extent that the poor work with capital equipment—a transfer of income from the rich to the poor can conceivably make the poor worse off, at least over a period of time, as the poor gradually have fewer capital assets to aid them in production.

The poor of today may be better off because they receive supplements to their income that are transferred by the government from the rich. The poor of the future may be worse off because the aggregate income of the society then will tend to be less because of reduced capital accumulation. In that event, the poor of the future will tend to earn less income (they will be less productive because they will have less capital with which to work), and the government will have less income to transfer from the rich to the poor. There is, therefore, at least some reason to doubt that Rawls's scheme would achieve the necessary agreement among all poor, those of today and those of all future generations (who will dominate the decisionmakers in Rawls's conceptual framework).

Indeed, Robert Nozick, another Harvard philosophy professor, has written a book that contains a major attempt to counter Rawls's basic arguments.[23] A basis thesis of Nozick's work is that the rich, who may be rich because of greater natural or acquired talents and who are more productive, benefit the poor by providing them with mutually beneficial opportunities for trade at

---

[23]Robert Nozick, *Anarchy, State, and Utopia* (New York: Basic Books, 1974).

lower prices than would otherwise exist. It is certainly doubtful that the poor would be better off if the rich did not possess their greater productive skills.

Richard Wagner goes even further and contends that adoption of Rawls's framework for establishing justice in the distribution of income may result in fewer income transfers from the rich to the poor than we now have.[24] Behind the veil of ignorance, people do not know their relative income position. In that state they will vote for income redistribution schemes that reflect their ignorance of their relative position and the fact that they have an equal chance of being in a high- or low-income bracket. When the veil of ignorance is lowered, however, they immediately become aware of their station in life — their present and expected future income. Wagner argues that in a world in which people are aware of their relative income standing, people with above-average income will vote for less equalization than formerly; those with below-average income will vote for more government transfers and greater equalization in income distribution.

Given the country's distribution of income, many more people have incomes below the average than above the average. This is because the relatively few people who have extremely high incomes pull the average income level upward to the point where more than 50 percent of the people have less than the average income. In the real world of practical politics, in which the veil of ignorance has been dropped and people know their relative position in the income distribution, Wagner argues that people will vote for more income transfer programs than they would adopt behind the veil of ignorance, where there is at least some possibility that they each will have an above-average income.

Rawls's theory of justice is based on the supposition than once the principles of justice are accepted, people will adhere to them. They will not change the rules of the game once the veil of ignorance is dropped. In the real world of practical politics, however, this condition, too, may rarely hold, or it may hold only to a very limited extent and for a relatively short period of time. Wagner's suggestion is that by using Rawls's veil of ignorance as a frame of reference in establishing justice in the distribution of income, the present distribution of income, which includes significant government transfers, may be unjust in the sense that there is too much rather than too little in the way of income transfers from the rich to the poor.

Finally, note that the Rawlsian justification for income redistribution does not necessarily imply that the poor in the United States would be, or should be, the recipients of large income transfers. The poor of this country are the relatively rich of the world, and there is no inherent reason why the Rawlsian theory of justice should be applied only within the boundaries of the United States. If taken seriously, the Rawlsian theory suggests that the income should

---

[24]Richard W. Wagner, "Politics, Bureaucracy, and Budgetary Choice: The Brookings Budget for 1974," *Journal of Money, Credit and Banking* (August 1974), 367-83.

be transferred from just about everyone in the United States to lower income people in the rest of the world.

Although Rawls's theory provides a basis for thinking through the complex issues of justice in the distribution of income from a noneconomic point of reference, it adds little to our understanding of how much government aid should be given to the poor. The argument can, with appropriate blinders to counterarguments, be used to justify more or fewer income transfers. Still, the one lesson from the give and take of this intellectual debate is that redistribution must be approached from a long-term constitutional perspective, with constitutional controls on government redistributive powers as the policy objective.

Income Redistribution as a Public Good

Poverty relief is said to be a public good. It benefits a large number of people more or less simultaneously, and the benefits of poverty relief, if relief is provided, are received by people who may not have contributed to the aid of the poor. In this regard, poverty relief is viewed by many people, including economists, as a legitimate government activity. Even Milton Friedman has recognized the public benefits that come from poverty relief and has justified some government redistribution programs on the grounds that private charities may generate less aid to the needy than is socially desirable:

> I am distressed by the sight of poverty; I am benefited by its alleviation; but I am benefited equally whether I or someone else pays for its alleviation; the benefits of other people's charity therefore partly accrue to me. To put it differently, we might all of us be willing to contribute to the relief of poverty, *provided* everyone else did. We might not be willing to contribute the same amount without such assurance.[25]

The usual presumption in such arguments is that collectivization of charity through redistributive programs will lead to more relief for the poor. This, however, will not necessarily be the case.[26] Standard public goods theory assumes that everyone in the relevant population knows how much of the public good is produced. If a unit of national defense, for example, is produced, then each person knows it and can assess the benefits he receives from that unit. Private poverty relief is different from national defense (and many other public goods) in one important respect: Both the recipient and the donor of aid may have an incentive to hide the amount of privately provided

---

[25]Milton Friedman, *Capitalism and Freedom* (Chicago: University of Chicago Press, 1962), 191.

[26]This argument is developed with graphic detail in Richard B. McKenzie, "A Note on the Construction of a Public Goods Demand Curve and the Theory of Income Redistribution," *Public Choice* 36 (1981), 337-44.

aid. The beneficiary of the aid may be embarrassed if others learn of the aid received and may understand that if he allows others to know of the aid received, others will reduce their giving. Beggars characteristically do not allow their cups to runneth over simply because they understand the effect it will have on potential contributors who pass them by. On the other side of the private transfer, the donor may give out of a sense of duty and respect for the recipient and, being concerned for the recipient's welfare, may keep his gifts secret. The end result may be, but not necessarily will be, that too much aid is given to the poor. Stated differently, collectivization of aid may let everyone know how much is given in total, a result that can lead to a contraction in (not necessarily an expansion of) the total amount of transfers. Although such a conclusion must be hedged on all sides, our critical consideration of the logic of the argument serves the very important purpose of suggesting that the conventional public goods argument for poverty relief is not a proof-positive case that public aid arrangements necessarily lead to more aid going to the poor.

In addition, if taken seriously and applied consistently (as we must presume it is intended to be), the argument may justify some rather peculiar and perverse transfers. The public goods argument for poverty relief assumes that all the externalities from the aid are positive—that is, that they give added satisfaction to all within the relevant community. Casual observation of people, however, instructs us differently; many have an abiding distaste for helping the poor, meaning that poverty relief has external costs for some as well as external benefits for others. If applied consistently, transfers would have to be made to those who have a distaste for public charity in order to compensate them for (or get their agreement on) the relief program. Such a system (which we do not endorse but point out only as a logical outcome of the public goods argument) seem bizarre but may partially explain the transfers incorporated in a wide range of government programs that benefit higher income groups.

The Fate of the Poor under Open-Ended Government

Our review of several theories of income justification teaches us that income transfers by way of government coercion are difficult to justify from philosophical, as well as economic, perspectives. Nevertheless, we venture to speculate that most people (including the authors) do sense a need or desire to transfer a limited amount of income to poor people over and above that which would be transferred by private actions of independent individuals, just as they have a need or desire to use government powers to transfer income to themselves (which is, perhaps, the dominant transfer motivation).

The question that constitutional economics must address is "What are the consequences of opening up the political process for the purpose of transfers?" Will the poor, who by most accounts tend to be politically impotent, benefit on balance from such an open-ended political process? And if they do not, are there ways of allowing people to express their well-intended desire to help the poor (the first transfer motivation mentioned above) without, at the same time, permitting them to use government to transfer income to themselves (the second motivation)?

The empirical work reviewed above on the net long-term impact of government poverty relief suggests a gloomy answer. The aid provided the poor does not appear to have materially affected the welfare of the poor. Further, such conclusions are drawn from studies that do not fully account for the full cost that the redistributive society imposes on the poor. Granted, the poor receive a share of the welfare benefits, which, we might add, tend to be open to political scrutiny. But they pay a share of the cost of government redistributive programs, much of which is hidden from political scrutiny, by way of sales and excise taxes, corporate income taxes passed on to consumers in the form of higher product prices, property taxes incorporated in rental payments, and higher prices brought on through a plethora of government programs (such as tariffs, building codes, zoning restrictions, and even market entry restrictions) designed to transfer income from everyone else to some particular middle-income and high-income group. In addition, many of the poor have become wards of the state through generations of dependency not on themselves and those who care about them but on the impersonal welfare state that measures success more by dollars spent than by accomplishments.

Constitutional economics addresses the issue of poverty relief from a system approach. It acknowledges that the poor (as well as any other identifiable interest group) would tend to prefer a political system in which they alone benefited from the transfer activity undertaken by the state. The question the poor must ask, however, is whether they would prefer a political system that allows transfers to themselves and at the same time gives everyone else the same opportunity to garner transfers. In the United States, the poor or their advocates can push for their own programs, but so can everyone else—as has almost everyone else.

Of course, while acknowledging the attractiveness of a closed-off welfare state, the poor are very reluctant to give up the government benefits at their disposal, just as everyone else is. This is because they know that without some broad-based restriction on the transfer activity of the government, the poor would, by relinquishing their benefits, place themselves in double jeopardy: They would incur the cost of other government programs (that would then be easier to secure when the poor withdrew from the political arena), and they would get little or nothing in return. The same sort of reasoning could be followed by all other groups, which is a fundamental explanation for why any contemplated withdrawal from the redistributive society must be approached by way of a broad-based constitutional proposal.

Further, the restriction on redistribution must be binding (not subject to change by way of short-term policy switches). Otherwise, over time the resistance to a reduction in the size of the redistributed state will be fortified. Each interest group will fear that if it lowers its guard against defending its program, at some time in the future it will be burdened with the costs of other welfare programs with little or no benefits for its own members.

Our concern about exactly how the poor would vote for government relief programs is made more problematic if we consider how all poor people, regardless of generation, would vote on the transfer issue. To the extent that current welfare programs redistribute income from the nonpoor to the poor, the current generation of poor may understandably be in support of a transfer arrangement. Such transfers can, however, reduce the incentive of current and future generations of poor and nonpoor alike to work, save, and invest, meaning that the poor of future generations can be harmed in two principal ways. First, the transfers can dampen the growth in the nation's income, which may mean that the poor of the future probably will be poorer (or less rich) than they otherwise would be. Second, government in the future will have lower revenues, because of lower national income, with which to help the poor than it would have had in the absence of the current transfer programs.

Would the poor, meaning all poor of all generations, vote for current poverty relief? A certain percentage of the current poor can be expected to vote in favor of it because they will likely be net beneficiaries. If all future generations of poor people are considered (and when we are conceptually assessing the issue of how the poor will vote, there is no reason to limit the analysis to the present generation of poor), it seems reasonable to conclude that those poor in the current generations voting for poverty relief programs will be an inconsequentially small percentage of all poor. This is because the poor and the would-have-been-poor of the future will be a very large number.

All this does not mean that if poverty relief were addressed as a constitutional question, it would be resoundingly defeated. It does suggest that the poor and the nonpoor probably would vote for a restricted welfare state, one that would attempt to limit transfers to the needy and preclude transfers to the nonpoor—if transfers were agreed on at all. The restrictions on the transfers would emerge as a compromise between the legitimate desire of people to help the needy and the legitimate need to preclude the possibility of the welfare state's degenerating into a redistributive society in which everyone is paying the cost of all programs, including the deadweight loss resulting from the government-created disincentives to work, save, and invest and the deadweight loss resulting from resources used to alter political outcomes. (Indeed, if we use the current open-ended redistributive state as a benchmark, the welfare benefits of the future could financed by the greater income generated by the reduced disincentives of the curtailed transfer programs that now benefit the nonpoor.)

Admittedly, our analysis is speculative, as it must be. Still, constitutionally restricted welfare programs may be just the sort of compromise that may be acceptable to all the factions now competing in the political process for a share of the transfer pie. To make such a restrictive operational, welfare expenditures would have to be restricted, say, to a certain percentage of the government budget that, in turn, would be tied to, for example, the national income level.

Concluding Comments

During the past decade or so, American society has gone through an almost unnoticed political metamorphosis. As Marc Plattner has poignantly observed, American society entered the 1960s as a "welfare state" and emerged in the late 1970s as, to a significant extent, a "redistributive society."[27] Plattner suggests that in a welfare state the poor may be aided through government programs. A common political assumption is that people who own their incomes pay a share of their incomes in the form of taxation to government for common expenses such as poverty relief. In a welfare state people perceive themselves as handing over to the government a part of what is presumed to be theirs.

In a redistributive society, however, individual incomes are presumed to be a part of a common income pool. Plattner writes that the redistributive view (in contrast to the welfare view) suggests that a person's income is not his own but rather that of the whole society. "Hence, in assessing the rate of tax on an individual," Plattner argues, "the government is deciding not on how much of his own income it will require him to pay, but how much of the society's income it will allow him to keep." If an individual is permitted to keep a portion of his income, it is because the government has determined that the greater portion "will promote a more efficient and more productive national economy—not because the more productive citizen is in any way *entitled* to a larger income."[28]

The redistributive view has two important implications. First, as Plattner and we have argued, it undermines the moral basis of individualism: "The moral and political tradition that animates liberal democracy is founded on the notion that the rights of the individual are prior to the claims of the society—indeed, that the protection of those individual rights is the very goal

---

[27]Marc F. Plattner, "The Welfare State v. the Redistributive Society," *The Public Interest* (Spring 1979), 28-48.

[28]Ibid., 45. See also Arthur M. Okun, *Equality and Efficiency: The Big Trade-off* (Washington, D.C.: The Brookings Institution, 1975).

of political society."[29] Many redistributive government programs cannot be explained or rationalized very well, as we have shown, by conventional economic analysis. A major reason is that the concept of justice underlying traditional economic analysis is at odds with the concept of justice underlying many redistributive programs.

Second, the redistributive view of society makes the nation's income, to a significant extent, a common-access resource, as air, land, and water used to be. As tends to be true with all common-access resources, the competitive struggle for portions of this new common property should lead to abuse and misuse of the property. Given the different perception of justice that underlies the redistributive society, however, the inefficiencies that result from the competitive struggle are of little or no concern to many redistributionists. Still, the analysis is instructive because it suggests that to prevent the welfare state from being transformed into a redistributive society, constitutional barriers to the perversion of legitimate welfare concerns must be instituted.

---

[29]Plattner, "The Welfare State," 45.

10

Getting More with Less

That government is best which governs the least.
—Thomas Jefferson[1]

Much of this book has been critical of the activities of government. In this last chapter, we want to emphasize that this is not the same as being critical of government. Indeed, quite the contrary is true. Our view is that government is absolutely essential to a free and productive social order. Our productivity and our tolerance of individual freedom depends on the accountability that people assume for the consequences of their actions when certain general rules of social conduct are in force. In the absence of government enforcement of these general rules, they would not long remain in force.

It is precisely because of the importance of government that we have been so critical of many of the activities in which government engages. Government has increasingly become the tool by which those with political influence can acquire benefits by imposing costs on those without political influence. We are moving toward the point where almost everyone has political influence in a few areas and the political process is a free-for-all where little is produced but much is redistributed. As this happens, accountability and tolerance of the freedom of others are being eroded, and we are increasingly becoming a negative-sum transfer society.

Only government can convert this negative-sum activity into positive-sum activity. This conversion requires genuine power, but that power must be carefully regulated and limited in scope and discretion. As suggested by the title of the book, regulating government is the positive-sum solution. We get more from government with less government.

Major Questions and Answers

Do you want government to promote more social harmony and tolerance? The negative-sum transfer activity that invariably increases as the size of

---

[1]Found in Laurence J. Peter, *Peter's Quotations: Ideas for Our Time* (New York: William Murray and Co., 1977), 231.

government increases results in social hostility and intolerance. Negative-sum transfers are necessarily contentious because the gains to one group come at the expense of another group. In a politicized environment the best that each of us can do is to identify with groups that are engaging in political combat against other groups, which results in an unproductive struggle that on balance leaves everyone worse off. We would have a more cooperative and harmonious society if we would mutually disarm politically by constraining the transfer activity of government. A smaller government doing what only government can do (enforcing general rules, such as the rules of private property, and providing a few genuinely public goods) would give us more social harmony and tolerance.

Do you want the self-seeking behavior of businesspeople regulated so that they remain responsive to the interests of consumers? More government regulation of business has resulted in less real regulation of business. Organized business interests always dominate unorganized consumer interests when it comes to the specifics of government regulation. It should surprise no one that the power that has been concentrated in government to impose detailed regulations on business is a power that business has exploited to protect itself against the best protection the consumer can have—competition. A limited government with the power to enforce general rules of economic behavior but without the authority to impose detailed controls on particular businesses creates a competitive environment in which business is regulated by the demands of consumers.

Do you want government to promote more economic growth? Expanded government has increased the burden on the productive private sector of the economy and by so doing, has retarded economic growth. A larger government means more transfers that provide opportunities for advancing private interests by acquiring existing wealth rather than producing new wealth. A larger government means more regulations, controls, and protections that reduce both the incentive and ability of business to become more productive and innovative. A larger government means higher taxes reducing the return to productive activity. The only hope for a genuine supply-side economic policy consistent with long-term economic growth is to limit the size and discretion of government.

Do you want government to keep inflation under control? A larger government finds it inconvenient to cover all its expenses with taxes (see chapter 8). A politically attractive alternative to taxation is inflation, and this alternative usually becomes irresistible to a large government with discretionary control over the money supply (see chapter 6). Only by limiting government's ability to manipulate the money supply can we have any long-term hope of keeping inflation at bay.

Do you want government to help the poor? Granting government the power to take wealth from some for the express purpose of transferring it to deserving others is widely seen as the best way to help the poor. Unfortunately, the determination of who is deserving takes place through political competition, not through some objective evaluation of who is most needy. There is little reason to expect that the poor, who have not been successful at competing in the marketplace, will be any more successful at competing in the political arena, a major point of chapter 9. Indeed, the evidence indicates that increasing government transfers has not increased the share of the economic pie that goes to the poor. The overall distribution of income has changed little, if any, in response to a significant increase in the share of the national income transferred by government. This increase in government transfer activity has, however, reduced the size of the economic pie below what it would have been by retarding the growth in economic productivity.

The poor, receiving the same proportion of a smaller national income, have been made worse off by the escalation of government transfer programs, programs that are typically justified in the name of helping the poor. Over the long run the relatively poor would be better off if more constraints were imposed on the ability of government to redistribute income.

Despite the truth of our recurring theme that we get more from government with less government, the ever-present temptation is to try to get more from government by expanding government and unfettering its power. It is not difficult to understand the reasons for this temptation. It cannot be denied that wide-ranging government authority can promote specific outcomes that, viewed in isolation, are desirable. And those who benefit from these outcomes will view them in isolation because most of the costs will be borne by others. Even when the costs far exceed the benefits, as they often do, the costs will be so diluted over the general taxpaying public that they will be all but invisible politically (see chapter 2). It is also the case that many of the benefits a larger government can generate are received immediately, while the costs are delayed.

This sequence of benefits and costs will provide a strong motivation for expanding government because of the tendency for political decisionmakers to emphasize short-term consequences and ignore long-term ones. As former British Prime Minister Harold Wilson supposedly said, "In politics a week is a long time." When the immediate benefits are concentrated on the few and the delayed costs are spread over the many, the temptation to expand government is further strengthened. Unfortunately, yielding to the temptation to attempt to get more from government by unleashing its power is a sure prescription for getting less from government as more government leads to more negative-sum political activity (see chapter 3).

Constitutional limits on government overcome the constant pressure to expand government. When harmful long-term consequences will be the result of decisions that are sure to be made if discretion is allowed in the face of short-term temptations, the case is strong for committing to self-denying restrictions that cannot be easily neglected. If we are to get more benefit from our government, it will require constitutional reform that reimposes genuine constraints on the size and scope of government. The necessary restraint is simply not possible relying only on the incentives and pressures of day-to-day politics.

Needed: A Constitutional Perspective

This is not a call for throwing out the existing U.S. Constitution or even for making major revisions in it. It would be presumptuous in the extreme to suggest that we could make major improvements over the work of James Madison, Alexander Hamilton, George Wythe, Benjamin Franklin, George Washington, and their colleagues at the 1787 Constitutional Convention in Philadelphia. What is needed is not a new constitution but a return to the constitutional understanding that the American public had for so long and that has been an essential ingredient in the success of the U.S. Constitution.

With this understanding, our existing Constitution would once more become an effective barrier to government excesses. Without this understanding, no constitution will be more than ink on parchment. A constitution can serve effectively to guard against only those abuses of government power that are widely recognized as abuses. If battered by the force of public approval of particular government practices, constitutional barriers against those practices soon will be breached. As observed by Henry Simons,

> Constitutional provisions are no stronger than the consensus that they articulate. At best, they can only check abuses of power until moral pressure is mobilized; and their check must become ineffective if often overtly used.[2]

There can be little doubt that constitutional barriers against government involvement in the economy have in recent decades been breached as public opinion has shifted to the view that expanded and discretionary government power is a major force for social progress.[3] In writing this book, it is our hope to improve the level of constitutional understanding and in so doing, strengthen the regulation of government and move us toward a positive-sum solution.

---

[2]Henry C. Simons, *Economic Policy for a Free Society* (Chicago: University of Chicago Press, 1951), 20.

[3]See Bernard H. Siegan, *Economic Liberties and the Constitution* (Chicago: University of Chicago Press, 1980). See also Richard A. Epstein, *Takings: Private Property and the Power of Eminent Domain* (Cambridge, Mass.: Harvard University Press, 1985).

Index